THE
SPORTS INJURIES
HANDBOOK

I would like to dedicate this book to my beloved wife Maria and our fantastic children Sarah and William, who make life so full of meaning, joy and inspiration.

I also dedicate the book to my dear friend and mentor, Sir Gareth Roberts (1940–2007), former Vice-Chancellor of Sheffield University and thereafter President at Wolfson's College, Oxford University, for his bravery and foresight in inviting me to the first Founding Clinical Chair in Sports Medicine in the UK, and for his great support to me and my family during our stay here.

THE
SPORTS INJURIES
HANDBOOK
Diagnosis and Management

CHRISTER ROLF

A & C Black • London

Note: It is always the responsibility of the individual to assess his or her own capability before participating in any training or other related activity. While every effort has been made to ensure the content of this book is as technically accurate as possible, neither the author nor the publishers can accept responsibility for any injury or loss sustained as a result of the use of this material. Anyone who uses this book without specific medical background or expertise should see it only as a reference and guide. All treatment of injuries should be handled by recognised sports injury experts.

Published in 2007 by A & C Black Publishers Ltd
38 Soho Square, London WID 3HB
www.acblack.com

Copyright © 2007 Christer Rolf

ISBN 9780713679502

A CIP record for this book is available from the British Library.

A & C Black uses paper produced with elemental chlorine-free pulp, harvested from managed sustainable forests.

Inside design by Andrew Barker
Cover design by James Watson
Cover photographs © iStock / Oxford Designers and Illustrators / PhotoDisc / Christer Rolf

Typeset by Palimpsest Book Production Limited, Grangemouth, Stirlingshire

Printed and bound in China

CONTENTS

PICTURE ACKNOWLEDGEMENTS

The publishers would like to thank the following for the permission to reproduce material:

Illustrations on pp. 34, 47, 54, 56, 57, 68, 72, 73, 94, 96, 104, 107, 111, 112, 130, 135, 137, 139, 142, 143, 153, 154, 157, 164, 165, 166, 172, 177–7, 203, 205, 210, 212 © Oxford Designers and Illustrators

Photographs on pp. 15, 19 and 152 © Corbis
Photographs on pp. 20–23 and 130 © iStock
Photographs on pp. 148 and 157 © PAPhotos
Photographs on p. 203 © PhotoDisc
Photographs on pp. 79 and 160 © Shutterstock

All other images courtesy of the author, reproduced by kind permission.

Injury management, rehabilitation and exercise 'on prescription'

This book is a practical and comprehensive view of what you as a physician, physiotherapist, fitness trainer, coach, manager or athlete need to know to be able to understand, diagnose and manage the most commonly occurring injuries in sport, up to specialist level. It aims to help you address the ordinary questions that occur in relation to sport injuries: 'What do I do now?'; 'Can I continue exercising?'; 'Must I rest completely?' This book outlines the benefits and risks of common training methods and their indications and contra-indications in relation to familiar sports injuries.

Note! As an individual, the management of your injury, exercise prescription and specific training for rehabilitation should always be guided by experts who know your circumstances, strengths and weaknesses and the details of your injury. However, by learning more you can take more responsibility for your training and have more fruitful discussions with experts, even if you have no medical background. This is particularly important, since sports medicine is not in the curriculum of most medical schools and therefore many doctors may lack the specific skills required. Also, managers, fitness trainers and coaches may sometimes push athletes back too early or rest them unnecessarily when they are injured.

Team medics, coaches and fitness trainers have a responsibility to their teams. Training errors can cause injuries and these need to be identified and altered. Managers need to understand that players may be fit to train but not to play. Even though you have to produce results under your contract and improve your team's position in the league, coming back to the sports field too early after an injury is, in most cases, not beneficial to anyone. Unfortunately, it is often proclaimed in the media that players continue to play despite their injuries, but in most cases an injured player cannot perform at their best and the long-term consequences may be dire. In my clinic, I often see players of 20 years of age or younger who retire from professional sport due to their injuries. Exercise and sport is, nevertheless, important for us all whether we are professionals or recreational athletes.

The first part of this book describes sports which may be recommended as exercise 'on prescription' both for injured elite athletes and for those suffering chronic ailments such as diabetes, obesity, osteoporosis, high blood pressure, heart insufficiency, asthma and so on. Physical activity levels have dropped dramatically in schools and in the daily routines of many people, leading to an increased incidence of obesity and poor fitness levels even in young, otherwise healthy, individuals. For them, exercise may make the difference between a healthy and prosperous life and development of ailments and early death. Depending where you are on that scale and what basic performance level you have, exercise can make a huge difference to your quality of life. However, too much intensity or too fast a progression in training, unrealistic ambitions or inappropriate advice can cause injury or other complications. Always make sure that you are fit enough for your chosen sport. Never exercise or compete when you are unwell. If you are in any doubt, or if you take regular medication, see your GP or team doctor for advice. This book does not cover exercise on prescription for ailments other than injuries and focuses on the musculo-skeletal effects more than on general physiological and cardiovascular adaptations, even though these are just as important for general well-being.

The second part of the book introduces some common sports injuries. The approach is problem-oriented and summarises the current understanding of best practice. For each injury, I begin with its location in the body and its associated symptoms and signs. Each page takes you through the consensus and controversies in understanding the mechanism of the injury; provides guidance on reaching a diagnosis; explains how this injury is clinically examined; describes the value of common investigations; enables you to refer it to an appropriate level of expertise; and guides you through rehabilitation on the way back to full sporting performance. After each section there is a traffic light chart that outlines what kind of training you should or should not do when you are injured.

Each injury and diagnosis is described systematically:

- Symptoms and location

- Mechanism of the injury

- Clinical signs and appropriate clinical tests

- Management of the injury

- Relevant investigations and considerations

- Referrals and specific questions

- Exercise on prescription and principles of rehabilitation

- Evaluation of treatment

- Return to sport and long-term prognosis

The location of each injury is provided by an anatomical photo or illustration as a starting point. Look at your injury, identify the injured area and check on the anatomical picture to see if its location fits. Basic clinical examinations, specific for various diagnoses and tests are discussed for the foot, ankle, lower leg, knee, hip, groin, hand, wrist, elbow and shoulder. For each diagnosis, there are warnings with reference to important differential diagnoses – possible alternative injuries to consider and test for, so as to avoid incorrect diagnosis and prescription of treatment that will worsen the injury. I cover rehabilitation principles, specific training for different injuries and ways of monitoring outcomes before resuming full pre-injury levels of activity.

The injuries in this book are grouped by their location. This avoids the difficulty of looking in the index when you don't know what the injury is! On pp. 25–6 there is a full listing of injuries, arranged in alphabetical order within each section for ease of use. There is also a colour-coding system to help you turn directly to the appropriate section. Also, at the back of the book, there is a glossary giving a brief definition of the medical terminology used in the book.

CHAPTER 1

What is a sports injury?

A 'sports injury' can be defined as an injury that occurs during sporting activities or exercise. This can be broadened to include injuries affecting participation in sports and exercise and affecting athletes of all ages and all levels of performance. Patients who seek medical attention at sports injury clinics represent the spectrum from top professional to recreational athletes. Even though we can identify the mechanism of an injury and its pathoanatomical correlate or diagnosis, its consequences may be very different for different athletes. If you are a professional player, there may be loss of earnings and the risk of losing your contract and even your career. If you are a club manager, it may mean losing an important player, perhaps at a crucial time, and the financial costs of a replacement player. If you are the team doctor, physiotherapist, fitness trainer or coach, you will want to know how the injury will affect your plans for the players' ongoing dietary and physical training programmes. If you are the medic in charge, it will mean having to convince not only the player but also the club's other staff that you have the situation under control. The stakes are high. If a player goes back too early, they risk relapse or further injury but if they are held back, they might ask for a second opinion.

For younger athletes trying to establish themselves in their sport, an injury can result in major family-related conflicts. Over-ambitious or over-protective parents and pressure from coaches and team-mates can put stresses on to a young athlete not able to participate in their sport. For recreational athletes, injuries may mean loss of regular physical and social activities and problems with general health, such as blood pressure, insulin control or secondary problems to the lower back from limping. A shoulder injury from squash may cause difficulties for a builder or plumber with their own business or raise concerns about the safety of a police officer or firefighter. Completely irrational charity bets – 'I must run the London Marathon in a few months even though I have never run more than three miles because my honour is at stake' – are another issue.

The importance of sport and exercise and the consequences of an injury must be emphasised by whoever provides treatment and advice. They must appreciate and understand but provide evidence-based advice. To tell a keen recreational tennis or golf player that they have to stop playing because of an injury must be thoroughly considered advice. There are very often a number of options for consideration during recovery from even a very serious injury. Complete rest is seldom motivating and may be ill-advised because of the detrimental effect rest has on tensile tissue strength and general fitness, and such rest's potentially fatal consequences for some patients. An 80-year-old keen, regular golfer, suffering from a painful knee due to a meniscus tear, could die from the inactivity caused by the injury. With arthroscopy, that knee could be operated on and fixed within fifteen minutes, allowing him to play golf a week or two later; it would be a shame and very wrong to tell him to stop playing golf.

For doctors, the keys to success are: consulting evidence-based criteria for the definition and diagnosis of an injury; using reliable examination techniques; considering the background and fitness level of the patient; and being prepared to admit to a lack of knowledge and to refer the patient to someone who may know more. They must recognise the changes and developments that are occurring in sports medicine and the cultural differences that exist in the management of these injuries. Doctors should not take the view that sports injuries are self-inflicted and tell their patients to 'stop doing these silly things'. In societies threatened by obesity, osteoporosis and a general decline in fitness due to inactivity, exercise and sport are potent means of keeping the population fit and healthy.

Most sports injuries are specific to the sport and the level of participation: for example, 70 per cent of keen runners will be affected by a lower limb injury during their career, usually through over-use; soccer players have a high risk of traumatic ankle or knee injuries from tackles. The incidence of injury in soccer is between 15 and 20 injuries per thousand activity hours, with the highest risk during games. The figures are somewhat higher for rugby: between 20 and 40 injuries per thousand activity hours and with higher risks of upper limb injuries, in particular those of the shoulder joint. Golf is a low-risk sport but a knee or shoulder injury can affect performance and the ability to walk a five kilometre course. Within any particular sport, different positions and roles carry different risks. For example, in cricket a fast bowler may struggle to perform with a minor knee injury to his stance leg or a fielder may be hampered by a minor shoulder injury, while a batsman can perform well with both these injuries.

We must all, athletes, administrators and medical personnel alike, educate ourselves about the principles of exercise on prescription and different training methods and improve our understanding of the demands and impact inflicted by different sports. Thus, injured athletes can have an individualised recovery programme, based on current concepts and based on evidence. I hope this book will help.

CHAPTER 2

Diagnosis, Diagnosis, Diagnosis!

The principles of injury management rely on the premise that we know what we are treating. Diagnosis is the key to success. We must differentiate injuries such as 'knee sprain', 'muscle strain' and 'bruises' from the corresponding pathoanatomical diagnoses: 'rupture of the anterior cruciate ligament', 'grade II muscle rupture' or 'intra-muscular haematoma'. In some cases, the diagnosis is obvious from the person's history, symptoms, signs and clinical tests; in others an X-ray, MRI scan or second opinion from a general surgeon, rheumatologist or other specialist will be required. Even when the diagnosis is clear, opinions may vary as to the most appropriate treatment. There are consensuses and controversies that change over time and depend on routines, skills and resources. For example, an anterior cruciate ligament rupture of the knee can be treated with physiotherapy, with or without surgery, depending on the patient and other factors. With the rapid and improved access to information offered by the Internet, many patients do their homework before they arrive at the sports clinic, although the material they find may need careful interpretation. The results of studies may be interpreted in different ways, depending on the quality of the study and the patients studied. For example, non-active patients who sprain their knee and rupture their anterior cruciate ligament do very well without surgical reconstruction, while a professional footballer's career would be ended without surgery. We need to know how best to read and understand the literature to reach an informed decision to the benefit of the injured athlete.

With the technical wizardry available to healthcare professionals today, it is easy to forget the importance of hands-on skills. Clinical symptoms and signs, combined with a thorough history of the patient can, in the majority of cases, give a clear lead to the correct diagnosis, providing the professional knows how to test and what to ask. Leading questions are usually unsuccessful: simply asking the injured athlete to describe what happened and their symptoms is usually more fruitful. Diagnoses can then be confirmed with a clinical test, or perhaps an X-ray or scan, before treatment. Thorough inspection and palpation and passive and active mobility and resistance tests of dynamic muscle function, comparing the healthy and injured sides is also very important.

In a general clinical practice, examination of a knee or shoulder injury cannot, for practical reasons, take more than ten to fifteen minutes, which is sometimes inadequate. In a sports injury clinic like mine, we usually allow 30 to 45 minutes for the initial consultation, including the clinical examination. For most acute limb injuries, this is adequate but for chronic problems arising from over-use, two or more sessions may be required before a diagnosis can be reached.

The main, and most crucial, question to ask any injured person is: can you please demonstrate and describe, in your own way, what happened? Many athletes will be able to demonstrate and explain in such detail that they provide the diagnosis as if from the text book. Before rushing to carry out detailed specific tests, the doctor should evaluate posture and gait, look for signs of pain or discomfort and remember that most musculo-skeletal injuries to a limb or joint will reduce the athlete's range of motion and control, which could cause muscle atrophy. Ask if the athlete has taken painkillers, which may blur your findings, and perform basic functional tests on the relevant part of the body.

Inspection and palpation of the injured area can identify signs of inflammation, such as oedema (swelling around the joint), effusion (fluid within the joint), tenderness, increased temperature, redness, impairment of function or bruising. Let the injured athlete demonstrate the movements that cause the problem. Muscle resistance tests can identify weakness or pain and should be done manually on all the relevant muscles, comparing the injured and non-injured sides. Joint laxity tests and specific injury tests are crucial for the diagnosis of many of the most common injuries. They are not always easy to perform and require years of training.

CHAPTER 3

Exercise 'on prescription'

Close collaboration between well-educated rehabilitation staff and coaches is vital to the successful outcome of treatments. Advisors have to provide appropriate indications and restrictions. Professional teams have fitness trainers and physiotherapists; for recreational athletes, membership of a fitness centre with recognised instructors is a good alternative. It is important that everyone concerned has a basic understanding of different training methods. The skills and knowledge of the instructor are far more important than their equipment. For most injuries, a progressive training programme, which enables monitoring over time, is needed. A simple training diary is very important and can help to explain why training did not have the expected effect or perhaps caused further injury.

Exercise is a very efficient treatment if it is prescribed and performed appropriately and correctly, with clear and realistic targets. However, it can cause further injuries if misused. The aim of exercise and training during convalescence from an injury is to minimise any decline in the muscle function and tensile strength of the injured area. It also counteracts the negative effect an injury has on posture, core stability, general fitness levels and sport-specific techniques.

Decreased muscle function or muscle weakness can be caused by:

- Muscle atrophy, following the immobilisation of a limb. Progressive strength training is needed to restore muscle strength and volume.

- Impaired neuro-muscular control, following immobilisation. Proprioceptive and neuro-muscular control training is needed to restore muscle and joint control.

- Muscle fatigue and poor endurance after immobilisation. Aerobic and anaerobic exercises are needed to restore muscle performance.

- Reduced mobility after immobilisation. Restricted mobility can be passive, where mechanical factors, such as scarring, adhesions or joint injuries, limit the range of motion; mobilisation or even surgery may be needed. Stiff muscles may need stretching.

- An underlying functional instability of the joint, when proprioceptive and functional training is the key.

- Structural instability, where taping, support or stabilising surgery is required.

- Pain, or fear of pain. Understanding the source and character of the pain and controlling it is vital.

Muscle training can activate muscle groups or single muscles. Closed chain exercises are important in the early stages of the healing of ligament ruptures and during rehabilitation after ligament reconstruction. (A closed chain exercise is one in which the end of the limb is firmly fixed, for example bicycling or leg presses. An example of open chain training is leg extension exercises in a sitting position.) Most rehabilitation plans combine specific training for the injured area with more functional training for the rest of the body.

Prescribed exercise needs to be well-balanced to achieve the best outcome. Objective and subjective scoring of function, comparing the injured with the non-injured side, is vital and usually requires qualified assistance from a physiotherapist or sports therapist. The ultimate functional test is when the injured athlete returns to sport-specific training and games, monitored by their team medics.

CONSIDER AND NOTE

Even though most musculo-skeletal problems in athletes are caused by injuries, the following warning signals should not be neglected. Even though the athlete may have a history of trauma during sport and have a swollen joint or limb, an orthopaedic injury is not the only cause to consider:

- Muscular and neurological diseases can result in muscle atrophy and dysfunction.

- Infectious diseases can lead to local inflammatory signs and problems. A swollen joint can be the first sign of a systemic or local disease such as gout, ulcerous cholitis or diabetes.

- In an elderly athlete, the sudden onset of pain and swelling of a joint can be an early sign of a looming septic arthritis.

- In a young athlete, the sudden onset of pain and swelling of a joint can be an early sign of osteomyelitis.

- Referred pain from the spine can cause radiating pain and dysfunction of a limb.

- Vascular diseases, or deep vein thrombosis, can result in localised swelling and dysfunction.

- Tumours can cause musculo-skeletal symptoms.

I must reiterate the importance of a well-defined diagnosis and a mind open to re-evaluation if the prescribed exercise and training does not result in the expected outcome or if the symptoms persist or worsen.

Unexpected consequences of training must sometimes be explained since, from the athlete's perspective, some of the effects may be considered unwanted or adverse. For example, in the calf muscles, strength training with heavy weights leads to an increase in volume that is hardly noticeable. This is a well-known dilemma for body builders. Equivalent training for the quadriceps muscles (at the front of the thigh) may result in an increase in volume that makes trousers feel too tight. A functionally excellent outcome of rehabilitation for knee problems may thus result in an unhappy patient who has to buy larger-sized trousers!

Compliance with a defined rehabilitation programme is extremely important. Athletes and other people involved must understand the reason for the exercises prescribed and how to achieve the wanted effect. Highly motivated athletes may overdo the training, while cautious patients may not want to do an exercise because it could be painful. If, three months after rehabilitation starts, there is still obvious muscle atrophy and persistent symptoms, the athlete's compliance with the scheduled training programme must be questioned. If they have complied well, the diagnosis may have been wrong or complications may have occurred.

PRINCIPLES OF BASIC TRAINING METHODS

STRENGTH TRAINING

Muscle strength and endurance training can be controlled movement (machines), semi-controlled (cross wires) or free weights (dumb-bells or body weight). The choice of training method depends on the athlete's aims and training background and the character of the injury. Free weights are more difficult to control than fixed movement training machines but add more stress to muscle and joint control. Complex muscle groups are more effectively trained using free weights, while isolated muscle groups may be efficiently trained using machines.

To achieve an increase in muscle strength and volume, progression in training may be guided by the Repetition Maximum (RM) method. One RM is the maximum resistance the athlete can manage once, in a controlled manner or specific movement. If the movement can be performed up to, but not more than, 10 times it is called 10RM. A 10RM movement will result in increase in muscle strength and volume if performed for six weeks or more. Before initiating heavy resistance training such as this, the instructor must emphasise the importance of warming up and learning the correct techniques for the method and apparatus used for each muscle group. The initial increase in performance after this kind of training is neuromuscular: the athlete learns how to use existing muscle fibres. To achieve a true increase in muscle volume and muscle hypertrophy, at least three months of regular training is required.

Training with lighter resistance and more repetitions will improve muscle strength and endurance. This type of training predominantly uses slow-twitch fibres but, if performed at higher speeds, fast-twitch fibres will be used. Muscular endurance is defined as the ability to perform dynamic muscular work, with constant generation of power, over a limited time. If using resistance training to achieve this effect in a specific muscle group, more than 15 repetitions in sets of three to five are recommended. Other types of endurance training include running, bicycling, skiing, cross-training and sport-specific activities. Endurance training can be performed daily providing its intensity and duration is progressively and reasonably increased. Most injuries due to over-use are caused by 'too much too soon'.

Strength training is best done not more than two to three times a week, with at least one day of rest between each session, but endurance strength training can be done daily. Most muscle strength and muscle endurance exercises are a combination of controlled, slowly executed concentric (where the muscles are shortened and contracted) and eccentric (where the muscles are extended and contracted) muscle contractions. Athletes must rest properly between each set of repetitions.

Eccentric muscle strength is about 40 per cent greater than concentric. Concentrating on eccentric muscle training can increase resistance and enhance the effect of training. An athlete who can perform an eccentric manoeuvre three to five times can perform the same manoeuvre concentrically without ever having trained for it. This kind of training has been shown to be effective for over-use injuries such as chronic Achilles tendinosis.

FLEXIBILITY TRAINING

Flexibility is defined as the active or passive range of motion of a muscle group. A limitation in muscle flexibility can be due to muscle tightness, cramps or a restriction of joint motion. The underlying cause of restricted flexibility or joint motion must be defined before a treatment can be recommended.

The normal flexibility of different muscle groups is sport-specific. For example, a ballet dancer can usually take their foot, with the leg straight, right up to their shoulder, while a marathon runner may be able to lift the straight leg to only 60 degrees. Symmetrical, bilateral apparent muscle tightness, which does not cause symptoms, may be considered as a functional adaptation to the sport being performed. However, if there is an obvious asymmetric flexibility or the athlete's movements are painful, mobilisation or other treatments may be indicated. Tight thigh muscles (hamstring) and hip-flexing (iliopsoas) muscles can not only cause pain in those muscles but also back problems, disturbed core stability and similar symptoms. Tight calf muscles may prevent squats, whereby weight will be transferred to the lower back, causing pain there. Chronic muscle tightness can cause fatigue, pain and dysfunction. However, hypermobility and excessive unrequired flexibility is not to be preferred: stretching can cause as many problems as it can solve. There are different types of stretching but the difference in effect among the various methods is small. The most important thing to make the stretching as effective as possible is that the injured player 'finds' the middle of the muscle bulk they need to stretch. Stretching in this position should be held for about 10 to 15 seconds, followed by a few seconds of relaxation, repeated two to three times. (Interestingly, animals like dogs regularly stretch their legs for one to two seconds only.) Stretching should always be performed in warmed-up muscles.

PROPRIOCEPTIVE TRAINING AND CORE STABILITY TRAINING

Co-ordination, balance, proprioception and core stability are terms frequently used in sport but rather difficult to define. They involve the ability to perform, or regain, controlled movements, in a sport-specific, safe and precise way. We cannot pin-point each and every control mechanism but there is lots of experience to apply to sport. *Tai chi* is an excellent example of a method that aims completely to regain full body and mind control, so essential for elite sports. Martial arts and dancing focus on this type of training, which is a key to successful performance. Unfortunately, most contact sports such as soccer, rugby and ice hockey often neglect this type of training. For years I have tried to convince physiotherapists and coaches to learn from this: not only would it reduce the number of injuries and their consequences, but it would enhance performance and their players' ability to undertake effective rehabilitation when injured.

SPORT-SPECIFIC TRAINING

The aim of rehabilitation is to restore a sport-specific function to, or above, pre-injury levels. In cricket it could be the perfect bowling action, in tennis the serve, in baseball the throw, in football ball control or in gymnastics landing. This type of training requires knowledge and understanding of the sport's specific demands and is usually prescribed and supervised by a sports therapist in close collaboration with a coach. After surgery or long immobilisation, this final stage of rehabilitation training is the most time-consuming and risky. In the final stage of rehabilitation after healing of an injury, functional training back to full performance level must be gradual, over a period of time that corresponds to the functional requirements of the muscles and the healing process of the underlying injury. This period could vary from a few weeks after a simple ankle sprain to a year after complicated knee surgery. The training has to be specific and, preferably, performed in a controlled environment. Returning too soon to full-time play will inevitably result in further or new injuries.

Objective performance scores, specific for the sport, are very valuable but poorly developed. I have tried to develop such scores for professional rugby and soccer and their validity is improving. One of the main reasons for the difficulties of objective scoring is that the functional scores used by orthopaedic surgeons or physiotherapists are developed for the general population, ranging from recreational athletes of all age groups to elite athletes from varying sports. A high shoulder or knee score compared to the general population may not indicate it is safe for a professional soccer or rugby player to return to the game. Another reason is that a goalkeeper or striker in soccer, a winger, prop or full-back in rugby or a bowler or batsman in cricket may perform on the same level in the same team but the consequence of a low or high score may be very different for each of them.

The evaluation of training outcomes is currently being investigated intensively. Hopefully, more specific scoring systems for different injuries and sports will soon be available. Until then, we have to trust in our experience and in close collaboration between the parties involved.

CHAPTER 4

Sport 'on prescription'

RUNNING ON A HARD SURFACE

Running is one of the most popular sports in the world. This not only covers marathons and track and field running – running is also part of the training in vir-

tually all other sports, including soccer, rugby, handball and triathlon. Running is a very efficient method for maintaining or improving cardiovascular, respiratory and musculo-skeletal fitness and increasing the structural strength of the musculo-skeletal system. It is also an effective way of improving the tensile strength of the lower limbs. Modified levels and intensities of running can also be used as alternative training for most athletes with certain types of injuries. However, before running on a hard surface, such as roads or astroturf, the patient must be able to withstand

Despite its popularity, running on asphalt is very demanding

the repetitive eccentric impact to the lower limbs, as each stride will create an impact force of five to ten times body weight for a fraction of a second. Since each stride stresses the same structures, their tensile strength and endurance lie between positive training effects and injury.

Running can be over a distance, in a variety of intervals or as a varied running-jogging-walking programme. The intensity and the distance must be proportionate to the runner's ability and objectives. Running on a hard surface mainly loads the lower limbs, where 90 per cent of running injuries are found. The most common error an inexperienced runner makes is to run too fast and too long too early, so that training causes new injuries instead of promoting the healing of another. It is important to use common sense when prescribing hard-surface running. For an inexperienced runner the safest way to build up performance after an injury is a slow and steady running tempo, including a proper warm-up.

The best test of improvement in running capacity is repeatedly to measure the runner's effort and time in a simple test race. For a fairly unfit but otherwise healthy person who wants to improve their general fitness and aerobic performance, running can be recommended as part of a progressive programme. From a reasonable starting point, such a programme would usually increase less than 15 per cent in distance and intensity per year. An elite marathon runner with an over-use injury may simply reduce their running time from two hours to one hour per day; not pushing over the pain threshold but gradually increasing the time day by day. A 130 kg rugby player, even though extremely fit, is not a good candidate for long-distance or road running. Their knees will undoubtedly say 'no!' to this madness. This type of exercise also cannot be recommended for obese or generally unfit recreational athletes or people with structural knee or hip problems, such as osteoarthritis. A reasonable running tempo that can be maintained for 30 minutes is essential for a persistent training effect. Runners should aim for a pace at which they can chat with a running mate while breathing almost normally; this is equivalent to 60 to 70 per cent of maximum aerobic capacity. The subjective experience of running is far more important than the heart frequency, which is not directly proportionate to the runner's feeling. Even with the same heart frequency, for example 160 beats per minute, running can be very easy one day and very uncomfortable the next.

The subjective experience of training is very important for a non-runner's motivation. Since the surface is consistent for each stride the same structures in the lower limbs will be put under repeated stress. While this leads to a functional adaption of the strength of the structures it can also lead to injuries in the short term. This also highlights the importance of proper, comfortably fitting running shoes with a cushioned sole, which can reduce the impact from touchdown in the stride, distribute the forces and provide stability to the ankle and foot. The commercial running shoe market is unfortunately mainly fashion-orientated and new models are pumped out every six months. Despite improved biomechanical knowledge, which manufacturers claim has revolutionised the market, and lighter high-quality materials and technology within the sole to compensate for different individual factors, modern running shoes do not last long. It may also be questioned whether they have reduced the incidence of injuries. When Arthur Lydiard introduced his running shoes around 1970, I could hardly run out a pair in two years' intensive running, and new soles could be reattached at least once before the shoe broke up. Today, most running shoes are worn down by regular running within 6–12 months. Regular runners will soon find their own style, but might have more trouble getting a consistent style of footwear.

Most running injuries are caused by training errors. In some cases, bio-mechanical factors, such as excessive pronation, contribute to the injury. If such factors are suspected, an experienced podiatrist may be able to help.

Running on a hard surface is a very efficient training method but as a primary alternative training form for the untrained, overweight or those with major injuries to the lower limbs, it should be prescribed with care.

RUNNING ON SOFT SURFACES

Running on soft surfaces maintains or increases fitness and tensile strength of the lower limbs and with less eccentric impact compared to running on hard surfaces. A well-balanced running programme over moors, in parklands or in forests can be recommended as a primary alternative training for most runners and other athletes with over-use injuries, even those of the lower limbs. People with mild or moderate knee or hip osteo-arthritis, who struggle to run 500 m on the road, may be able to jog a 5 km orienteering course without adverse effects.

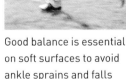

Good balance is essential on soft surfaces to avoid ankle sprains and falls

A varied and soft running surface creates a lower impact on the musculo-skeletal system, due to the longer time for shock absorption from each stride and the wider distribution of forces over the kinetic chain. On the other hand, the runner is forced to work harder, from a muscular point of view; they need to lift the knees higher when running uphill or over obstacles on the ground like vegetation. This consumes more energy and, all in all, uses more muscle groups than running on hard surfaces. (Running in forests consumes up to twice as much energy per kilometre as road running.) Running on soft surfaces is less demanding for the lower limbs but, due to the increased energy demand, puts more stress on the cardiovascular and respiratory system and so is good for weight reduction and general fitness.

There are risks in the prescription of this type of training. Over uneven terrain, the risk of ankle sprains and falls increases. Even though temporarily running on soft surfaces can be recommended for a marathon runner with over-use injuries of the lower limbs, they must be aware of the increased risks. Proprioceptive ankle training and core stability training must accompany alterations in running type. Older athletes, or fragile patients with osteoporosis or disabling injuries, may jog or walk on softer surfaces instead of running.

WALKING

Walking has been recommended by doctors for rehabilitation since the eighteenth century. Long walks were used as regular training by established marathon runners as long ago as the nineteenth century. It is a natural way of exercising, which does not require any special preparation, equipment or clothing (except clothes suitable for the climate). This low-intensity and low-impact exercise produces increased tensile strength of the lower limbs for a relatively low cardiovascular effort. It is a training form that can be prescribed to almost everyone, except people on crutches who cannot bear their weight fully. Even very unfit, elderly or obese patients may benefit from walking slowly and for reasonable distances. It is well documented that ageing of muscles and skeleton in the locomotor system can be altered with low-intensity regular physical activity.

A dog is an excellent incentive for taking a 30-minute walk every day

This kind of training can be done in the same way as running, with varying distances and speeds. While Olympic athletes can walk 10,000 metres in less than 40 minutes, most people wouldn't be able to run it in that time. To increase energy consumption at low walking speeds, a rucksack or weight belt may be carried. Walking in forest, parklands or the beautiful countryside is an extremely popular weekend activity for a great many British people: a day out can be a great experience as well as excellent exercise. To help city dwellers and single elderly people who may not dare to walk alone, walking clubs are springing up in most cities. These clubs organise walks in small groups, which also has a positive social effect. We should not underestimate the effect of daily walking, even in big cities. A modern shopping or outlet centre can provide kilometres of walking. Red 'SALE' signs will enhance the pace of walking for most visitors! The effect of this kind of exercise for general health is substantial – as long as we walk somewhere, it doesn't matter how or where.

WATER EXERCISES AND WATER RUNNING

Exercising in water can be done during convalescence from most injuries

Water exercises may be prescribed as rehabilitation and alternative training for most injuries, unless the person has wounds, eczema or other skin disorders. Usually, a surgical wound requires two weeks of healing and any stitches to be removed before starting water exercises, due to the risk of infections. Water exercising allows an athlete to maintain or improve aerobic and anaerobic capacity if suffering injuries that do not allow full impact on hard surfaces. Water running and work-out exercises can be used as alternative training for most types of injuries, as you can see from the frequent green light in the 'exercise on pre-scription' summaries in chapter 4. An athlete who is immobilised in one limb can have a plastic brace, which allows water training, instead of a plaster one. Water exercising can improve the endurance and flexibility of asthmatic athletes and people with different disabilities. It is a superb alternative training method for disabled or elderly patients, where large muscle groups can be trained without impact. The low resistance of water creates a low eccentric impact on the lower limbs.

In principle, everything you can do on a floor you can do in water. It is important to devise a programme – not just jump in the water and tumble around. Use either a floating device or jacket that allows the athlete to concentrate on the exercises, rather than on floating; they are therefore able to run even in deep water, without touching the floor. This is quite difficult to start with but after some training to find their balance, it is great. Even better for most injuries is to run on the floor of more shallow water, since the athlete is 'pushing off', albeit with a slight delay – like 'space walking'. This allows training without a float jacket but I recommend some thin shoes to avoid blisters. An athlete can burn as much energy in water exercises as in any other training but must be careful to control dehydration, which may not be felt in the same way as when running on a road.

Water exercising is recommended for obese unfit people but they may not wish to join a group of people dressed in swimsuits, so their likely compliance must be considered. However, with the huge number of public pools around the country this type of training is accessible to most.

SWIMMING

Swimming is often recommended as an alternative training method for people with injuries of the lower limbs and back problems, but for upper limb injuries and neck injuries it may be contra-indicated.

The technique of swimming is very demanding and often hampers its aerobic and anaerobic effects and thus the time spent in the water. To swim for 30 minutes requires a well-developed technique. Even though there is no direct impact, swimming may cause problems if the training is not precisely defined: it is important to recommend or restrict different techniques of swimming for different injuries. For example,

95-year-old Ann-Margret does not need a gym. She has taken a swim in this Swedish lake almost every day for more than 70 years

swimming the breaststroke can exacerbate knee injuries such as medial meniscus tears, osteoarthritis, anterior knee pain and most shoulder injuries. Most swimming techniques will provoke sub-acromial impingement and patients with multi-directional instability in the shoulder should not be prescribed swimming. Low back pain and neck pain may well be aggravated if the athlete does not lower the head down into the water in the swimming stride but looks up, protecting the face or eyes from the chlorine but hyper-extending the cervical and lumbar spine. Such simple mistakes often mean that the athlete does not comply with the programme.

The advice to include swimming in a training programme must be supported by a detailed history of the injured athlete's abilities and restrictions. For an elderly elite swimmer or a triathlete with an Achilles tendon injury, swimming is an excellent alternative to running on roads.

BICYCLING

Cycling, either on a stationary or a normal bicycle, can maintain and improve aerobic and anaerobic endurance and muscle strength in the legs, with

Few injuries prevent you from cycling, which can be enjoyed in many ways

low eccentric impact. It is a good way of initiating a fitness programme for untrained, elderly and overweight patients. Cycling can be prescribed for injuries where running is impossible. The leg muscles will be trained differently, depending on the saddle height, pedal position and handlebar shape and position. Varying these factors will stress specific muscle groups: for example, an athlete with a cast on a lower limb, perhaps for Achilles tendon repair, can place the pedal under the heel and cycle. People with femuro-patellar pain or hip osteoarthritis will often require a higher saddle, while those suffering a rupture of the hamstring muscles or back pain will need an upright position and a higher handlebar, and those with carpal tunnel syndrome must avoid gripping the handlebar too hard. A stationary bicycle at a sports clinic makes it possible to test and adjust seating position, and advise on training individually.

There are very few injuries where you cannot cycle and cycling is a very good training alternative for all ages. Cycling can be done over a distance, in intervals, in classes or individually; resistance and pace can be altered to suit most athletes. Cycling in the countryside is lovely but can be more demanding, depending on the terrain, weather and traffic conditions. As for other exercise prescriptions, the programme and progression must be detailed.

MOUNTAIN BIKING

Mountain biking is an advanced form of cycling training that can be recommended to some more adventurous athletes. For young and fit cyclists, orienteerers, skiers and players in most team sports, mountain biking is an excellent choice when suffering most types of injuries. Both the leg and arm muscles will be put under very high stress when riding in hilly terrain but the eccentric impact is low. Mountain biking will maintain or increase aerobic and anaerobic endurance, muscle strength in the legs, arms and upper part of the body and general balance.

Mountain biking is an excellent alternative to running for maintaining leg strength and general fitness

The position of the handlebar and the saddle height is somewhat limited by the fact that the cyclist must have a low centre of gravity; toe clips are often necessary. Mountain biking has its limitations: the bike is expensive and town dwellers may not have access to appropriate and available countryside. It is also slightly dangerous for inexperienced cyclists – most injuries are caused by falling off the bike. It is very important for the cyclist to adapt their speed to their capacity.

Cycling in hilly terrain gives mountain biking a natural interval training profile but it is physically very demanding. Helmet, gloves, appropriate clothing and knee protection should always be worn and the bike must be good–quality, with efficient brakes.

SKATEBOARDING, ROLLER-SKATING AND WIND-SURFING

These activities can help athletes maintain or increase body posture, proprioception, core stability and muscle function with low impact, subject to good technique and the avoidance of new injuries from unnecessary falls. These kinds of activities have become very popular for younger people and must be considered as alternative training methods for fit athletes.

This is advanced core stability, and balance training requires lots of practice!

The equipment is quite expensive but can be rented. These activities require very good co-ordination and muscle strength and should be prescribed to already fit individuals, for example soccer or rugby players, but cannot be recommended for those with poor balance and co-ordination. For example, for those with shin splints or who are recovering from knee surgery, as an alternative to bicycling and running, roller-skating is very efficient endurance training to develop quadriceps muscle strength. For ice-hockey players, roller-skating is a natural way of exercising during pre-season training. Both skateboarding and wind-surfing are excellent balance exercises for different seasons for injured martial arts athletes and gymnasts. All these sports should preferably be performed in controlled environments, with instructors.

CROSS-TRAINING

Cross-training refers to varied training, combining different sports like cycling, running, swimming, skiing, skating and workouts and gives all-round training. Any of these sports can be left out if necessary for rehabilitation. A six-month programme, mixing these activities in reasonable proportions over each week, with gradual progression, will give efficient fitness training.

Cross-training is a great way to regain functional fitness at the end of rehabilitation

TENNIS AND OTHER RACKET SPORTS

Racket sports, such as tennis, squash, racketball and badminton can sometimes be prescribed as alternative training for general fitness development and during convalescence for a number of injuries. Modifications may be required: for example, a sore knee may allow baseline tennis play on grass but not allow sprints and turns on a hard court. A stiff shoulder may not allow overhead serves but be perfectly all right for baseline play. Elbow injuries, such as lateral epicondylitis, may require double backhands to avoid pain. Double or mixed games do not involve the same amount of running as singles. Squash is more demanding for the wrist and elbow than the shoulder; badminton is very demanding for the Achilles tendon but may be played with a non-dominant shoulder injury. Thus, instead of resting completely, a keen player can maintain parts of their play until treatment and rehabilitation is completed. Meeting and playing with friends is also very important for encouraging the return to sport.

Maintain a 'not too much too soon' policy and most racket sports are fairly risk free

GOLF

Golf is excellent, low-impact exercise for all age groups, providing a pleasant social environment and general well-being. Golf can be prescribed during convalescence from most injuries and disorders that only allow walking. Even with severe hip osteoarthritis, a motorised cart may be used to cover the main bulk of the distance. A left knee injury may require the golfer to open their stance slightly. A painful shoulder may decrease the power at tee-off but perhaps precision will improve. People with back injuries should take individual advice, since the rotational movements are quite demanding.

The five-kilometre walk, combined with the thrill of hitting the ball over varied courses, excites most people. Technique is important and most club professionals will assist with advice. Professional players in many sports play golf and courses can be found everywhere.

Golf is a great 'lifestyle' sport where you can keep fit and socialise at the same time

SOCCER, RUGBY AND OTHER CONTACT SPORTS

Most contact sports have an undeserved reputation for being dangerous. Even though injuries do occur and are sometimes severe, especially in the professional game, the rate of injury per hour of training and playing is relatively low. At a recreational level, players can agree to avoid unnecessary and dangerous body contact: choosing non-contact netball instead of basketball, agreeing to keep hockey sticks below the waist, using proper protection and so on, can keep the injury rate low.

It can be difficult safely to stage the return to playing: being out of rugby for six months and then playing a full 80-minute game is very risky. Going back must be stepped: running in a straight line, then faster running, side-stepping, turning, improving core stability and posture, light contact and passing, full contact, playing the last 20 minutes in a reserves' game and so on. Such staging requires good teamwork but is more difficult for recreational players who have no access to coaches or team medics.

Ball sports have an unfair reputation as more risky, but there are only more injuries because these sports are so popular

Many of the injuries we see in contact sports are caused by insufficient rehabilitation from previous injuries. The aim must first be to restore balanced limb performance and then an appropriate and sport-specific level of fitness. One way to achieve this is to compile a functional score, which includes a subjective score, an objective examination and the results of simple functional tests. The problem is that each sport and each level of performance requires its own score.

WORKING-OUT AND GYM TRAINING

Working-out, aerobics and similar activities are excellent, and often essential, rehabilitation methods and useful alternatives during rehabilitation of many injuries. Gym training, with a variety of fixed stations for weight training, has become popular recreational exercise. It is also used for basic pre-season training in almost every sport. There is no better way to learn functional anatomy than to work-out the muscle groups step by step in a gym.

No equipment is better than the skills of the instructor. Working-out with weights is technically difficult and there are lots of pitfalls that need to be considered in close collaboration with a licensed instructor and access to appropriate training equipment. Training should start with an objective function test, so a reasonable measure of progress can be made. Beginners usually start with an individual training programme based on six to ten exercises. After working-out a few times at low resistance and learning the specific movements, the training is documented, including what kind of equipment is used, how many repetitions and sets and how much resistance. Warming up, on a bike or treadmill, is essential before strength training. Depending on any underlying problems, such as osteoporosis or injury, such as a temporary fragile cruciate ligament graft, the programme must be modified over time.

Fitness centres are all over the place. Remember, the instructor is the best equipment!

HIDDEN HOME EXERCISES

Even for the general, sedentary, non-sporty population, exercise is an essential part of well-being. Exercise is also the 'drug' prescribed for a number of major health problems such as high blood pressure, heart insufficiency, diabetes, asthma, obesity, osteoporosis, rheumatoid arthritis and multiple sclerosis. Although for each of these disorders there are exercise alternatives that may be prescribed under the close supervision of a specialist doctor, we should be wary of sending unmotivated people to gyms or fitness centres where they feel out of place and uncomfortable. We should not underestimate the negative effects of how modern society has turned many into crisp-eating, soap-watching, coach potatoes.

On the other hand, we should not underestimate the positive effect of everyday activities. For example (and this applies to both sexes), one to two hours of vigorous weekly cleaning of a normal house will force a middle-aged sedentary

Who needs a gym if you have a garden?

Cleaning windows is excellent training for shoulder muscles and posture

Vacuum cleaning is excellent core-stability training

person to use 70 to 80 per cent of their maximal oxygen uptake, equivalent to running for 45 minutes at a good pace. Cleaning windows manually is excellent rotator cuff training after shoulder injuries; vacuum cleaning requires core stability and posture; washing dishes in warm water is excellent for a healed radius fracture. There are many, many other examples: running up and down stairs, standing on one leg on a wobble board while brushing your teeth, stretching out in the shower, cutting the hedges, mowing the lawn, walking or jogging the dog, jumping off the bus one stop away from the office, using stairs instead of lifts. We neglect many of these things (if we can) during the week, then we spend money and energy on a one-hour run on a treadmill and gym training. Who needs a gym if there is a garden to attend to? Who needs exercise if you are running after three small children all day or taking the dog out once a day?

Exercise on prescription is not new. A Swedish doctor who lived in Enkoping in the early twentieth century gave detailed prescriptions: six walks a day around the park, three sit-downs and stand-ups from each of the park benches and so on. In ancient literature, from the Egyptians and Greeks to the Chinese, exercise is named as a basic and essential ingredient of life. If we sit still we die!

Without sounding like an old schoolmarm, I do think we should go back to some of these basic ideas, to avoid further deterioration of sedentary people's fitness levels and help motivate injured athletes by prescribing a balanced diet of alternative exercises.

INJURIES TO THE FOOT

Fracture of metatarsal bones
Hallux rigidus
Hallux valgus
Morton's neuroma
Plantar fasciitis
Sesam bone stress fractures
Stress fractures of the foot
Sub-talar instability and pain
Tarsal coalition
Turf toe

INJURIES TO THE ANKLE

Anterior impingement syndrome
Cartilage injury of the talus dome
Lateral ankle ligament ruptures
Multi-ligament ruptures of the ankle
Peroneus tendon dislocation
Peroneus tendon rupture
Posterior impingement of the ankle
Syndesmosis ligament rupture
Tarsal tunnel syndrome
Tibialis posterior syndrome

INJURIES TO THE LOWER LEG

Achilles tendon rupture
Achilles tendinopathy
Achilles tendinosis
Achilles paratenon disorders
Anterior chronic compartment syndrome
Anterior tibia stress fractures
Apophysitis calcaneii
Medial tibia stress syndrome
Rupture of the gastrocnemius
    or soleus muscles
Stress fracture of fibula
Stress fracture of posterior tibia

INJURIES TO THE KNEE

Anterior cruciate ligament tear (ACL)
Anterior knee pain
Cartilage injuries
Chondromalacia patella
Gout: arthropathies
Iliotibial band friction syndrome
Lateral collateral ligament tear (LCL)
Medial collateral ligament tear (MCL)
Medial plica syndrome
Meniscus tear
Osgood-Schlatter's disease
Osteoarthritis
Osteochondritis dissecans (OCD)
Patella dislocation
Patella tendon rupture
Patellar instability or mal-tracking
Patellar tendinosis
Popliteus tenosynovitis
Posterior cruciate ligament tear (PCL)
Posterior lateral corner injuries
Posterior medial corner injuries
Prepatellar bursitis
Rupture of the quadriceps or
    hamstring muscles
Tibial spine avulsion fracture

INJURIES TO THE THIGH AND GROIN

Adductor tendonitis/tendinosis
Hip joint labral tears
Hip joint osteoarthritis
Iliopsoas-related groin pain
Nerve entrapment causing groin pain
Rupture of the rectus femoris muscle
Stress fracture of the femur neck
Stress fracture of the pelvis
Symphysitis

INJURIES TO THE WRIST

Baseball mallet finger
Bowler's thumb
Carpal tunnel syndrome
De Quervain's tenosynovitis
Dislocation of finger joint
Handlebar palsy
Hypothenar syndrome
Rugby finger
Scaphoid fracture
Skier's thumb
Stress fracture of the radial epiphysis
Squeaker's wrist
Tenosynovitis of the extensor carpi ulnaris
Wartenberg's syndrome

INJURIES TO THE ELBOW

Cartilage injury and loose bodies
Distal biceps tendon rupture
Golfer's elbow

Lateral epicondylitis (tennis elbow)
Olecranon bursitis
Pronator teres syndrome
Radial tunnel syndrome
Triceps tendon rupture

INJURIES TO THE SHOULDER

Acromio-clavicular dislocation
Anterior shoulder dislocation
Biceps tendon rupture
Clavicle fracture
External impingement
Frozen shoulder
Internal impingement syndrome
Multi-directional instability
Pectoralis muscle rupture
Posterior shoulder dislocation
Post-traumatic shoulder stiffness
Referred pain from the cervical spine
Referred pain from the upper back
Rotator cuff rupture
SLAP tear
Subscapularis tendon rupture
Thoraco-scapular muscle insufficiency

Foot injuries are very common but have been neglected for many years in sports medicine. The developments of podiatry and foot surgery as orthopaedic specialities have dramatically improved our knowledge and the possibility of assisting in the treatment of these sometimes disabling injuries. Foot injuries are common in virtually all sports and at all ages.

The below figures show the anatomical appearances of the foot from different angles with arrows indicating the locations of presenting injury symptoms.

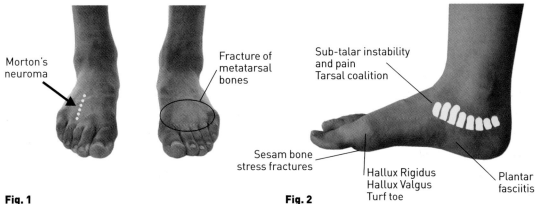

Morton's neuroma

Fracture of metatarsal bones

Sub-talar instability and pain
Tarsal coalition

Sesam bone stress fractures

Hallux Rigidus
Hallux Valgus
Turf toe

Plantar fasciitis

Fig. 1

Fig. 2

1. FRACTURE OF METATARSAL BONES

SYMPTOMS There is a sharp localised exercise-induced pain over a metatarsal bone. Most commonly, MT IV or V are affected, often after a previous sprain or after a direct impact injury.

AETIOLOGY The injury is either caused by direct impact, for example from football boot studs, or by excessive repetitive stress from forefoot running or jumping, sometimes due to faulty shoes or inlays with the breaking point of the sole over the mid-part of a metatarsal.

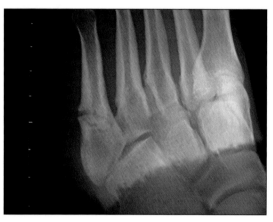

Fig. 3 MT V stress fractures should be treated with caution, since healing is often prolonged

CLINICAL FINDINGS There is swelling and distinct tenderness on palpation over the fractured metatarsal bone.

INVESTIGATIONS X-ray can be mistaken for normal if the stress fracture is undisplaced until there is callus formation, which occurs within a few weeks. MRI shows localised bone oedema very early. CT scans can disclose the fracture line. Displaced fractures, which are rare, are diagnosed directly by X-ray.

TREATMENT This depends on the location of the fracture. While MT IV fractures usually heal with the use of non-weight-bearing boots and modifications in training within four to eight weeks, MT V fractures can be hazardous if displaced or unstable, leading to non-union and long-term problems, independent of treatment. Immobilisation in a non-weight-bearing boot or surgery may be indicated. Stress fractures to the first and second metatarsal bones are more uncommon in athletes.

REFERRALS Refer to orthopaedic surgeon for consideration of immobilisation or surgery with screw fixation.

EXERCISE PRESCRIPTION Rest will not help so allow all kinds of non-impact sporting activities using well-fitting shoes, non-weight-bearing boots or strapping and avoiding impact. Suggest low-impact activities such as cycling and swimming.

EVALUATION OF TREATMENT OUTCOMES
Monitor decrease of clinical symptoms and signs and X-ray showing healed fracture.

PROGNOSIS Excellent-Good in most cases but may be career-threatening for professional players, due to long healing times.

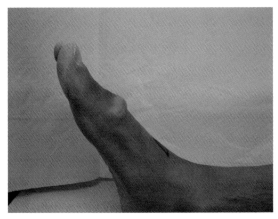

Fig. 4 Clinical presentation of advanced Hallux Rigidus

SYMPTOMS There is increasing stiffness and exercise-induced pain around MTP I without preceding trauma, usually affecting adult athletes. This condition can be mistaken for 'turf toe', which is common in young footballers.

AETIOLOGY The aetiology is unclear but there is a possible genetic predisposition.

CLINICAL FINDINGS There is decreased active and passive range of motion, most notably in extension and flexion of the MTP I to the degree that the joint freezes. There is localised swelling, effusion and tenderness on palpation over the MTP I joint. The condition is often bilateral.

INVESTIGATIONS X-ray is initially normal. In later stages there is typically a decreased joint space, dorsal exostoses and sub-chondral sclerosis.

TREATMENT Initially try individually adapted orthotics combined with stretching of the flexor and extensor muscles of MTP I. NSAID or cortisone injections into MTP I can give short-term relief. Surgery with osteotomy and excision of exostoses may be indicated to increase the mobility of the joint in severe cases but should be performed with caution on athletes since outcomes are sometimes unpredictable. Full weight bearing is usually allowed within six weeks of surgery.

REFERRALS Refer to podiatrist or physiotherapist for mild symptoms and to orthopaedic surgeon if there are severe or progressive symptoms.

EXERCISE PRESCRIPTION Rest will not help, so allow all kinds of sporting activities using well-fitting shoes. If there is pain on impact, suggest cycling, swimming or other low-impact sports as alternatives to running and jumping.

DIFFERENTIAL DIAGNOSES Osteoarthritis, which usually does not give the typical stiffness and X-ray appearance; turf toe, which is post-traumatic intra-articular stiffness due to capsule and cartilage damage.

EVALUATION OF TREATMENT OUTCOMES Monitor decreased clinical symptoms and signs and expect a normal X-ray around 12 weeks from surgery.

PROGNOSIS Good-Fair. Many of these conditions lead to an immovable joint, in the long term preventing running and jumping on the forefoot.

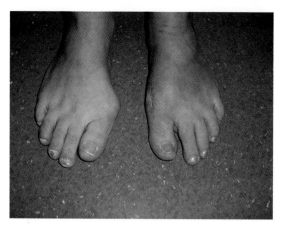

Fig. 5 Clinical presentation of Hallux Valgus before surgery (patient's right foot) and after surgery (left foot)

SYMPTOMS Increasing stiffness, aching pain and typical deformation of MTP I without preceding trauma. Often the symptoms are bilateral. This condition is commonly presented by middle-aged recreational athletes or sedentary people, predominantly female, but it can occur in younger individuals.

AETIOLOGY The aetiology is unclear but there is possibly a genetic predisposition to this disease, which causes a typical mal-alignment of MTP I with secondary bursitis and joint degeneration. Asymptomatic hallux valgus does not need treatment.

CLINICAL FINDINGS Hallux valgus is diagnosed when there is more than 10 degrees of malformation, with adducted distal phalanges and localised swelling, redness and tenderness on palpation over the MTP I joint.

INVESTIGATIONS X-ray confirms the diagnosis and indicates the extent of mal-alignment, subluxation and lateralisation of the MTP I joint. Usually there is a degree of osteoarthritis.

TREATMENT Try individually made orthotics in the shoes to support the anterior arch, combined with stretching of the MTP I adductor muscles. NSAID or local cortisone injections can give short-term relief. Surgery with correction of the mal-alignment (osteotomy of the bone and screw fixation in a straight position) is indicated in severe and progressive cases and has excellent outcomes. Full weight bearing is usually allowed at an early stage.

REFERRALS Refer to podiatrist or physiotherapist for mild symptoms and to orthopaedic foot surgeon if severe or deteriorating symptoms and severe mal-alignment.

EXERCISE PRESCRIPTION Rest will not help, so allow all kinds of sporting activities using well-fitting shoes. If pain is aggravated on impact suggest cycling, swimming or similar low-impact sports as alternative to running and jumping sports.

DIFFERENTIAL DIAGNOSES Osteoarthitis that usually does not give the typical deformation.

EVALUATION OF TREATMENT OUTCOMES Monitor the decrease of clinical symptoms and signs, the pain should disappear and a new X-ray should be normal, with healed osteotomy, six to twelve weeks after surgery. The screw that fixes the osteotomy can be removed later if symptoms occur.

PROGNOSIS Excellent with appropriate treatment. Untreated hallux valgus can lead to severe mal-alignment, MTP I osteoarthritis and pain. If the bone becomes too osteoporotic, surgery may be difficult.

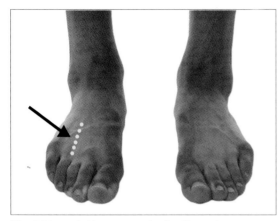

Fig. 6 Morton's Neuroma typically affects the nerve between MTIII and MTIV

SYMPTOMS Sharp radiating exercise-induced pain or dysaestesia between two metatarsal bones, most often between MT III and MT IV, without obvious preceding trauma. There are often bilateral symptoms. Usually it occurs in adults and particularly in middle-aged recreational athletes who wear tight shoes.

AETIOLOGY This syndrome is caused by entrapment of an inter-digital nerve between two metatarsal bones arising from a local neuroma or synovitis.

CLINICAL FINDINGS There is distinct tenderness on palpation and a positive Tinel's sign. Squeeze test is positive. Squeezing the toes together while holding the metatarsals parallel causes a typical local sharp pain reaction.

INVESTIGATIONS Injection of 1-2 ml of local anaesthetic around the tender spot gives immediate pain relief. MRI can confirm the diagnosis and its cause.

TREATMENT Initially try orthotics to support and lift the anterior foot arch. NSAID or local cortisone injections can give short-term relief. Surgery for excision of the neuroma is indicated in severe cases and shows excellent outcomes. However, the patient will then lose sensation in the area distal to the neuroma, which could be slightly disabling. Surgery is done as a day case and full weight bearing is often allowed within two to four weeks.

REFERRALS Refer to podiatrist or physiotherapist for mild symptoms and to orthopaedic surgeon if the symptoms are severe or progressing.

EXERCISE PRESCRIPTION Rest will not help so allow all kinds of sporting activities using well-fitting shoes.

DIFFERENTIAL DIAGNOSES Stress fracture of metatarsal with synovitis.

EVALUATION OF TREATMENT OUTCOMES Monitor a decrease of clinical symptoms and signs. Tinel's sign and Squeeze test should be negative.

PROGNOSIS Good-Fair. The pain, which disappears with treatment, is replaced with lack of sensation, which some athletes retrospectively feel is worse than the initial pain.

Fig. 7 Palpating the insertion of the plantar fascia while stretching the toe extensors causes sharp localised pain. This is a positive Plantar Fasciitis test

SYMPTOMS There is increasing sharp or aching localised pain around the insertion of the plantar fascia at the anterior inferior part of the calcaneus, without preceding trauma. This condition commonly occurs in middle-aged athletes who run or jump repeatedly on the forefoot but is also common in manual workers who stand on hard surfaces in poor shoes.

AETIOLOGY The aetiology is unclear but in the literature a chronic inflammatory process from overuse/stress to the insertion is often suggested. Strangely, when biopsies are taken from operated fasciitis there are no inflammatory cells. The name of this condition could thus be challenged.

CLINICAL FINDINGS There is intense localised tenderness on palpation over the insertion, which is aggravated on extension of the plantar fascia by **dorsi-flexion** of the ankle and the toe extensors.

INVESTIGATIONS X-ray often shows a bony spur in chronic cases, which is not correlated to the symptoms but rather indicates a chronic reaction caused by repetitive strain to the insertion.

TREATMENT Initially try orthotics to support the foot arch, which provides improved shock absorption/padding of the insertion area combined with stretching of the plantar fascia. NSAID or local cortisone injections can give short-term relief. Surgery is seldom indicated.

REFERRALS Refer to podiatrist and physiotherapist for mild symptoms and sports physician if the symptoms are severe.

EXERCISE PRESCRIPTION Rest will not help so allow all kinds of sporting activities, with well-fitting shoes. If there is pain on impact, suggest low-impact alternatives such as cycling and swimming.

EVALUATION OF TREATMENT OUTCOMES
Monitor the decrease of clinical symptoms and signs. Symptoms can last for one to two years.

DIFFERENTIAL DIAGNOSES A plantar fascia rupture can give the same symptoms and occur on the same location but with sudden onset and collapse of the foot arch. Ultrasound or MRI can help to differentiate. This condition occurs either while landing from a jump or in a running stride and is often associated with a previous cortisone injection for plantar fasciitis. Tarsal tunnel syndrome can cause radiating pain from nerve branches below the medial malleoli towards the insertion of the plantar fascia. Often the Tinel's sign is positive and local anaesthetic injected around the Tarsal tunnel (not the plantar fascia insertion) immediately relieves symptoms.

PROGNOSIS Excellent but with long duration of symptoms.

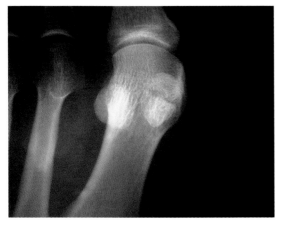

Fig. 8 Sesam bone fractures are uncommon but very difficult to treat

SYMPTOMS There is gradually increasing exercise-induced pain and swelling around and below MTP I or diffuse pain in the forefoot on forefoot landings and running.

AETIOLOGY This injury is usually caused by excessive direct impact from landing on the forefoot on hard surfaces.

CLINICAL FINDINGS There is distinct tenderness on palpation over the medial or lateral sesam bones during forced dorsi-flexion of toe extensors. Jumping and landing on the forefoot is very painful.

INVESTIGATIONS X-ray is often normal until later stages or if avascular necrosis or sclerosis occurs. MRI may show oedema in and around the sesam bone and occasionally, in late stages, avascular necrosis. CT scans can sometimes show the fracture line.

TREATMENT Initially try orthotics or soft padding to take the load off the sesam bones. NSAID or local cortisone injections can give short-term relief. Surgery for excision of the fractured fragments or of the fractured bone may be necessary.

REFERRALS Refer to podiatrist or physiotherapist for mild symptoms and to orthopaedic foot surgeon if symptoms become severe.

EXERCISE PRESCRIPTION Rest will not help so allow all kinds of sporting activities using well-fitting shoes and avoiding impact to the forefoot. Suggest low-impact activities such as cycling and swimming.

EVALUATION OF TREATMENT OUTCOMES Monitor decrease of clinical symptoms and signs.

PROGNOSIS Excellent if treated appropriately but duration of symptoms can be long after surgery.

7. STRESS FRACTURES OF THE FOOT

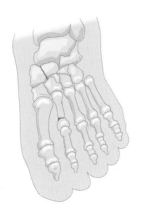

Fig. 9 Navicular bone stress fractures can be career threatening

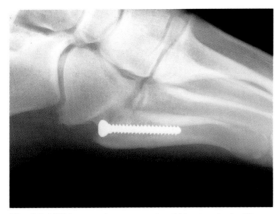

Fig. 10 MT V stress fractures should be treated with caution, since healing is often prolonged and this injury often requires surgery

SYMPTOMS There is increasing localised pain over a bony prominence, often with no direct preceding trauma. The start of symptoms can be acute. There is often a history of suddenly increased training intensity or jumping or running on hard surfaces. A number of famous footballers' metatarsal stress fractures have figured in the media over the last few years.

AETIOLOGY A stress fracture is preceded by an imbalance in impact/loading and adaptive bone turnover. 'Too much too soon' is the typical cause in the healthy young athlete; in elderly athletes osteo-porosis may play a role; in younger athletes who have been temporarily immobilised inactivity-related osteopenia can play a role.

INVESTIGATIONS X-ray confirms the diagnosis around three weeks from onset when there is callus formation. MRI and bone scans pick up this injury within a few days from onset and can be recom-mended in unclear cases.

TREATMENT Initially modify the training avoid-ing or decreasing impact to the foot. The location of the stress fracture is important for outcomes. There are a few stress fractures that need to be treated with utmost caution: MT V, the Navicular bone and talus, calcaneus and sesam bone fractures adjacent to MTP I. These may need immobilisation or some-times surgery. Most other stress fractures, unless with underlying bone problems, will heal within six to twelve weeks by just modifying activities.

REFERRALS Refer to podiatrist and physiotherapist for mild symptoms and to orthopaedic foot surgeon if stress fractures on the above locations.

EXERCISE PRESCRIPTION Rest will not help so allow all kinds of sporting activities using well-fitting shoes and decrease impact to fractured area. A non-weight-bearing boot can be used temporarily. If there is pain on impact, suggest cycling, water exercises or swimming as alternatives to running and jumping sports.

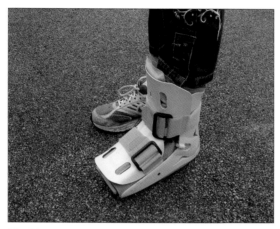

Fig. 11 A range of boots is commercially available for stability or 'non weight-bearing'

EVALUATION OF TREATMENT OUTCOMES

Monitor the decrease of clinical symptoms and signs and take an X-ray six to twelve weeks after onset to monitor healing. Beware the risk of avascular necrosis or non-union in bones with persistent symptoms. These injuries often require surgery and can be career-threatening.

DIFFERENTIAL DIAGNOSES Skeletal tumours often present with resting pain, night pain and general feeling of unease. X-rays usually detect such tumours; osteoporotic fractures or suspected bone tumours should always be referred to an orthopaedic specialist. All stress fractures in anorexic young athletes should be referred to psychologists and other specialists in this condition. Usually an anorexic athlete's stress fractures affect the flat bones (pelvis, spine, etc) first. If there are general signs of infection or previous surgery in the affected area, rule out bone infections, such as osteomyelitis.

PROGNOSIS Excellent in most cases but some cases may be career-threatening with or without surgery.

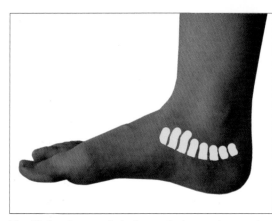

Fig. 12 Persistent pain in the marked area after previous sprain can be caused by this syndrome

SYMPTOMS There is increasing stiffness or sense of instability combined with diffuse aching pain around and below the talo-tibial ankle joint, often occurring after previous sprain.

AETIOLOGY The aetiology is unclear but the trauma may have caused structural damage to the region that can be missed.

CLINICAL FINDINGS There is tenderness on palpation over the sub-talar joint (sinus tarsi) during forced inversion. Occasionally there is a combined sub-talar and tibio-talar laxity that makes the diagnosis difficult.

INVESTIGATIONS X-ray is often normal. MRI may show oedema and swelling in the sub-talar joint.

TREATMENT Initially try orthotics to support the foot arch. NSAID or local cortisone injections can give short-term relief. Surgery is seldom indicated.

REFERRALS Refer to podiatrist or physiotherapist for mild symptoms and to orthopaedic surgeon if there are severe or progressing symptoms.

EXERCISE PRESCRIPTION Rest will not help so allow all kinds of sporting activities, using well-fitting shoes and avoiding impact. If there is pain on impact suggest non-impact activities such as cycling and swimming as alternatives.

EVALUATION OF TREATMENT OUTCOMES Monitor the decrease of clinical symptoms and signs.

DIFFERENTIAL DIAGNOSES Tarsal coalition; tumour (X-ray and MRI will differentiate); stress fracture (X-ray and MRI will differentiate); osteomyelitis (signs of infection, fever, positive blood tests for CRP, ESR); OCD (X-ray and MRI will differentiate); osteid osteoma (X-ray and MRI will differentiate).

PROGNOSIS Good-Fair. The symptoms can be prolonged with or without surgery.

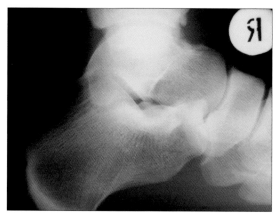

Fig. 13 Coalition between two nearby bones in this area can cause pain and stiffness, severely affecting jumping and running

SYMPTOMS There is diffuse exercise-induced aching pain around the sub-talar joint, sometimes after previous sprain.

AETIOLOGY The aetiology is unclear. Sub-talar structures fuse over time by fibrosis or callus formation.

CLINICAL FINDINGS There is tenderness on palpation over the sub-talar joint (sinus tarsi), decreased mobility and swelling.

INVESTIGATIONS X-ray may show talo-navicular coalition; talo-calcaneal coalition requires MRI or CT scans.

TREATMENT Initially try orthotics to support the foot arch. NSAID or local cortisone injections can give short-term relief.

REFERRALS Refer to podiatrist or physiotherapist for mild symptoms and to orthopaedic surgeon if symptoms are severe. Surgery may involve fusing the joints or excision of fibrosis but is not always successful.

EXERCISE PRESCRIPTION Rest will not help so allow all kinds of sporting activities, using well-fitting shoes and avoiding impact. If there is pain on impact suggest low-impact activities such as cycling and swimming.

EVALUATION OF TREATMENT OUTCOMES Monitor the decrease of clinical symptoms and signs.

DIFFERENTIAL DIAGNOSES Tumour (X-ray and MRI will differentiate); Stress fracture (X-ray and MRI will differentiate); Sub-talar pain syndrome.

PROGNOSIS Good-Fair with or without surgery.

10. TURF TOE

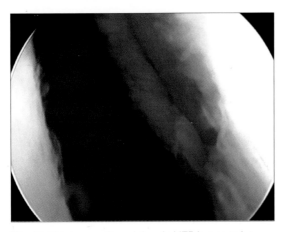

Fig. 14 This is a cartilage injury in MTP I as seen by arthroscopy. A typical cause of turf-toe syndrome

SYMPTOMS There is a gradually increasing stiffness and diffuse aching pain around MTP I. Commonly affects team sports players who wear studded shoes.

AETIOLOGY Common theories include repetitive minor trauma to the capsule and cartilage of MTP I from ill-fitting shoes, direct impact and playing on hard turf with shoes that get stuck. The name refers to an injury that dramatically increased in frequency when new artifical turf on all-weather football pitches became common.

CLINICAL FINDINGS There is tenderness on palpation, swelling, effusion and redness over MTP I. Decreased active and passive flexion and extension of MTP I.

INVESTIGATIONS X-ray is often normal in early stages but can later show bony intra-articular fragments. MRI may show effusion, oedema and swelling around MTP I.

TREATMENT Initially try orthotics and stretching of the structures around MTP I. NSAID or local cortisone injections can give short-term relief.

REFERRALS Refer to podiatrist and physiotherapist for mild symptoms and to orthopaedic foot surgeon if symptoms become severe. Surgery can be carried out, arthroscopically, to remove loose intra-articular bodies and **debride** the joint.

EXERCISE PRESCRIPTION Rest will not help so allow all kinds of sporting activities, using well-fitting shoes and avoiding impact. If there is pain on impact suggest low-impact activities such as cycling and swimming.

EVALUATION OF TREATMENT OUTCOMES Monitor the decrease of clinical symptoms and signs.

DIFFERENTIAL DIAGNOSES Stress fracture of sesam bones below MTP I (X-ray or MRI can differentiate); Hallux rigidus (X-ray and clinical picture differentiate).

PROGNOSIS Excellent-Good but there can be long duration of symptoms.

EXERCISE ON PRESCRIPTION DURING INJURY TO THE FOOT

This table provides advice on forms of exercise that may or may not be recommended for athletes with different injuries. The advice must be related to the severity and stage of healing and take the individual's situation into account.

- ⚫ This activity is harmful or risky.
- 🔘 This activity can be done but with care and with specific advice.
- ⚪ This activity can safely be recommended.

	Running	Walking	Water exercises	Bicycling	Racket sports	Golf	Contact sports	Working-out	Home exercises
HALLUX RIGIDUS	⚫	⚪	⚪	⚪	⚪	⚪	⚪	⚪	⚪
HALLUX VALGUS	⚫	⚪	⚪	⚪	⚪	⚪	⚪	⚪	⚪
FRACTURE OF METATARSAL BONES	⚫	🔘	⚪	⚪	⚫	⚪	⚫	⚪	⚪
MORTON'S NEUROMA	⚪	⚪	⚪	⚪	⚪	⚪	⚪	⚪	⚪
PLANTAR FASCIITIS	⚫	⚪	⚪	⚪	⚫	⚪	⚪	⚪	⚪
SESAM BONE STRESS FRACTURES	⚫	🔘	⚪	⚪	⚫	⚪	⚫	⚪	⚪
STRESS FRACTURES OF THE FOOT	⚫	⚪	🔘	⚪	⚫	⚪	⚪	⚪	⚪
SUB-TALAR IN STABILITY AND PAIN	⚪	⚪	⚪	⚪	⚪	⚪	⚪	⚪	⚪
TARSAL COALITION	⚪	⚪	⚪	⚪	⚪	⚪	⚪	⚪	⚪
TURF TOE	⚪	⚪	⚪	⚪	⚪	⚪	⚪	⚪	⚪

ii ANKLE INJURIES

Ankle injuries are among the most common injuries in sport. 'Ankle sprain' (which is a mechanism rather than a diagnosis) is the most common injury in virtually all epidemiological studies. Being the first part of the kinetic chain to withstand the impact of running, twisting, pushing off and landing, the ankle and foot must, within fractions of a second, distribute the impact higher up the chain in complex flexion, extension, eversion and inversion movements of the talo-crural joint and supination and pronation at the mid-foot. The faster the movement, the more important is the balancing act and proprioceptive function of the ankle. In contact sports, such as soccer and rugby, direct impact injuries from studded shoes or opponents' legs are very common.

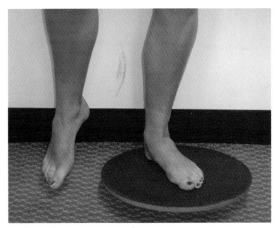

Fig. 15 Proprioceptive skills and core stability are essential to prevent and rehabilitate ankle injuries

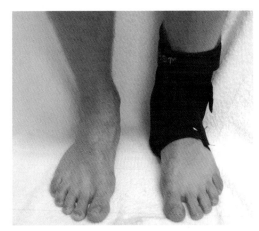

Fig. 16 Ankle braces are useful in prevention and reha- bilitation, but cannot replace functional training

SPECIFIC TRAINING AFTER INJURY TO THE FOOT OR ANKLE

In principle, training should include strength and flexibility training in flexion, extension (dorsi-flexion), pronation and supination and proprioceptive training on wobble boards or trampettes and functional train- ing, including running, side-stepping, jumping and landing exercises. Temporary strapping or bracing may be needed. A functional ankle-scoring system adapted to the sport in question can be used to evaluate when rehabilitation is complete and return to sport is safe, by comparing the injured and non-injured sides.

TRAINING OF THE LOWER LEG MUSCLES

Injuries to the lower leg or immobilisation of the ankle joint often lead to atrophy of the lower leg muscles and reduced power output in ankle plantar flexion with straight knee (m gastrocnemius) and with flexed knee (m soleus, m tibialis posterior, m flexor hallucis longus, m flexor digitorum longus) and in dorsi-flexion (m tibialis anterior and m extensor digitorum). The lower leg muscles are of vital importance for activities like jumping, running on hard surfaces and most ball sports. Strength training of the calf muscles can be performed with toe raises in standing or sitting positions, with both straight and flexed knees.

Muscle endurance can be trained by cycling with the pedal under the forefoot, with a high saddle (m gastrocnemius), with a low saddle (m soleus and other deep flexors), with a step machine, on a treadmill or in a cross-trainer.

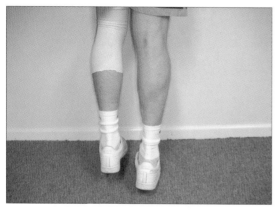

Fig. 17 Toe raises with straight knee predominantly train the gastrocnemius muscles

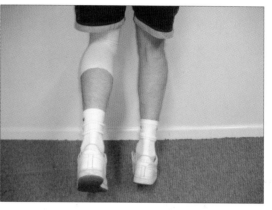

Fig. 18 Toe raises with flexed knee predominantly train the deep plantar flexors and the soleus muscle

Fig. 19 Stretching of the calf muscles does not require specific equipment (straight knee for gastrocnemius, flexed knee for soleus muscle)

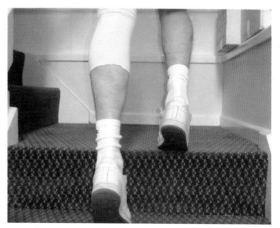

Fig. 20 A simple step-up test can be valuable for testing endurance, strength and function

Fig. 21 A stationary bike is an essential tool in all rehabilitation

Flexibility can be achieved by stretching of the calf muscles and is performed standing, with a flexed knee for m soleus and other deep flexors or a straight knee for m gastrocnemius.

Proprioceptive training can be done with classical ballet training at a *barre* or by using a more demanding standing surface, such as a wobble board. This training is essential, as different parts of the Achilles tendon and the calf muscles are being trained during different parts of the ankle movement.

Functional training of the calf muscle should be done individually depending on the patient's needs.

The figures below show the anatomical appearances of the ankle from different angles, with arrows indicating the locations of symptoms of the injuries.

This chapter deals with some of the more common ankle injuries but it should be stressed that there are a number of other injuries that require specialist advice from a foot surgeon or podiatrist.

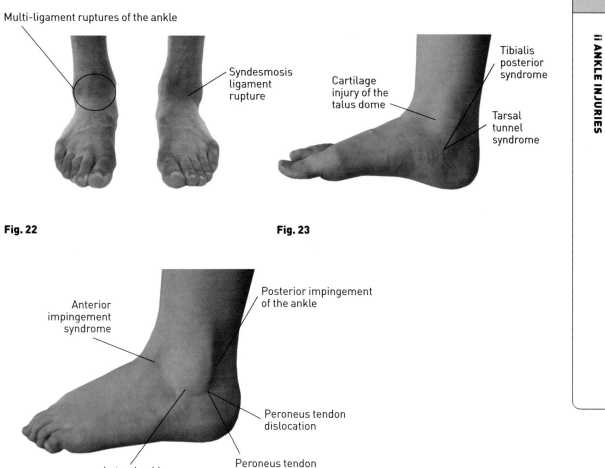

Multi-ligament ruptures of the ankle

Syndesmosis ligament rupture

Fig. 22

Cartilage injury of the talus dome

Tibialis posterior syndrome

Tarsal tunnel syndrome

Fig. 23

Anterior impingement syndrome

Posterior impingement of the ankle

Peroneus tendon dislocation

Peroneus tendon rupture

Lateral ankle ligament ruptures

Fig. 24

1. ANTERIOR IMPINGEMENT SYNDROME

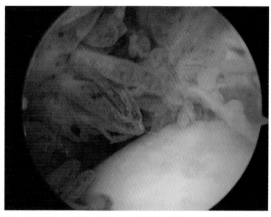

Fig. 25 View of the talocrural joint where synovitis causes anterior impingement and pain

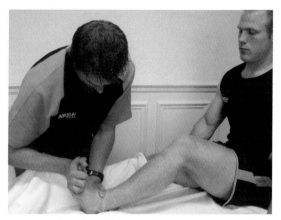

Fig. 26 Pain on forced dorsiflexion while compressing the anterior compartment of the ankle is a positive anterior impingement test

SYMPTOMS There is a gradually increasing stiffness of the ankle and exercise-induced pain around the anterior part of the ankle joint, often after previous sprain.

AETIOLOGY Impingement syndrome is not a diagnosis but a symptom and may be caused by repetitive trauma to the anterior ankle joint, for example from striking footballs, recurrent sprains causing fibrosis or chondral damage, or be secondary to a chondral injury to the talus dome or caused by loose bodies. Several underlying pathoanatomical factors can cause impingement, including loose bodies, fibrosis, chondral flap tears, synovitis and impinging soft tissue flaps.

CLINICAL FINDINGS There is effusion and localised tenderness on palpation over the anterior talus dome during forced dorsi-flexion while compressing the extensor tendons and capsule. This is the 'anterior impingement test'.

INVESTIGATIONS X-ray can show intra-articular loose bodies or osteophytes. MRI may show sub-chondral oedema of the talus and effusion. Clinical findings and

patient history are more important for clinical decisions. MRI often misses superficial cartilage injuries.

TREATMENT NSAID can give short-term relief, as can intra-articular cortisone injections. If there are persistent or severe symptoms, arthroscopy with debriding and excision of impinged structures is recommended and curative.

REFERRALS Refer to orthopaedic ankle surgeon for consideration of arthroscopy.

EXERCISE PRESCRIPTION Rest will not help so allow all kinds of sporting activities using well-fitting shoes. If there is pain on impact suggest low-impact activities such as cycling and swimming.

EVALUATION OF TREATMENT OUTCOMES Monitor decrease of clinical symptoms and signs. The anterior impingement test should be negative.

DIFFERENTIAL DIAGNOSES As mentioned above, several underlying problems can cause impingement, including loose bodies, fibrosis, chondral flap tears, synovitis or impinging soft tissue flaps.

PROGNOSIS Excellent if treated properly.

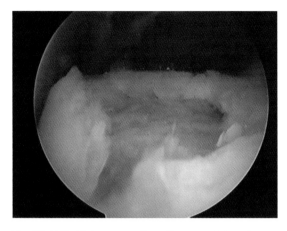

Fig. 27 Full-thickness cartilage flap tear of the talus dome, as seen by arthroscopy

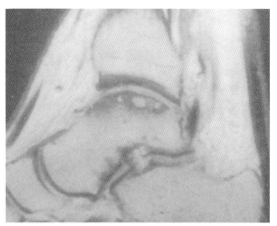

Fig. 28 MRI often under-represents or does not reveal superficial cartilage tears of the ankle but sub-chondral oedema and cystic formations (as above) should raise this suspicion

SYMPTOMS The patient presents with stiffness, diffuse exercise-induced aching or occasional sharp pain, clicking, locking and effusion of the ankle joint, most often after a severe previous sprain or recurrent instability.

AETIOLOGY The aetiology is direct or indirect trauma to the talus dome cartilage, often occurring in contact sports like soccer and rugby. This is the most common cause for ankle pain persisting for more than three weeks after an ankle sprain.

CLINICAL FINDINGS There is effusion and tenderness on palpation over the talus dome. Plantar flexion provides better access to the dome. Sometimes the anterior impingement test is positive. Occasionally there is combined pain and instability of the ankle joint after a previous sprain that makes the diagnosis difficult. Instability from insufficient lateral ligaments seldom causes pain, however when the syndesmosis ligament is damaged pain can be the predominant symptom.

INVESTIGATIONS X-ray is often normal. MRI may show sub-chondral oedema and effusion in the joint but cartilage injuries are often missed on MRI. When there is a bony component (osteochondral injury) MRI often underestimates the extent of the injury.

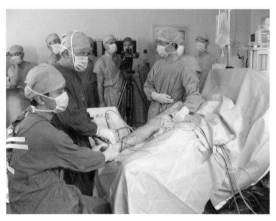

Fig. 29 Arthroscopy of the ankle can be done as an outpatient procedure and is very useful in diagnosing and treating inter-articular ankle injuries

TREATMENT NSAID can give short-term relief but arthroscopy is usually indicated and curative. Loose bodies are excised, cartilage defects are trimmed and underlying bone is sometimes micro-fractured. Direct weight bearing is usually allowed.

REFERRALS Refer to podiatrist and physiotherapist for mild symptoms and to orthopaedic ankle surgeon if symptoms are severe or when there is persistent pain, effusion and the above signs more than one month after a severe ankle sprain.

EXERCISE PRESCRIPTION Rest will not help so allow all kinds of sporting activities using well-fitting shoes and avoiding impact. If there is pain on impact suggest low-impact activities such as cycling and swimming.

EVALUATION OF TREATMENT OUTCOMES Monitor decrease of clinical symptoms and signs.

DIFFERENTIAL DIAGNOSES OCD, which has a typical appearance on MRI but is treated in the same manner, with arthroscopy.

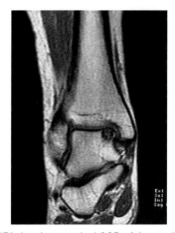

Fig. 30 MRI showing a typical OCD of the medial talus dome which usually requires surgery

PROGNOSIS Excellent-Good. Osteoarthritis of the ankle joint after mild to moderate cartilage injuries is rare.

SYMPTOMS The patient refers to a sudden sharp tearing pain around the lateral aspect of the ankle joint after an acute inversion sprain or, on occasions, of recurrent instability after previous sprains.

not required for the diagnosis, but rather to rule out associated injuries to other major structures.

TREATMENT After an acute sprain rest, ice, compression, elevation (RICE) is advocated. Early proprio-

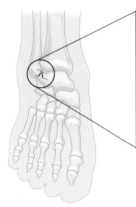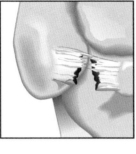

Fig. 31 Anterior view of the ankle, illustrating the anterior talofibular ligament (ATFL)

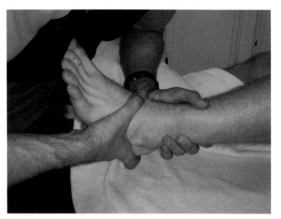

Fig. 32 Anterior drawer test (ATFL rupture); tibia is fixed with one hand, the other hand grips as shown and pulls the foot anteriorly. If there is increased laxity and no distinct endpoint the test is positive

AETIOLOGY The anterior talo-fibular (ATF) and fibulo-calcanear (FC) ligaments are the most commonly damaged structures in uncomplicated inversion-plantar flexion ankle sprain. Most of these ruptures heal well within three months but recurrent instability develops in around 20 per cent of cases.

CLINICAL FINDINGS After an acute episode there is tenderness on palpation over the lateral ligaments, localised bruising or swelling and/or haemarthrosis/ effusion of the joint if both ligaments rupture. Positive anterior drawer (ATF) and talar tilt (FC) tests are typical for these two ligament ruptures.

INVESTIGATIONS X-ray is often normal but should be taken to rule out fractures, in particular in growing athletes with open growth plates and in elderly athletes when osteoporosis is suspected. MRI may show localised oedema over the lateral ligaments though is

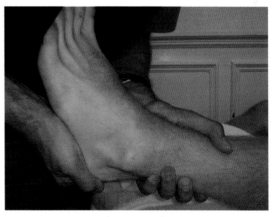

Fig. 33 Talar tilt test (FC rupture); tibia is fixed with one hand. The foot is tilted and translated medially with the other hand. If there is increased laxity and no distinct endpoint the test is positive. Compare with the other ankle

3. LATERAL ANKLE LIGAMENT RUPTURES *Cont.*

ceptive training and weight-bearing exercises are often recommended. Rehabilitation is usually curative and the athlete can resume sport within two to three weeks, occasionally using a brace or strapping during the first 12 weeks. If there is persistent pain or effusion after three weeks, suspect associated injuries to cartilage or other structures. Reconsider the pathoanatomical diagnosis.

REFERRALS Refer to physiotherapist for mild symptoms and to orthopaedic surgeon if there is severe pain or effusion persists for more than three weeks.

EXERCISE PRESCRIPTION Rest will not help so allow all kinds of non-impact sporting activities using well-fitting shoes. During the convalescence and early return to sport an ankle brace or strapping may be used. Suggest low-impact activities such as cycling and swimming.

EVALUATION OF TREATMENT OUTCOMES
Monitor decrease of clinical symptoms and signs. Anterior drawer and talar tilt tests should be negative. However it is important to differentiate joint laxity from joint instability. Thus, these two tests may well reflect increased laxity, while the player does not experience subjective or functional instability. Compare with the non-injured side. There are different functional tests for ankle stability for different kinds of sports.

Fig. 34 Strapping the ankle is very useful in the early period after returning to play, to avoid re-injury, but it cannot replace proper training

DIFFERENTIAL DIAGNOSES Syndesmosis ligament tear (positive syndesmosis test); intra-articular cartilage injuries (pain and effusion); dislocation or longitudinal tear of the **peroneus** tendons (positive peroneus test); MT V fracture (localised pain on palpation); infection (increased temperature); tumour (X-ray); inflammatory diseases (gout, rheumatoid arthritis, systemic diseases etc).

PROGNOSIS Usually excellent or good. More than 80 per cent of these injuries fully heal within a few weeks. Of the 20 per cent remaining, some may require surgery, but it is unlikely any will lead to long-term sequelae.

SYMPTOMS Almost immediate effusion/ haemarthrosis after severe inversion or eversion or hyper-extension/flexion sprain, sometimes complicated by direct impact from a block tackle, which is common in contact sports.

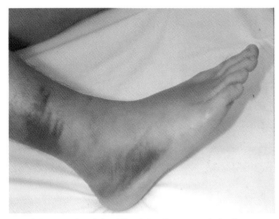

Fig. 35 Ankle bruising like this after a spain indicates a severe ligament injury or fracture, and also shows that acute compression and ice have not been applied

AEATIOLOGY This injury may cause ruptures of anterior talo-fibular and fibulo-calcanear ligaments in combination with deltoid or syndesmosis ligament ruptures or posterior capsule injuries with or without fracture of the ankle.

CLINICAL FINDINGS In the acute phase there is haemarthrosis and or bruising if the capsule has torn. There is tenderness on palpation over the affected ligaments. There is often a combination of positive tests, such as positive anterior drawer and talar tilt tests, combined with positive reverse talar tilt and syndesmosis tests. Often gross multidirectional laxity can be identified.

INVESTIGATIONS X-ray must be undertaken to rule out fracture but may be normal. MRI may miss

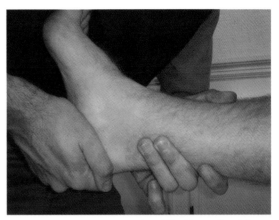

Fig. 36 If the calcaneus can be shifted laterally while fixating the lower leg, this indicates a deltoid ligament tear. This is a positive reverse talar tilt

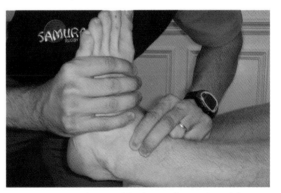

Fig. 37 If a forceful dorsiflexion and eversion of the ankle causes pain over the anterior syndesmosis that is palpated, it indicates injury to this very important stabiliser

the ligament injuries in the initial phase, due to extra- and intra-articular bleeding. This injury must be investigated through the mechanism of injury, the forces involved and clinical signs.

TREATMENT In the acute phase RICE, crutches and non-weight-bearing exercise should be advised until the extent of the injury is determined. Initial rehabilitation aims to control and reduce swelling to

4. MULTI-LIGAMENT RUPTURES OF THE ANKLE *Cont.*

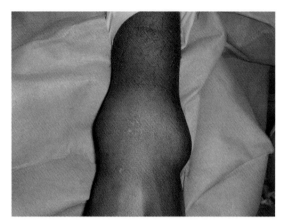

Fig. 38 This is the clinical apperance of an acute ankle injury with haemarthrosis, caused by a severe deltoid ligament and syndesmosis ligament tear, but no fracture

allow a thorough examination of the joint. Early arthroscopy and examination under anaesthesia is sometimes indicated, with or without surgical stabilisation of the affected ligaments. The deltoid and lateral ligaments often heal without surgery and can be dealt with at a later stage if symptoms persist. These injuries can take the athletes out from sport for 12 to 26 weeks. Occasionally they may need bracing or strapping during the first weeks after the return to sport. These injuries are often combined with intra-articular cartilage injuries that increase the need for early surgical intervention.

REFERRALS Preferably refer to orthopaedic surgeon directly after injury for detailed investigations and treatment.

EXERCISE PRESCRIPTION Immobilisation of the ankle in a non-weight-bearing boot is indicated for a number of weeks, with or without stabilising surgery. Therefore exercise must maintain general fitness of the rest of the body, before specific training of the injured leg can be allowed. Core stability exercises must be done whenever weight bearing is allowed.

EVALUATION OF TREATMENT OUTCOME Monitor decrease of clinical symptoms and signs. Normal clinical laxity tests of the ankle should result. Full strength, RoM and proprioception, compared with other leg should be expected. Functional ankle scores and core stability must be tested at the end of an often long rehabilitation period before resuming full sport.

DIFFERENTIAL DIAGNOSES Extra-articular injuries such as dislocation of peroneus tendons or fracture. Clinical picture, X-ray and MRI will differentiate.

PROGNOSIS Good-Poor. This can be a career-threatening injury.

SYMPTOMS In the acute phase, there is sharp pain and swelling/bruising over the lateral, posterior part of the ankle and distal fibula, after previous sprain. The patient will have a sense of weakness and instability of the ankle and may recall one or two snapping sounds from the time of the injury. If there was one snap, it may be a tear. If there were two, dislocation and reposition of the tendon should be suspected.

AETIOLOGY The peroneus brevis and/or longus can dislocate over the tip of the lateral malleoli from its groove during an inversion-plantar flexion ankle sprain. In the acute situation, a tear of the overlying retinaculum will cause sharp pain and a snapping sound and the tendons can rupture longitudinally while dislocating over the malleoli. The dislocation can be permanent but often the tendons reposition themselves spontaneously, which makes the diagnosis difficult.

CLINICAL FINDINGS There is distinct tenderness on palpation posterior to the tip of the lateral malleoli over the peroneus retinaculum and localised bruising and swelling, sometimes effusion. Rarely, the dislocated tendon can be palpated on the lateral malleoli.

INVESTIGATIONS X-ray is normal. MRI may show localised oedema and swelling over the lateral retinaculum or occasionally a tear in one of the tendons. Longitudinal tendon ruptures may be difficult to see unless there is a complete tear, which is very unusual in athletes. Ultrasound examination is very valuable, since a dynamic assessment is possible and subluxation can be provoked by plantar flexion-eversion.

TREATMENT In the acute phase RICE is advocated. An athlete with a dislocated tendon can hardly walk. Early proprioceptive training and weight-bearing exercise is sometimes allowed. Rehabilitation is usually curative and the athlete can resume sport

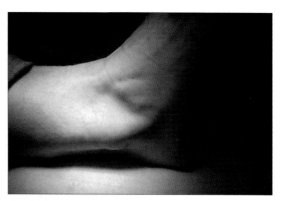

Fig. 39 This photo demonstrates a dislocated peroneus tendon which has to be repositioned and surgically repaired

within two to three weeks, occasionally using a brace or strapping for the first six to twelve weeks. In professional athletes with high demands, surgery may be indicated, including inspection and treatment of ruptures and fixing of the retinaculum, since chronic subluxations can disable the athlete for a long time. Six to twelve weeks after surgery, the athlete can return to sport, using a brace.

REFERRALS Refer to an orthopaedic ankle surgeon for early consideration of surgery or immobilisation preferably while the injury is acute or within two weeks.

EXERCISE PRESCRIPTION Rest will not help so allow all kinds of sporting activities using well-fitting shoes but avoiding impact, such as running and jumping.

EVALUATION OF TREATMENT OUTCOMES Monitor decrease of clinical symptoms and signs.

DIFFERENTIAL DIAGNOSES Syndesmosis ligament tear (positive syndesmosis test); MT V fracture (tenderness on palpation, positive X-ray; Fibula fracture (positive X-ray).

PROGNOSIS Excellent-Good.

6. PERONEUS TENDON RUPTURE

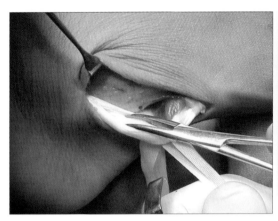

Fig. 40 Surgical presentation of peroneus tendon rupture

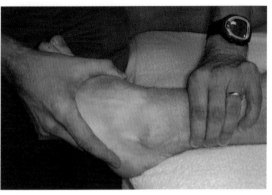

Fig. 41 Peroneus tendon strength can be tested by asking the patient to do a resisted plantar flexion and eversion. Compare with the other side

SYMPTOMS The patient presents with a history of sharp pain over the lateral posterior part of the ankle joint, often mistaken for a sprain. Sometimes the athlete refers to a 'pop' when the tendon ruptures or dislocates. Two snaps are typical for dislocation-repositioning.

AETIOLOGY Peroneus tendon rupture is uncommon in young athletes but can occur if previous cortisone injections have weakened the tendon. A complete rupture is usually associated with degeneration in systemic diseases such as diabetes with arthropathy or after cortisone treatment. Usually one of the two tendons (brevis or longus) is intact, which makes the diagnosis even more difficult.

CLINICAL FINDINGS There is tenderness on palpation over the peroneus retinaculum or along the peroneus tendon and weakness on a resistance test with active plantar flexion-inversion. Compare with the other ankle.

INVESTIGATIONS MRI or ultrasound may show localised swelling and can often identify a rupture.

TREATMENT In the acute phase RICE is advocated. Surgery is usually required to repair a ruptured tendon followed by eight to twelve weeks partial immobilisation.

REFERRALS Refer to orthopaedic surgeon for consideration of surgery.

EXERCISE PRESCRIPTION Rest will not help so allow all kinds of sporting activities using well-fitting shoes and avoiding impact. A brace restricting plantar flexion and eversion-inversion can be used, allowing weight bearing but protecting the repair.

EVALUATION OF TREATMENT OUTCOMES Monitor decrease of clinical symptoms and signs. Regained strength in plantar flexion-inversion and proprioception should be monitored. Compare with other ankle.

DIFFERENTIAL DIAGNOSES Syndesmosis ligament tear (positive syndesmosis test), dislocation of peroneus tendons; MT V fracture or lateral malleoli fracture (positive X-ray).

PROGNOSIS Excellent-Good, but the delay in diagnosis is often substantial leading to a long convalescence.

SYMPTOMS There is a gradually increasing stiffness of the ankle and exercise-induced pain around the posterior part of the ankle joint, sometimes after previous sprain. This injury often affects footballers and ballet dancers.

AETIOLOGY Impingement syndrome is not a diagnosis but a symptom and may be caused by repetitive injury to the posterior ankle joint, for example from repetitive plantar flexions striking footballs or dancing on tiptoe thus compressing the posterior compartment. Several underlying pathoanatomical factors can cause posterior impingement, including fibrosis, synovitis or an Os Trigonum.

CLINICAL FINDINGS There is sometimes effusion and localised tenderness on palpation over the posterior ankle deep in front of the Achilles tendon. It is provoked during forced plantar-flexion.

INVESTIGATIONS X-ray can show an Os Trigonum. MRI may show soft tissue oedema sometimes around the Os Trigonum.

TREATMENT Orthotics and adjustment in techniques may be tried. NSAID can give short-term relief, as can a local cortisone injection. If there are persistent or severe symptoms, surgery with excision of impinged structures is recommended and curative.

REFERRALS Refer to orthopaedic surgeon in difficult cases.

EXERCISE PRESCRIPTION Rest will not help so allow all kinds of sporting activities using well-fitting shoes. If there is pain on impact suggest low-impact activities such as cycling and swimming.

EVALUATION OF TREATMENT OUTCOMES Monitor decrease of clinical symptoms and signs.

DIFFERENTIAL DIAGNOSES Several underlying problems can cause posterior impingement, including loose bodies, fibrosis, chondral flap tears, synovitis or impinging soft tissue flaps or conditions around the Achilles tendon such as bursitis or tendinosis.

PROGNOSIS Excellent if treated properly.

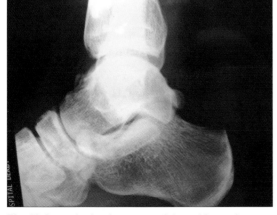

Fig. 42 Posterior impingement of the ankle can be caused by an inflamed area around the Os Trigonum

8. SYNDESMOSIS LIGAMENT RUPTURE

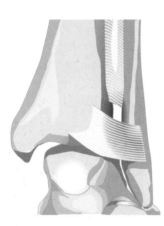

Fig. 43 Syndesmosis ligament tear, anatomic view

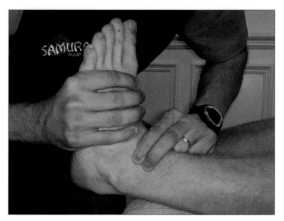

Fig. 44 If a forceful dorsiflexion and eversion of the ankle causes pain over the anterior syndesmosis that is palpated, it indicates injury to this very important stabiliser

SYMPTOMS There is a severe sharp pain around the anterior tibio fibula junction, haemarthrosis and sense of ankle instability after a severe hyperflexion-inversion or eversion ankle sprain. A player cannot continue and will limp off the pitch. This injury is well-known in association with a fracture but occurs frequently in isolation in contact sports such as football and rugby.

AETIOLOGY There is an anterior, mid and posterior portion of the syndesmosis ligament, the midportion being the interosseous membrane. All these structures can be damaged individually or in combination. Even though these injuries are fairly rare they must not be missed.

CLINICAL FINDINGS There is tenderness on palpation over the anterior syndesmosis ligament and bruising/swelling-haemarthrosis. There is an increased laxity which is sometimes mistaken for positive anterior drawer and talar tilt tests. Perform a forced dorsi-flexion and eversion while palpating the anterior syndesmosis. Pain indicates a positive syndesmosis test and a tear

of the ligament. If there is a complete tear of the three structures, the fibula can be translated both anteriorly and posteriorly without resistance holding fibula between the thumb and index finger.

INVESTIGATIONS X-ray is often normal unless taken in the weight-bearing position when there is a complete rupture of all three components. MRI may show localised oedema and effusion over the syndesmosis ligament but as a static examination it cannot fully show the extent of the instability that this injury causes. Clinical findings are most import.

TREATMENT In the acute phase RICE and non-weight bearing is advocated until the full extent of the injury is defined. A non-weight-bearing boot or crutches with non-weight-bearing should be used. In partial ruptures, proprioceptive training and partial weight-bearing exercises are often allowed after four to six weeks. Rehabilitation is usually curative

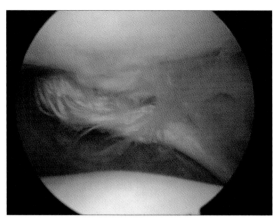

Fig. 45 Arthroscopic photo of a ruptured posterior syndesmosis ligament

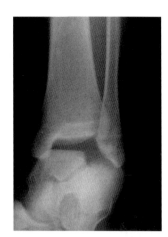

Fig. 46 This is a weight-bearing X-ray of a missed syndesmosis ligament tear causing severe dysfunction and pain two years after injury, requiring major reconstructive surgery

in mild cases and the athlete can resume sport within eight to twelve weeks, using a brace or strapping during the first weeks. In complete ruptures and multi-ligament injuries, surgery to stabilise the ligament, followed by a few weeks immobilisation, is usually necessary. In such cases six months absence from sport can be expected.

REFERRALS Refer to orthopaedic surgeon as soon as possible after the injury for consideration of surgery.

EXERCISE PRESCRIPTION Since non-weight bearing is advocated for a long period, exercise should focus on general low-impact fitness training until healed.

EVALUATION OF TREATMENT OUTCOMES

Monitor decrease of clinical symptoms and signs and negative laxity tests. At the end of rehabilitation core stability and functional ankle tests must be done before resuming full sport.

DIFFERENTIAL DIAGNOSES Fracture (X-ray will exclude).

PROGNOSIS Excellent-Good if appropriate treatment is given but long-term consequences can be dire if the diagnosis is missed.

9. TARSAL TUNNEL SYNDROME

SYMPTOMS There is aching or sharp pain around the medial part of the foot and ankle joint, often radiating along the medial or the lateral part of the foot, or towards the plantar fascia insertion.

AETIOLOGY This syndrome is caused by trapping of the posterior tibia nerve or any of its branches in the tarsal tunnel, most often after scarring from trauma. Other non-traumatic aetiology, such as varicose veins, neuroma or tumours, may also trap the nerve.

CLINICAL FINDINGS There is tenderness on palpation over the tarsal tunnel and a positive Tinel's sign is typical. Dysaestesia along the nerve branch distribution is also a common finding.

INVESTIGATIONS X-ray is usually normal. MRI may show localised oedema in or around the tarsal tunnel and may, if present, identify some causes for the entrapment such as varicose veins or tumours. Nerve conduction tests can show decreased nerve conduction in chronic cases but can be normal in early cases.

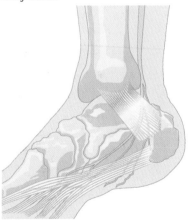

Fig. 47 Tarsal tunnel syndrome, medial view

TREATMENT Direct friction over the tarsal tunnel should be minimised by using well-fitting shoes or soft padding. NSAID or a local injection of cortisone may decrease symptoms in mild cases. In chronic cases surgery may be necessary to release the nerve.

REFERRALS Refer to orthopaedic foot surgeon if the pain is persistent or is getting worse, to investigate the underlying cause of entrapment and for consideration of surgery. In mild cases, the surgeon may suggest orthotics to start with.

EXERCISE PRESCRIPTION Even though exercise often worsens the symptoms, rest will not help, so allow all kinds of sporting activities using well-fitting shoes but avoiding unnecessary impact.

EVALUATION OF TREATMENT OUTCOMES Monitor clinical symptoms, which should disappear. Tinel's sign should be normal. Note that even after successful surgery it can take a very long time (months to a year) before nerve function is normal.

DIFFERENTIAL DIAGNOSES Plantar fasciitis (entrapped nerve branch may cause radiating pain to insertion of plantar fascia); Deltoid ligament tear (acute injury); OCD of the talus dome (ache, no radiating pain, joint effusion). Note! Tarsal tunnel syndrome may be associated with metabolic diseases such as diabetes or malignant tumours.

PROGNOSIS Usually good–fair. If symptoms persist over several months, surgery may be indicated. Again the underlying cause of the nerve compression is more important for outcome than the syndrome itself. Even after successful surgery symptoms may persist over one to two years.

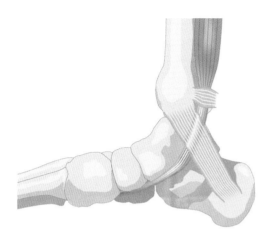

Fig. 48 The posterior tibial tendon is most often injured between the position posterior to the medial malleoli and the distal insertion

SYMPTOMS Gradually increasing exercise-induced pain around the posterior medial part of the ankle joint, often after previous sprain. It is common in middle-aged or elderly athletes.

AETIOLOGY This is a tenosynovitis and or partial rupture of the posterior tibial tendon. If the tendon ruptures completely, a fairly discrete acquired flat foot can result after a long time of diffuse symptoms.

CLINICAL FINDINGS There is tenderness on palpation over the posterior tibial tendon.

INVESTIGATIONS MRI or ultrasound may show localised oedema or swelling around the tendon. Sometimes a rupture can be seen.

TREATMENT Early proprioceptive training and weight-bearing exercises are usually recommended. Rehabilitation is usually curative and the athlete can resume occasional sport within six to twelve weeks, using well-fitting shoes, with or without orthotics.

REFERRALS Refer to physiotherapist for mild symptoms and to orthopaedic surgeon if pain is unclear or severe.

EXERCISE PRESCRIPTION Rest will not help so allow all kinds of sporting activities using well-fitting shoes and avoiding impact. Suggest low-impact activities such as cycling and swimming.

EVALUATION OF TREATMENT OUTCOMES Monitor decrease of clinical symptoms and signs.

DIFFERENTIAL DIAGNOSES Stress fracture of the navicular bone (X-ray or MRI will differentiate).

PROGNOSIS Excellent-Good but in rare cases an acquired flat foot can occur, requiring permanent orthotics in shoes.

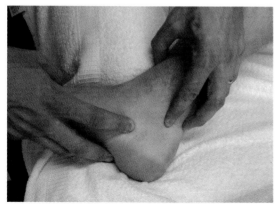

Fig. 49 Tenderness on palpation over the tendon during a weak-resisted plantar flexion and inversion may indicate injury to this tendon

EXERCISE ON PRESCRIPTION DURING INJURY TO THE ANKLE

This table provides advice on forms of exercise that may or may not be recommended for athletes with different injuries. The advice must be related to the severity and stage of healing and take the individual's situation into account.

● This activity is harmful or risky.

◐ This activity can be done but with care and with specific advice.

○ This activity can safely be recommended.

	Running	Walking	Water exercises	Bicycling	Racket sports	Golf	Contact sports	Working-out	Home exercises
ANTERIOR IMPINGEMENT	○	○	○	○	○	○	○	○	○
CARTILAGE INJURY	●	○	○	○	●	○	●	○	○
LATERAL ANKLE LIGAMENT RUPTURES	○	○	○	○	○	○	○	○	○
MULTI-LIGAMENT RUPTURES OF THE ANKLE	●	●	○	○	●	○	●	○	○
PERONEUS TENDON DISLOCATION	●	○	○	○	●	○	●	○	○
PERONEUS TENDON RUPTURE	●	○	○	○	●	○	●	○	○
POSTERIOR IMPINGEMENT OF THE ANKLE	○	○	○	○	○	○	○	○	○
SYNDESMOSIS LIGAMENT RUPTURE	●	●	○	○	●	○	●	○	○
TARSAL TUNNEL SYNDROME	○	○	○	○	○	○	○	○	○
TIBIALIS POSTERIOR SYNDROME	●	○	○	○	○	○	○	○	○

iii LOWER LEG INJURIES

Injuries to the lower leg are very common in sports where running and jumping on hard surfaces are important parts of training and competition. This area is affected first in beginners trying to improve their general fitness. Most of these injuries are caused by poor planning and over-ambitious training.

The figures below show the anatomical appearances of the lower leg from different angles, with arrows indicating the locations of symptoms of particular injuries.

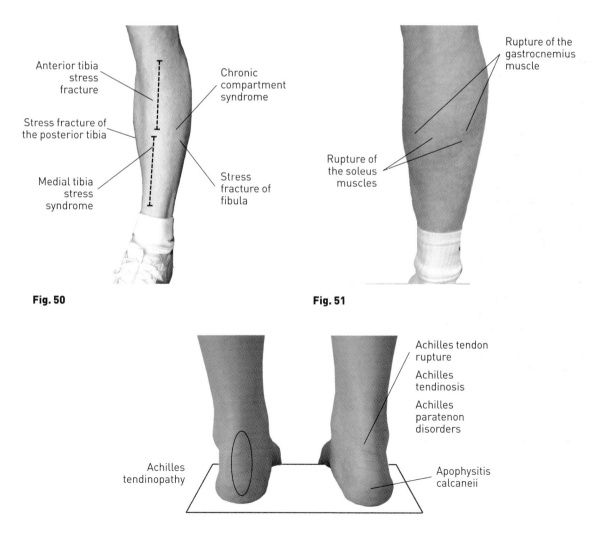

Anterior tibia stress fracture

Chronic compartment syndrome

Stress fracture of the posterior tibia

Medial tibia stress syndrome

Stress fracture of fibula

Fig. 50

Rupture of the gastrocnemius muscle

Rupture of the soleus muscles

Fig. 51

Achilles tendinopathy

Achilles tendon rupture

Achilles tendinosis

Achilles paratenon disorders

Apophysitis calcaneii

Fig. 52

1. ACHILLES TENDON RUPTURE

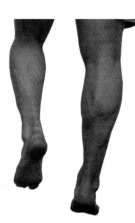

Fig. 53 A simple toe raise is impossible with an Achilles tendon rupture

SYMPTOMS A sharp sudden pain in the Achilles tendon during activity, often recognised by the patient and people around as a loud snap, followed by the inability to continue. Often the patient believes somebody has hit them over the calf. It is most common in middle-aged recreational athletes in impact sports such as badminton or soccer.

AETIOLOGY This is a complete rupture of the Achilles tendon, two to six centimetres proximal to the distal insertion. In most cases the tendon is not healthy before the rupture but suffers from tendinosis changes (see Achilles tendinosis).

CLINICAL FINDINGS There is local tenderness on palpation over the tendon, swelling/bruising, a palpable gap in the tendon and a positive squeeze test often referred to as Thomson's or Simmond's test. The patient lies prone with the ankle outside the stretcher. Squeeze the calf muscle; normally, the ankle should plantar flex but if the tendon is ruptured nothing will happen. To confirm the diagnosis, add resistance to an active plantar flexion. The

injured patient will not be able to apply any force. Compare to the other side. Note that an active plantar flexion can be achieved by plantaris longus, despite a complete Achilles tendon rupture. However, on adding an active toe raise, the diagnosis is clear since the injured athlete is unable to stand up on their toes, due to weakness.

INVESTIGATIONS Ultrasound or MRI will show the bleeding and rupture but often underestimate the extent of the injury. With the history and signs above this is always a complete rupture even though some fibres may look intact.

TREATMENT In the acute phase RICE is advocated. Surgery with anatomical reconstruction is recommended for sporting people, due to lower **morbidity** and an earlier return to sport. Surgery is followed by a few weeks' partial immobilisation and rehabilitation before resuming sport. Early weight-bearing is allowed, if protected by an ankle brace.

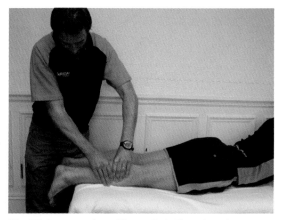

Fig. 54 Squeeze the calf muscle bulk and apply some resistance to the forefoot. If the Achilles tendon is ruptured there is no consequential plantar flexion of the ankle. Compare with other side

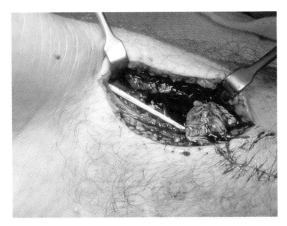

Fig. 55 Even with a complete Achilles tendon rupture, the tiny plantaris longus tendon allows active plantar flexion, which can fool the examiner, but with resistance there is very little force

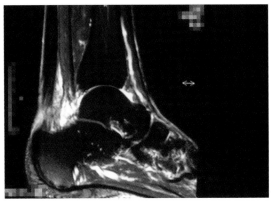

Fig. 56 MRI showing a complete disruption of the Achilles tendon. This is an unnecessary examination in most cases, since the diagnosis can be confirmed clinically

Non-surgical treatment, with eight to twelve weeks cast or brace treatment, can be sufficient for less active people or others with ailments contra-indicating surgery. The risk of re-rupture is higher for non-operated cases.

REFERRALS Refer to orthopaedic surgeon for consideration of surgery. Refer to physiotherapist for planning of a three to six months' gradual return programme.

EXERCISE PRESCRIPTION Cycling and swimming (when the wound is healed) are good alternatives to keep up general fitness.

EVALUATION OF TREATMENT OUTCOMES
Monitor clinical symptoms and signs. The tendon will remain thicker than normal after complete healing. Calf muscle strength should be similar to the other side. Objective tests with resisted toe raises are strongly suggested before resuming sport.

DIFFERENTIAL DIAGNOSES With the typical history and clinical findings above, the diagnosis should be clear. Despite this, many of these injuries are missed in clinical practice.

PROGNOSIS Excellent-Good. Fewer than 3-4 per cent of injured athletes complain of persistent symptoms or re-rupture after surgery but in the non-operated group this figure is higher.

2. ACHILLES TENDINOPATHY

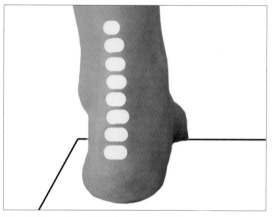

Fig. 57 Area typically affected by Achilles tendinopathy

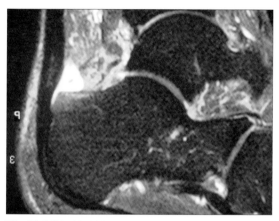

Fig. 58 MRI of Achilles tendinopathy showing retrocalcaneal bursitis as a common cause

SYMPTOMS The athlete complains of gradual onset of diffuse exercise-induced pain or ache around the Achilles tendon. This is common in runners and in players during pre-season training in soccer, rugby and similar sports.

AETIOLOGY 'Tendinopathy' is a broad definition, encompassing a number of ailments that cause pain in this region. From the anatomical and clinical point of view it is important to differentiate insertional problems from free tendon or paratendon ailments.

CLINICAL FINDINGS There is local tenderness on palpation over the tendon or its insertion, which often is thicker, with or without localised nodules. Occasionally there are inflammatory signs with redness and increased temperature. Compare to the other side.

INVESTIGATIONS Ultrasound or MRI will differentiate between intra-and extra-tendinous ailments.

TREATMENT Management and advice depend on underlying pathoanatomical diagnosis. Paratendinous ailments are the most benign, usually treatable with modification in training, correction of shoes and local anti-inflammatory medication. If they become chronic, surgery may be necessary to release constrictions and adhesions between the skin and tendon sheath. Temporary adaptation of training is usually required; Free tendon and insertion ailments (partial ruptures, tendinosis and tendonitis and bursitis) – see specific sections for detailed treatment. Cortisone injections should be administered only in rare cases, due to the high risk of later tendon rupture. Surgery, followed by a few weeks' partial immobilisation and rehabilitation before resuming sport, may be necessary if conservative treatment fails. Weight bearing is usually allowed early if the injury is protected by an ankle brace.

REFERRALS Refer to orthopaedic surgeon for consideration of surgery. Refer to physiotherapist for planning of a three to six months' return programme.

EXERCISE PRESCRIPTION Cycling and swimming (when wound is healed) and closed chain strength exercises, are good alternatives to keep up general fitness.

EVALUATION OF TREATMENT OUTCOMES Monitor clinical symptoms and signs. The tendon may remain thicker than normal after healing. Calf muscle strength should be similar to the other side. Objective tests with resisted toe raises are suggested.

DIFFERENTIAL DIAGNOSES Tendinosis, tendonitis, bursitis, para-tendinosis, para-tendinitis, posterior impingement, tarsal tunnel syndrome.

PROGNOSIS Excellent-Good.

3. ACHILLES TENDINOSIS

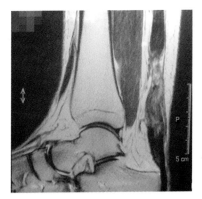

Fig. 59 This MRI shows serious tendinopathy, with a thick tendon (normally black) with grey and white areas of fibrotic in-growth, neo-vascularisation, and a rupture in the proximal end

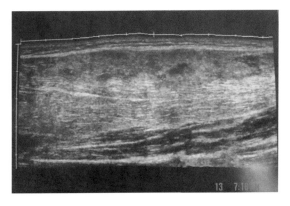

Fig. 60 This is the same tendinotic tendon seen by ultrasound

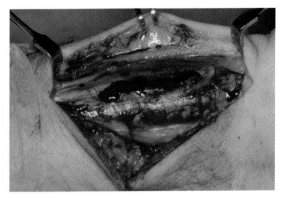

Fig. 61 This demonstrates the hypervascularity of tendinosis, contrary to common beliefs that there is poor blood supply in the tendon. A healthy tendon does not bleed like this

SYMPTOMS Gradual onset of diffuse exercise-induced pain or ache around the Achilles tendon. Often the athlete has noted a tender nodule at the mid-portion of the Achilles tendon. It is most common in middle-aged runners and recreational athletes.

AETIOLOGY 'Tendinosis' is defined from histopathological findings as a free tendon condition with an altered collagen structure, thickening of the tendon, re-vascularisation and increased cellularity. It can be looked upon as a 'blocked' early healing stage and is a continuing process, not a degenerative condition. This condition may or may not be symptomatic. A majority of complete Achilles tendon ruptures have these changes in the tendon.

CLINICAL FINDINGS There is tenderness on palpation over the tendon, which often is thicker, with or without localised nodules. Occasionally there are inflammatory signs with redness and increased temperature. Compare to the other side.

INVESTIGATIONS Ultrasound or MRI will show typical intra-tendinous findings.

TREATMENT This often chronic ailment may respond to conservative treatment in early stages, including modification of training and calf muscle strengthening exercises that can be tried over three months. If this regime is not successful surgery may be necessary to release any constrictions and adhesions between the skin and excise abnormal parts of the tendon. Cortisone injections should be administered only in rare cases, due to the high risk of later tendon rupture. Indeed, cortisone injection and frequent use of NSAID are possible causes of this ailment. Surgery is followed by a few weeks' partial immobilisation and rehabilitation before resuming sport. Weight bearing is usually allowed soon after surgery, if the injury is protected by an ankle brace.

REFERRALS Refer to orthopaedic surgeon for consideration of surgery. Refer to physiotherapist for planning of a three to six months' return programme.

EXERCISE PRESCRIPTION Cycling and swimming (when the wound is healed) and closed chain training are good alternatives to keep up general fitness.

EVALUATION OF TREATMENT OUTCOMES
Monitor clinical symptoms and signs. Note that the tendon will remain thicker than the non-injured side. Calf muscle performance should be similar to the other side. Objective tests with, for example, maximum numbers of resisted toe raises are strongly suggested.

DIFFERENTIAL DIAGNOSES Tendinosis, tendinitis, bursitis, para-tendinosis, para-tendonitis (see tendinopathy).

PROGNOSIS Good-Poor; in some cases this condition can be the beginning of the end for an elite athlete's care.

4. ACHILLES PARATENON DISORDERS

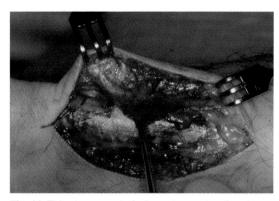

Fig. 62 This shows a relatively acute paratendinosis with adhesions to the skin

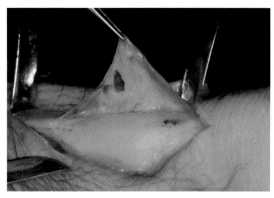

Fig. 63 This is a chronic fibrotic tendon sheath overlying a severe and chronic tendinotic tendon

SYMPTOMS There is gradual onset of diffuse exercise-induced pain or ache and swelling around the Achilles tendon, often around the mid-portion. It is common in runners and during pre-season training in soccer, rugby and similar sports.

AETIOLOGY Para-tendinosis is defined from histopathological findings as a paratenon condition with an initial inflammation, changing into fibrosis, thickening of the tendon sheath and adhesions. This condition may or may not be symptomatic. It can be caused by increased friction from ill-fitting shoes, strapping or braces.

CLINICAL FINDINGS There is tenderness on palpation over the tendon, which may feel spongy and thicker, with or without inflammatory signs and with redness and increased temperature. Compare to the other side. This condition may occur simultaneously as tendinosis with or without a nodule (see Achilles tendinosis).

INVESTIGATIONS Ultrasound or MRI may show typical extra-tendinous findings and confirm or rule out intra-tendinous ailments.

TREATMENT This often chronic ailment may respond to conservative treatment, including modification of training and calf muscle strengthening exercises that can be tried over three months. It is also important to reduce friction against the tendon by adjusting shoes or technique. If this regime is not successful, surgery may be necessary to release any constrictions and adhesions between the skin and paratendon, which in severe cases needs to be excised. Cortisone injections should be administered only in rare cases, due to the high risk of consequential tendon rupture. Surgery is followed by a few weeks' partial immobilisation and rehabilitation before resuming sport. Weight bearing is usually allowed early on.

REFERRALS Refer to orthopaedic surgeon for consideration of surgery. Refer to physiotherapist for planning of a one to two months' return programme.

EXERCISE PRESCRIPTION Cycling and swimming (when wound is healed) are good alternatives to keep up general fitness.

EVALUATION OF TREATMENT OUTCOMES
Monitor clinical symptoms and signs. Note that the tendon may remain thicker than normal. Calf muscle performance should be similar to the other side. Objective tests with maximal number of resisted toe raises are strongly suggested before resuming full sport.

DIFFERENTIAL DIAGNOSES Tendinosis, tendinitis, bursitis, para-tendinosis, para-tendonitis.

PROGNOSIS Excellent-Good.

5. ANTERIOR CHRONIC COMPARTMENT SYNDROME

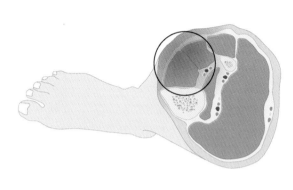

Fig. 64 The anterior lateral compartment of the lower leg, which is affected in chronic compartment syndrome

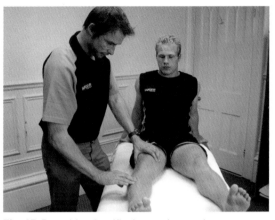

Fig. 65 Repetitive dorsiflexion against resistance causes severe pain and a very tender muscle bulk

SYMPTOMS There is a gradual onset of diffuse exercise-induced pain on the anterior lateral aspect of the lower leg. It is common in fairly short but muscular 'bulky' athletes. The pain becomes so great that continued sport is not possible. The athletes complain that the muscles feel like they are bursting. Rest, with the legs elevated, usually relieves the symptoms within minutes.

AETIOLOGY There is an increased intra-muscular pressure within the peroneus and tibialis anterior muscle bulks causing ischaemic pain. This can be due to increased muscle volume from intensive strength training but the true aetiology is unclear. The condition is often bilateral.

CLINICAL FINDINGS There is intense tenderness on palpation over a very firm muscle bulk. The typical pain and swelling can be provoked by repetitive ankle dorsi-flexions against resistance.

INVESTIGATIONS Ultrasound or MRI is normal. Intra-muscular pressure measurements during exercise can be made but are not necessary for the diagnosis.

TREATMENT This condition may respond to conservative treatment including modification of training and stretching exercises (stretching of the ankle-calf-hamstrings-quadriceps-hip muscle complex) that can be tried over three months. If this regime is not successful surgery may be necessary to release the fascia (fasciotomy). Surgery is followed by a few weeks of rehabilitation before resuming sport. Weight bearing is usually allowed a few days after surgery.

REFERRALS Refer to orthopaedic surgeon for consideration of surgery. Refer to physiotherapist for planning of a few weeks' return programme back to full sport.

EXERCISE PRESCRIPTION Cycling and swimming (when wound is healed) are good alternatives to keep up general fitness.

EVALUATION OF TREATMENT OUTCOMES
Monitor clinical symptoms and signs. The symptoms are usually completely gone after surgery. Note that the muscle bulk will be more prominent than the other side after fasciotomy.

DIFFERENTIAL DIAGNOSES Muscle rupture (sudden onset on one leg, localised pain, ultrasound will differentiate), DVT (developing after long-haul flights or surgery, pain and swelling of the entire leg, resting pain).

PROGNOSIS Excellent-Good but if not treated properly it may be the end of the career of an elite athlete.

6. ANTERIOR TIBIA STRESS FRACTURE

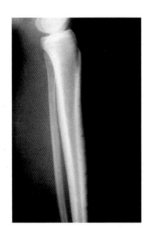

Fig. 66 This X-ray shows 11 anterior stress fractures in an athlete who tried to avoid pain by changing his jump-off technique

SYMPTOMS There is a gradual onset of localised exercise-induced pain at the anterior edge of the tibia, often affecting ballet dancers and athletes in jumping or running sports with high-impact forces or when plyometric training is involved (e.g. basketball, high jump or long jump). Initially, the symptoms may be vague but gradually they become so severe that they prevent jumping or running.

AETIOLOGY This is a tension-side stress fracture that does not heal bone to bone, since fibrosis grows into the fracture site, causing non-union that gets worse over time. When the anterior cortical bone becomes thicker the fibrosis growth in the fracture line makes bone-to-bone healing impossible.

CLINICAL FINDINGS There is tenderness on palpation and localised swelling over the fracture site.

INVESTIGATIONS X-ray is negative until several weeks after onset of symptoms due to the lack of callus formation. CT scans or MRI may disclose the diagnosis earlier. In later stages, an X-ray will show a 'shark bite appearance' of the anterior cortex in lateral view.

TREATMENT This stress fracture may initially respond to conservative treatment including modification of training and avoiding jumping and running for three months. Unfortunately the diagnosis is often delayed and the condition turns chronic. Surgery may be necessary to stimulate bone healing but this injury halts many athletes. Surgery is followed by a long period of partial immobilisation and rehabilitation before resuming sport.

REFERRALS Refer to orthopaedic surgeon for consideration of surgery. Refer to physiotherapist for planning of six to twelve months' return programme.

EXERCISE PRESCRIPTION Cycling and swimming and any other low-impact activities are good alternatives to keep up general fitness.

EVALUATION OF TREATMENT OUTCOMES Monitor clinical symptoms and signs. Note X-ray can show the typical appearance in non-symptomatic athletes. Often the athlete changes stance or jumping technique, altering the site of stress and causing a new fracture at another site.

DIFFERENTIAL DIAGNOSES Shin splints (pain more diffuse; MRI can indicate); Chronic anterior compartment syndrome (pain in the muscle bulk); Posterior tibia stress fracture (location of symptoms medial posterior edge; X-ray and MRI differentiate); Tumour (X-ray differentiates).

PROGNOSIS Fair-Poor; this injury halts the careers of many top athletes.

Fig. 67 Let kids play! Apophysitis calcaneii can be similar to Osgood-Schlatter's disease and causes discomfort over a period of time for the young athlete

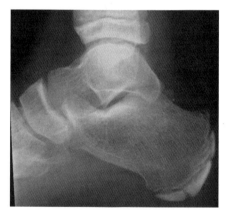

Fig. 68 As soon as the apophysis closes, the problem is solved and the pain is gone

SYMPTOMS There is gradual onset of diffuse exercise-induced heel pain or ache around the insertion of the Achilles tendon, most commonly in very young growing athletes of six to twelve years old.

AETIOLOGY This is a growth-related condition around the vertically positioned apophysis on the calcaneus, where the Achilles tendon inserts. It often affects active children but can cause pain in non-active children as well. It is induced by a local growth spurt in this area but symptoms are made worse by jumping and running. It is often bilateral, sometimes with a time delay between left and right.

CLINICAL FINDINGS There is tenderness on palpation over the posterior calcaneus and Achilles tendon insertion. Occasionally there are inflammatory signs with redness and increased temperature. Compare to the other side.

INVESTIGATIONS X-ray is often normal but can sometimes show a fragmented apophysis and should be compared with the other foot. MRI will show bone oedema but is usually not required for the diagnosis.

TREATMENT This often long-duration ailment responds to conservative treatment including modification of training, gentle heel lifts and natural healing by closing of the apophysis.

REFERRALS Refer to physiotherapist for advice of alternative training regime for an early return to sport.

EXERCISE PRESCRIPTION Cycling and swimming and most low-impact activities are good alternatives to keep up general fitness. This is an injury where you can play sports with minor pain in most cases. It is important to inform parents carefully about this condition and not discourage them from letting their child play sports.

EVALUATION OF TREATMENT OUTCOMES Monitor clinical symptoms and signs.

DIFFERENTIAL DIAGNOSES Bone tumour (X-ray differentiates); Osteomyelitis (signs of infection such as increased temperature and increased CRP/ESR).

PROGNOSIS Excellent.

8. MEDIAL TIBIA STRESS SYNDROME

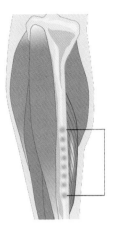

Fig. 69 The area usually affected by medial tibial stress syndrome

SYMPTOMS There is gradual onset of diffuse or localised exercise-induced pain at the posterior medial aspect of the mid and distal tibia. This condition is common during pre-season training. It typically occurs as a result of sudden changes in training habits, such as increase in intensity or amount of impact.

AETIOLOGY This is a stress reaction of the tibia to excessive jumping or running exercises. The location of pain is around the origin of the flexor digitorum longus or posterior tibial muscles at the medial posterior part of the tibia. The anatomy can vary substantially between the left and right leg. Symptoms can also therefore vary correspondingly.

CLINICAL FINDINGS There is tenderness on palpation over the posterior medial tibia along the the tibial border over the site of origin of the above-mentioned muscles. Pain can be provoked by repetitive jumping on the forefoot on hard ground.

INVESTIGATIONS X-ray is normal. MRI may show sub-cortical oedema along the posterior medial tibia and can usually exclude a more localised stress fracture.

TREATMENT This injury most often responds to conservative treatment including modification of training and stretching exercises over three months. There is seldom any indication of immobilisation or surgery but if symptoms persist for more than three months a fasciotomy, releasing the tibial fascia overlying the flexor muscles from the tibial border may be indicated.

REFERRALS Refer to physiotherapist for planning of three months' return programme back to full sport. Refer to orthopaedic surgeon if non-operative treatment fails.

EXERCISE PRESCRIPTION Cycling and swimming and most other low-impact activities are good alternatives to keep up general fitness. Running on soft ground is usually acceptable.

EVALUATION OF TREATMENT OUTCOMES Monitor clinical symptoms and signs.

DIFFERENTIAL DIAGNOSES Posterior chronic compartment syndrome; Shin splints (superficial periostitis-cortical micro-fractures); Medial posterior tibia stress fracture (more localised pain and swelling, X-ray or MRI will differentiate).

PROGNOSIS Excellent but symptoms can last for months.

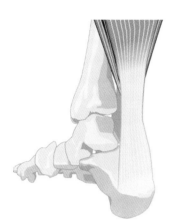

Fig. 70 Most ruptures occur in the musculotendinous junction

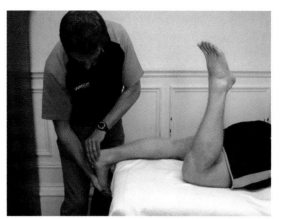

Fig. 71 Active plantar flexion with straight knee against resistance demonstrates the strength of the gastrocnemius and localised pain/weakness if there is a rupture

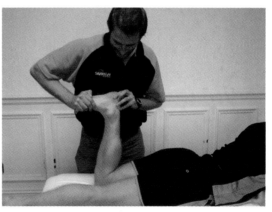

Fig. 72 Active plantar flexion with flexed knee against resistance demonstrates the strength of the soleus muscle and localised pain/weakness if there is a rupture

SYMPTOMS There is an acute onset of sharp tearing pain in the calf during activity. This injury often occurs in middle-aged recreational athletes in sports such as tennis or squash or other sprinting and jumping sports.

AETIOLOGY This is usually a partial (Grade I-II) rupture of the medial or lateral bulk of the gastrocnemius or soleus muscles. The rupture usually occurs at the musculo-tendinous junction. A complete (Grade III-IV) rupture on this location is rare.

CLINICAL FINDINGS There is tenderness on palpation over a localised area of the muscle bulk. Resistance tests of the muscle in question will cause further pain. Jumping and landing on the forefoot with a straight knee is most painful for a gastrocnemius rupture while landing with a flexed knee causes more pain if the deeper soleus muscle is ruptured.

INVESTIGATIONS This diagnosis is made from patient history and clinical findings. Ultrasound or MRI can demonstrate the rupture and haematoma. These investigations are important when the initial diagnosis has been missed, to rule out an intramuscular haematoma that may require surgical evacuation and to grade the rupture, which is important for rehabilitation and length of absence from sport.

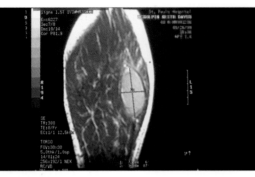

Fig. 73 This MRI demonstrates an intramuscular haematoma three months after the rupture. The tennis player can still not even jog

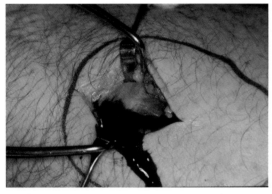

Fig. 74 The organised haematoma evacuated through a surgical incision with immediate improvement

TREATMENT This injury most often responds to conservative treatment including modification of training and strength exercises over three months, the usual healing time. Partial weight bearing is usually allowed.

REFERRALS Refer to orthopaedic surgeon for consideration of surgery if symptoms are severe or diagnosis is delayed. Refer to physiotherapist for planning of a three to six months' return programme back to sport.

EXERCISE PRESCRIPTION Cycling and swimming and other low-impact activities are good alternatives to keep up general fitness.

EVALUATION OF TREATMENT OUTCOMES Monitor clinical symptoms and signs. Strength and flexibility must be monitored objectively to be the same as the other leg at the end of rehabilitation or there is a high risk that the weaker muscle will re-rupture.

DIFFERENTIAL DIAGNOSES Achilles tendon rupture (different location); DVT (gradual onset but can be difficult to rule out if the patient has recently taken a long-haul flight or had surgery).

PROGNOSIS Excellent but re-ruptures are common following a too-early return to sport and insufficient rehabilitation.

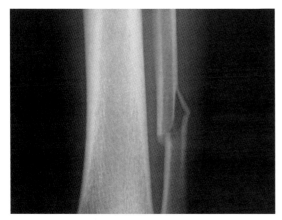

Fig. 75 Due to the rotational forces on the fibula, a stress fracture can displace, causing a lot of pain and requiring surgery

SYMPTOMS Gradual onset of localised exercise-induced pain on fibula. This injury is common in young athletes but less common than tibia stress fractures. It typically occurs as a result of sudden changes in training habits, such as increase in intensity or amount of impact.

AETIOLOGY This stress fracture is caused by excessive jumping or running exercises where rotation-pivoting landings are involved.

CLINICAL FINDINGS There is localised tenderness on palpation and swelling over the fracture site. Pain can be provoked by repetitive jumping on the forefoot on hard ground.

INVESTIGATIONS X-ray is normal until callus formation has started or fracture displaces. MRI will show sub-cortical oedema at the fracture site but can often not identify the line of the stress fracture. CT scans usually show the fracture line better.

TREATMENT This injury most often responds to conservative treatment including modification of training over three months when the fracture is healed. There is seldom an indication for immobilisation or surgery. An ankle brace, reducing the rotation of the ankle, will reduce the symptoms.

REFERRALS Refer to physiotherapist for planning of a three months' return programme back to sport. Note the errors in training that could have caused the injury and do not repeat.

EXERCISE PRESCRIPTION Cycling and swimming are good alternatives to keep up general fitness.

EVALUATION OF TREATMENT OUTCOMES Normal clinical symptoms and signs.

DIFFERENTIAL DIAGNOSES Bone tumour (X-ray will differentiate).

PROGNOSIS Excellent.

11. STRESS FRACTURE OF POSTERIOR TIBIA

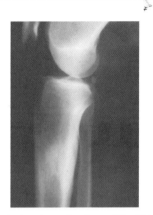

Fig. 76 A posterior stress fracture of the tibia will only be seen on an X-ray after callus is formed (three to six weeks). MRI or bone scintigram shows the fracture within days of onset!

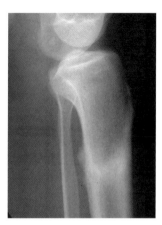

Fig. 77 This X-ray shows a rare case of a complete stress fracture through the tibia which has healed well

SYMPTOMS Gradual onset of localised exercise-induced pain at the posterior medial aspect of the tibia. This injury is common in young or adolescent athletes. It typically occurs as a result of sudden changes in training habits, such as increase in intensity or amount of impact.

AETIOLOGY This is a non-tension-side stress fracture, caused by excessive jumping or running exercises. The location usually correlates to the origin of the flexor digitorum longus or the posterior tibial muscle which can vary substantially between the left and right leg. Symptoms can therefore vary as well.

CLINICAL FINDINGS There is localised tenderness on palpation and swelling over posterior medial tibia over the fracture site. Pain can be provoked by repetitive jumping on the forefoot on hard ground.

INVESTIGATIONS X-ray is normal until callus formation has started. MRI will show sub-cortical oedema at the fracture site but can often not identify the line of stress fracture. CT scans usually show the fracture line better.

TREATMENT This injury always responds to conservative treatment including modification of training over three months when the fracture is healed. There is seldom a need for immobilisation or surgery.

REFERRALS Refer to physiotherapist for planning of a three months' return programme. Note the errors in training that could have caused the injury and do not repeat.

EXERCISE PRESCRIPTION Cycling and swimming are good alternatives to keep up general fitness. Running on soft surfaces is usually acceptable.

EVALUATION OF TREATMENT OUTCOMES Normal clinical symptoms and signs.

DIFFERENTIAL DIAGNOSES Posterior chronic compartment syndrome (similar condition but deeper and more resistant to pain); Shin splints (more diffuse pain along the tibia border).

PROGNOSIS Excellent.

EXERCISE ON PRESCRIPTION DURING INJURY TO THE LOWER LEG

This table provides advice on forms of exercise that may or may not be recommended for athletes with different injuries. The advice must be related to the severity and stage of healing and take the individual's situation into account.

● This activity is harmful or risky.

● The activity can be done but with care and with specific advice.

○ This activity can safely be recommended.

	Running	Walking	Water exercises	Bicycling	Racket sports	Golf	Contact sports	Working-out	Home exercises
ACHILLES TENDON RUPTURE	●	○	○	○	●	○	●	○	○
ACHILLES TENDINOPATHY	●	○	○	○	●	○	●	○	○
ACHILLES TENDINOSIS	●	○	○	○	●	○	●	○	○
ACHILLES PARA TENON DISORDERS	○	○	○	○	○	○	○	○	○
ANTERIOR CHRONIC COMPARTMENT SYNDROME	●	○	○	○	●	○	●	○	○
ANTERIOR TIBIA STRESS FRACTURE	●	○	○	○	●	○	●	○	○
APOPHYSITIS CALCANEII	○	○	○	○	○	○	○	○	○
MEDIAL TIBIA STRESS SYNDROME	○	○	○	○	○	○	○	○	○
RUPTURE OF THE GASTROCNEMIUS OR SOLEUS MUSCLES	●	○	○	○	●	○	●	○	○
STRESS FRACTURE FIBULA	○	○	○	○	●	○	●	○	○
STRESS FRACTURE POSTERIOR TIBIA	●	○	○	○	●	○	●	○	○

iv KNEE INJURIES

Knee injuries are very common, in particular in contact sports. A majority of the injuries that halt professional careers affect the knee. Before going into detail about these injuries I must emphasise the vital importance of the neuro-muscular control of the kinetic chain. Any weakness in that chain, such as poor ankles or poor core stability, can predispose to knee injuries.

The figures below show the anatomical appearances of the knee from different angles with arrows indicating the locations of symptoms from the injuries.

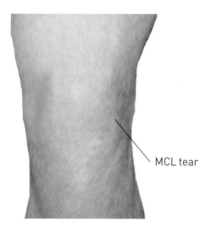

Fig. 78

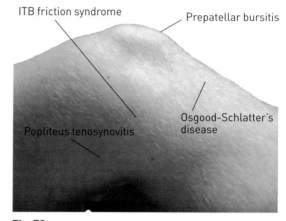

ITB friction syndrome

Prepatellar bursitis

Popliteus tenosynovitis

Osgood-Schlatter's disease

MCL tear

Fig. 79

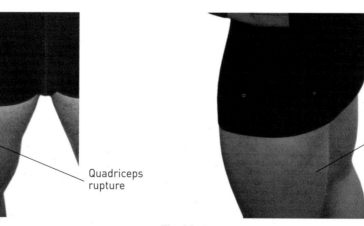

Quadriceps rupture

hamstring rupture

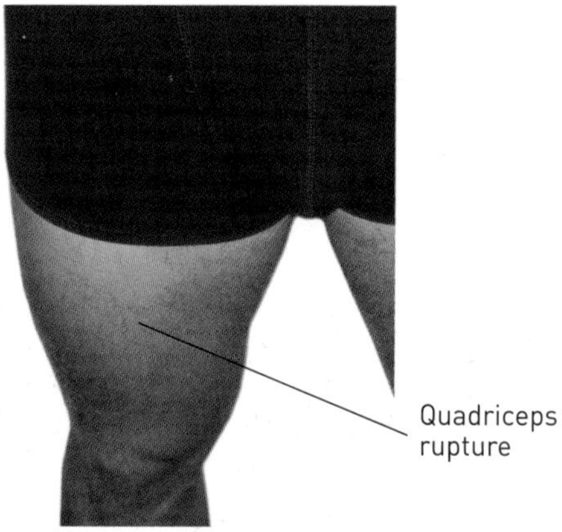

Fig. 80

Fig. 81

Fig. 82 Leg extension manoeuvres are closed chain exercises for the quadriceps muscles

TRAINING OF MUSCLES SUPPORTING THE KNEE

All strength exercises that aim to develop muscle power and volume should be performed slowly and in a controlled manner in concentric mode for one to two seconds and in eccentric mode for three to four seconds. The exercise should be performed with 8 RM for three sets to achieve muscle hypertrophy and increased strength. The injured leg must initially be trained separately from the non-injured.

Quadriceps muscle strength can be trained with leg press, squats or leg extension manoeuvres. The vastus medialis muscles require special attention after patella (kneecap) dislocation or in mal-tracking conditions that cause anterior knee pain. If the patella is subluxated or out of place and knee extensions cause pain, a soft knee brace can be useful and give very good results. The quadriceps muscles are essential for knee stability in activities such as jumping, sprinting, twisting and turning. The rectus femoris muscle, the most

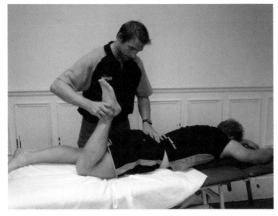

Fig. 83 Flexibility test for the quadriceps muscles

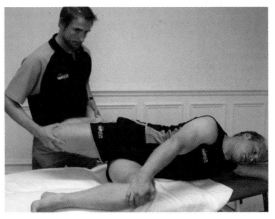

Fig. 84 Flexibility test for the rectus femoris muscle

powerful of the quadriceps, also controls hip flexion, together with the iliopsoas muscle. The flexibility of the quadriceps muscles is improved with stretching and can be performed in different ways.

Hamstring muscle strength is trained with knee flexion and hip extension exercises, standing or sitting, using wires with weights or specific machines allowing a hamstring curl. The hamstring muscles are particularly important in activities such as sprinting and turning and work against and with the quadriceps to stabilise the knee. The hamstring, despite being a hip extensor and knee flexor, extends the knee joint during the last 15 degrees of extension.

The endurance of the thigh muscles can be trained with 15–50 RM resistance for three sets, using a bicycle with the pedal under the heel or forefoot in either a forward-leaning or straight-up position or with running, if allowed. Flexibility is trained with stretching.

Good proprioceptive muscle function is vital to prevent further injuries. Co-ordination training can be done on wobble boards, initially in the static mode, followed by dynamic one-leg hops and controlled landings. A one-leg hop is a good test of the proprioceptive function of the leg.

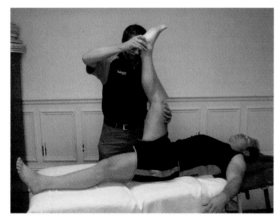

Fig. 85 Flexibility test for the hamstring muscles

Fig. 86 Stretching of the hamstring muscles

Fig. 87 Plyometric exercises are effective, but put the lower extremities under high-impact forces

Functional training depends on the patient's needs and may include running in a straight line, side-stepping, twisting, turning, jumping, landing and various forms of plyometric exercises. Knee function is dependent on the entire kinetic chain and posture; unstable or weak ankles or poor core stability will hamper knee function and may predispose to knee injuries. Core stability exercises should be included in all rehabilitation of injuries discussed in this book.

1. ANTERIOR CRUCIATE LIGAMENT TEAR (ACL)

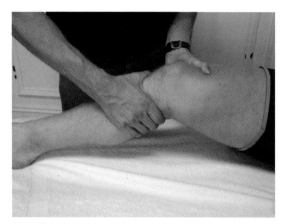

Fig. 88 Lachman's test is very effective for revealing an ACL rupture. Hold the thigh firmly with one hand. Knee should be slightly flexed. Move tibia anteriorly. If there is increased laxity and no firm endpoint the test is positive

Fig. 89 Anterior drawer test is another sensitive test for revealing an ACL tear. Sit gently on the patient's foot. Knee should be flexed around 90 degrees. Move tibia anteriorly. If there is increased laxity and no firm endpoint the test is positive

SYMPTOMS The symptoms are pain and immediate haemarthrosis, caused by bleeding from the ruptured ligament. This is an injury common in contact sports such as football, rugby and other high-intensity sports such as downhill skiing. There is often a 'pop' sound from the knee and an inability to continue.

AETIOLOGY The typical athlete suffers a hyper-extension or valgus rotation sprain. In many cases it is a non-contact injury, where the player loses balance and twists the knee. The ligament can rupture partially or completely. In growing athletes the bone insertion can be avulsed (tibia spine fracture). This injury is often associated with other injuries to cartilage, menisci, capsule or other ligaments.

CLINICAL FINDINGS There is intra-articular bleeding (haemarthrosis) in most cases. If there is a capsule rupture as well, blood can penetrate from the joint and cause bruising along the lower leg, so the

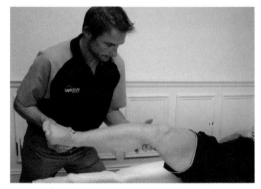

Fig. 90 The pivot shift test is difficult to do but, if positive, an ACL tear is confirmed

joint effusion does not look too severe. In rare cases, there is no haemarthrosis. The Lachman test is positive if the rupture is complete. This is the most sensitive test and can verify an anterior cruciate ligament rupture in more than 90 per cent of cases. Anterior drawer tests and pivot shift tests are complementary tests for the same purpose. Note! Since there are often associated injuries, the examination must include tests for collateral ligaments, menisci, cartilage and the capsular structures.

INVESTIGATIONS Clinical examination is the most important tool for diagnosis and should include tests for all ligaments and other structures in the knee. X-ray is valuable to rule out fractures, in particular in growing or elderly athletes. MRI can verify a complete ACL tear in most cases but is more important for evaluating associated injuries.

TREATMENT An athlete with haemarthrosis and a suspected ACL tear should be seen by an orthopaedic surgeon to consider an early arthroscopy. This procedure can verify the diagnosis and also deal with associated injuries that are often missed. Reconstruction of the ligament is recommended for active athletes in pivoting sports. Sedentary people and participants in non-pivoting sports may recover through rehabilitation only.

REFERRALS Refer to orthopaedic surgeon for further investigations to verify the extent of the injury. Physiotherapists will be involved in close collaboration with the surgeon.

EXERCISE PRESCRIPTION Cycling and swimming (not breast stroke) are good alternatives to keep up general fitness. Rehabilitation back to full sport usually takes around six months with or without surgery.

EVALUATION OF TREATMENT OUTCOMES
Monitor clinical symptoms and signs. Different functional knee scores for different sports are available to measure when the knee allows the return to full sport.

DIFFERENTIAL DIAGNOSES Posterior cruciate ligament rupture. Initial posterior sagging will give a sense of anterior translation of the tibia during a Lachman or anterior drawer test and mislead the examiner but the posterior drawer test is positive. Associated injuries, such as a bucket handle meniscal tear, can cause the knee to lock, and mask a positive Lachman test.

PROGNOSIS Surgery (ACL reconstruction) will allow return to professional sports in around six to nine months. The risk of re-rupture is about 5 per cent within five years. The reconstruction will protect the knee from further meniscus or cartilage injuries. However, reconstruction or not, the knee will be more vulnerable to stress and in the long term, 10 to 20 years, the risk of developing osteoarthritis is significant, compared to a non-injured knee.

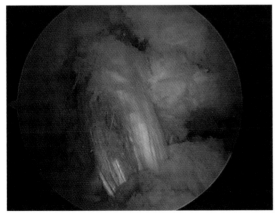

Fig. 91 Arthroscopic view of new patellar bone graft in an ACL reconstruction

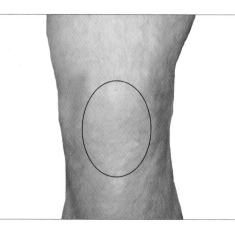

Fig. 92 Area affected by anterior knee pain

SYMPTOMS Gradual onset of diffuse or localised exercise-induced pain around the anterior part of the knee. Prolonged sitting or squatting often trigger the symptoms (positive 'movie sign' – so named because you are in the same position for a long period when watching a movie at the cinema) as can walking down stairs.

AETIOLOGY Anterior knee pain is not a diagnosis but a symptom that can be caused by a number of underlying pathologies. The correct diagnosis must be made before treatment can be successful. This condition often occurs as a result of sudden changes in training habits, such as increase in intensity or amount of impact.

CLINICAL FINDINGS This depends on the underlying diagnosis. If there is effusion, the cause is often intra-articular; if not, it is more likely to be extra-articular. If no structural pathologies can be found the problem can be functional, for example induced by poor core stability, pain referred from the back or poor ankle control. A systematic and thorough approach in the clinical examination is crucial for a successful outcome. Tests of core stability, proprioception, muscle strength and balance and flexibility of the entire kinetic chain must be thoroughly evaluated.

INVESTIGATIONS X-ray can exclude fractures, OCD, patella abnormalities, other osteochondral injuries and bone tumours. MRI can exclude soft tissue tumours and other localised soft tissue lesions such as the presence of medial plicae. It often under-estimates chondromalacia and other superficial chondral injuries as well as many meniscal tears and medial plica syndrome. CT scans can rule out severe patella mal-tracking. Ultrasound can be useful for evaluating functional tendons and ligament disorders such as jumper's knee or tendinosis around the knee. Arthroscopy is often an excellent diagnostic tool when clinical findings are vague.

TREATMENT Depends on the diagnosis.

REFERRALS These patients are very much helped by being evaluated clinically by their physician, surgeon and physiotherapist in close collaboration.

EXERCISE PRESCRIPTION Cycling and water exercises are good alternatives to keep up general fitness.

EVALUATION OF TREATMENT OUTCOMES Normal clinical symptoms and signs.

DIFFERENTIAL DIAGNOSES Meniscus tear, chondral injuries, OCD, medial plica syndrome, chondromalacia patellae, patellar instability or mal-tracking, quadriceps insufficiency, Sinding-Larsen's syndrome, synovitis, Pigmented Villonodular Synovitis (PVNS), patellar tendon disorders, referred pain, reactive arthropathies, secondary symptoms from ankle or back insufficiency, core instability and more.

PROGNOSIS Because many cases never reach an absolute diagnosis and correct treatment, anterior knee pain ends the career of many young athletes.

3. CARTILAGE INJURIES

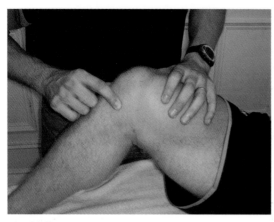

Fig. 93 Tenderness on palpation of the joint line indicates a local synovitis, often caused by an underlying cartilage or meniscal injury

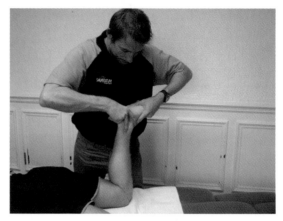

Fig. 94 Compression rotation test eliciting pain reflects a cartilage or meniscus injury

SYMPTOMS There is a gradual or acute on set of effusion and exercise-induced pain often combined with mechanical problems of locking, clicking, clunking or discomfort on impact (compression and rotation). This injury is common in sports such as football, rugby and other high-intensity contact sports but can also occur gradually in sports where hypermobility is important, such as ballet, gymnastics and martial arts.

AETIOLOGY In many cases this injury occurs from direct or indirect trauma or in association with other ligament injuries.

CLINICAL FINDINGS There is effusion in most cases. The compression rotation test is positive. There is often tenderness on palpation of the affected joint line and there are complementary tests for the same purpose. Since there are often associated injuries, examination must also include tests for ligaments, menisci and capsular structures.

INVESTIGATIONS Clinical examination is the most important tool for diagnosis and should include tests for all ligaments and other structures in

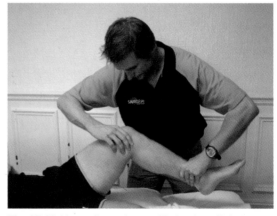

Fig. 95 McMurray's test is specific for a medial meniscal flap tear

the knee. X-ray is valuable to rule out fractures, in particular in growing or elderly athletes. Note! MRI can sometimes miss significant cartilage injuries but is valuable for evaluating associated injuries.

TREATMENT An athlete with effusion and suspected cartilage injuries should be seen by an orthopaedic surgeon to consider arthroscopy. This procedure can not only verify the diagnosis but also

Fig. 96 Grade IV osteoarthritis with complete loss of cartilage on weight-bearing areas

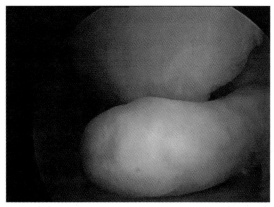

Fig. 97 Large loose body from old cartilage injury, now jamming the joint and causing pain and swelling

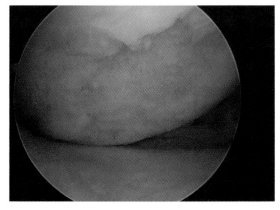

Fig. 98 Isolated, full thickness, localised cartilage injury on the femur condyle which is treated with micro-fracture

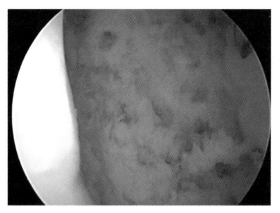

Fig. 99 Micro-fracture is done by drilling or punching small holes through the cortical bone to the subchondral area so bleeding can occur. This brings new cartilage producing cells to the surface

deal with associated injuries. Minor cartilage injuries are debrided or vaporised and loose bodies excised. Full-thickness cartilage injuries on weight-bearing surfaces can be micro-fractured to stimulate growth of fibro-cartilage, which fills the gap and provides reasonable support. Other, more complicated cartilage procedures, such as cell transplant procedures, are still experimental and their long-term outcomes are not superior to micro-fracture.

REFERRALS Refer to orthopaedic surgeon for further investigations to verify the extent of the injury. Physiotherapists will be involved in close collaboration with the surgeon.

3. CARTILAGE INJURIES *Cont.*

EXERCISE PRESCRIPTION Rest is only recommended temporarily. Cycling and swimming are good alternatives to keep up general fitness. Rehabilitation back to full sport usually takes a long time, up to 12 months or more.

EVALUATION OF TREATMENT OUTCOMES Monitor clinical symptoms and signs. Different functional knee scores for different sports are available to measure when the knee allows the return to full sport.

DIFFERENTIAL DIAGNOSES Meniscus injury, loose bodies, medial plica syndrome; all differentiated by arthroscopy.

PROGNOSIS Surgery will allow a return to professional sports in anything from two weeks to several months. The knee with serious cartilage damage is more vulnerable to stress and in the long term, 10 to 20 years, the risk of developing osteoarthritis is significant compared to a non-injured knee.

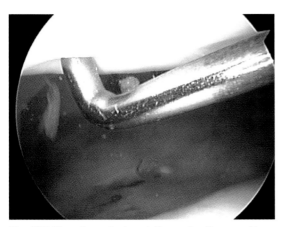

Fig. 100 Chondromalacia patella can be diagnosed by arthroscopic probing

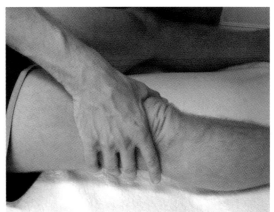

Fig. 101 Grinding test is positive if there is underlying chondromalacia, but this is also present in mal-tracking and other injuries

SYMPTOMS There is gradual onset of diffuse exercise-induced pain around the anterior part of the knee. Prolonged sitting or squatting often trigger the symptoms (positive movie sign). Walking down stairs is more difficult than up.

AETIOLOGY Chondromalacia means 'soft cartilage'. The exact aetiology is unknown. The correct diagnosis must be identified, by arthroscopic probing, before treatment can be successful, since this is only one of many diagnoses that result in anterior knee pain.

CLINICAL FINDINGS There is recurrent effusion and a positive grinding test. Tests of core stability, proprioception, muscle strength and balance and the flexibility of the entire kinetic chain must be thoroughly evaluated.

INVESTIGATIONS X-ray can exclude fractures, OCD, patella abnormalities, other osteochondral injuries and bone tumours. MRI can exclude soft tissue tumours and other localised soft tissue lesions but often underestimates chondromalacia and other superficial chondral injuries as well as many meniscal tears and medial plica syndrome. CT scans can rule out severe patella mal-tracking, which in some cases may be the cause of the chondromalacia. Ultrasound can be useful for evaluating functional tendon and ligament disorders such as jumper's knee or tendinosis around the knee. Arthroscopic probing is required for the diagnosis.

TREATMENT Long-term symptomatic and functional treatment by a physiotherapist is required.

REFERRALS These patients are very much helped by being evaluated clinically by their physician, surgeon and physiotherapist in close collaboration.

EXERCISE PRESCRIPTION Cycling and water exercises are good alternatives to keep up general fitness.

EVALUATION OF TREATMENT OUTCOMES Normal clinical symptoms and signs.

DIFFERENTIAL DIAGNOSES Meniscus tear, chondral injuries, OCD, medial plica syndrome, chondromalacia patellar, patellar instability or mal-tracking, quadriceps insufficiency,

4. CHONDROMALACIA PATELLA *Cont.*

Sinding-Larsen's syndrome, synovitis, PVNS, patellar tendon disorders, referred pain, secondary
symptoms from ankle or back insufficiency, core
instability and more.

PROGNOSIS Because many cases never reach an
absolute diagnosis and correct treatment, chondromalacia patella ends the career of many young
athletes.

SYMPTOMS There is a gradual or acute dramatic onset of effusion and often severe pain in the knee, without preceding trauma. This condition can affect virtually any joint but is common in the knee.

AETIOLOGY This is one of many types of arthropathies that can affect the joints and is often mistaken for an orthopaedic injury. A minor trauma can trigger an attack. Gout is caused by excessive outflow of uric acid, due to a metabolic imbalance. It was formerly called 'port wine toe' since it is most known for the dramatic red swelling in MTP I and correlated with alcohol intake.

CLINICAL FINDINGS There is painful, often massive, effusion and increased temperature of the knee.

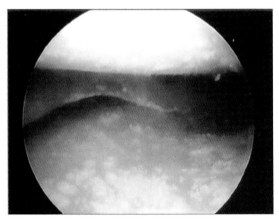

Fig. 102 Arthropathies like gout are often diagnosed by an arthroscopy on suspicion of a painful meniscal tear. The typical arthroscopic appearance is diagnostic

INVESTIGATIONS X-ray can exclude fractures, OCD, osteoarthritis, other osteochondral injuries and bone tumours. MRI can exclude soft tissue tumours and other localised soft tissue lesions. Serum levels of uric acid are elevated (more than 400) in most cases.

TREATMENT Nutritional advice is sometimes helpful, since these attacks are sometimes triggered by intake of specific food or drinks. Arthroscopic partial synovectomy is sometimes helpful in severe and chronic cases with mechanical block in movement. However, in many cases medication with NSAID for recurrent attacks and regular medication with Alopurinol for prevention of further attacks is required.

REFERRALS These patients are usually referred to their GP or a rheumatologist.

EXERCISE PRESCRIPTION Cycling and water exercises are good alternatives to keep up general fitness.

EVALUATION OF TREATMENT OUTCOMES Normal clinical symptoms and signs.

DIFFERENTIAL DIAGNOSES A variety of arthropathies, reactive arthritis, early stages of septic arthritis, PVNS etc.

PROGNOSIS This is one of many conditions, which can cause deterioration of the affected joint.

6. ILIOTIBIAL BAND FRICTION SYNDROME

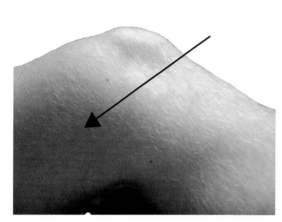

Fig. 103 Area affected by ITB syndrome

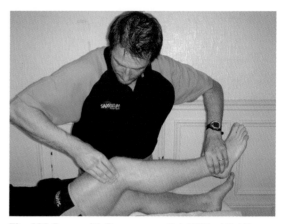

Fig. 104 Press with fingers over distal ITB whilst the player flexes and extends against resistance. If pain occurs the test is positive

SYMPTOMS Gradual onset of diffuse or localised exercise-induced pain at the lateral aspect of the knee without preceding trauma. It is most common in long-distance runners and is often labelled 'runner's knee'.

AETIOLOGY This is a stress reaction; periostitis often combined with bursitis at the insertion of the iliotibial tract at the distal lateral femur condyle from excessive jumping or running exercises. This condition typically occurs as a result of sudden changes in training habits, such as increase in intensity or amount of impact.

CLINICAL FINDINGS There is tenderness on palpation over the distal iliotibial tract at the distal lateral femur condyle, aggravated by pressing and flexing-extending the knee while pressing the insertion to the bone.

INVESTIGATIONS X-ray is normal. MRI may show superficial sub-chondral oedema or associated bursitis and can usually exclude a stress fracture. Ultrasound is also helpful in the

diagnosis. Repeating the clinical test before and after 1 ml of local anaesthetic is injected to the painful spot usually helps make the diagnosis clear.

TREATMENT This injury most often responds to conservative treatment including modification of training and stretching exercises of the iliotibial tract over three months. There is seldom any indication for immobilisation or surgery but if the symptoms persist for more than six months, a mini open release of the insertion and removal of the **bursa** may be indicated.

REFERRALS Refer to physiotherapist for planning of a three months' return programme back to sport. Refer to orthopaedic surgeon if non-operative treatment fails.

EXERCISE PRESCRIPTION Cycling and water exercises are good alternatives to keep up general fitness.

EVALUATION OF TREATMENT OUTCOMES

Normal clinical symptoms and signs.

DIFFERENTIAL DIAGNOSES Popliteus tenosynovitis (effusion, positive resistance test), stress fracture (MRI differentiates), lateral meniscus tear (effusion and positive compression test), posterior lateral corner instability (previous trauma).

PROGNOSIS Excellent.

7. LATERAL COLLATERAL LIGAMENT TEAR (LCL)

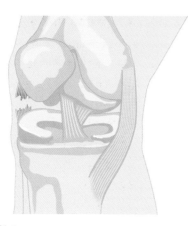

Fig. 105 LCL tear

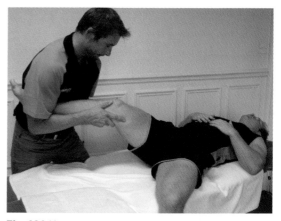

Fig. 106 Varus stress test

SYMPTOMS The symptoms are immediate haemarthrosis and pain in the lateral part of the knee. This injury is common in contact sports such as football, rugby and other high-intensity sports. LCL ruptures occur during a varus sprain and cause an inability to continue sport. The forces involved are high; since the lateral knee structures are stronger than the medial, these injuries are rare.

AETIOLOGY The ligament can rupture either partially (Grade I-II) or completely (Grade III-IV). Note! This injury is often associated with injuries to either the ACL, PCL, cartilage, menisci, capsule or the posterior lateral corner.

CLINICAL FINDINGS There is haemarthrosis in most cases. If there is a capsule rupture, blood can penetrate from the joint and cause bruising around the lateral part of the knee. The varus stress test is positive if the rupture is complete. This is the most sensitive test and can verify a lateral ligament rupture in most cases. The test should be done with a straight knee, which will show positive if there is a complete rupture, and with the knee flexed at 20–25 degrees. If the latter test is positive, this should raise suspicion of injury to the posterior lateral corner where the popliteus tendon is the predominant stabiliser. Dyer's test is valuable to evaluate the laxity caused by ruptures at the posterior lateral corner and this is indicated by an increased external rotation of the foot. Since there are often associated injuries, examination must also include tests for cruciate ligaments, menisci and cartilage.

INVESTIGATIONS Clinical examination is the most important tool for diagnosis and should include tests for all ligaments and other structures in the knee. X-ray is valuable to rule out fractures, in particular in growing or elderly athletes. MRI can verify the LCL tear in most cases but is also important for evaluating associated injuries.

TREATMENT An athlete with haemarthrosis and suspected LCL tear should be seen by an orthopaedic surgeon to consider MRI or arthroscopy. This procedure can verify the diagnosis and deal with associated injuries that are often missed. Grade I-II injuries are treated non-operatively but Grade III-IV may need surgery. Posterior lateral corner injuries are very difficult to treat and should be referred to a knee specialist. A brace is often recommended.

REFERRALS Refer to orthopaedic surgeon early for further investigations to verify the extent of the injury. Physiotherapists will be involved in close collaboration with the surgeon.

EXERCISE PRESCRIPTION Cycling and swimming are good alternatives to keep up general fitness. Varus stress to the knee should be avoided so breast stroke is not recommended. Rehabilitation back to full sport usually takes around six months.

EVALUATION OF TREATMENT OUTCOMES Monitor clinical symptoms and signs. Different functional knee scores for different sports are available to measure when the knee allows a return to full sport.

DIFFERENTIAL DIAGNOSES This is a difficult diagnosis and associated injuries to the capsule, menisci, cartilage or cruciate ligaments and fractures should always be borne in mind.

PROGNOSIS Appropriate treatment may allow a return to professional sport within six months. Some of these injuries are career-threatening for professional athletes.

8. MEDIAL COLLATERAL LIGAMENT TEAR (MCL)

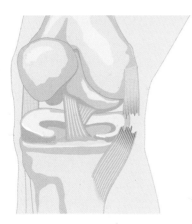

Fig. 107 MCL tear

SYMPTOMS The symptoms are immediate haemarthrosis and pain in the medial part of the knee. If only the external portion is ruptured there will be superficial bruising rather than haemarthrosis. This is an injury common in contact sports such as football, rugby and other high-intensity sports. The MCL ruptures during an excessive valgus sprain and usually causes the inability to continue sport.

AETIOLOGY In many cases this is a non-contact injury, where the player loses their balance and twists the knee. The ligament can rupture partially (Grade I-II) or completely (Grade III-IV), externally from its origin on the femur to its insertion on the tibia or internally at the insertion into the medial meniscus. This injury is, consequently, frequently associated with other injuries to cartilage, menisci, capsule or other ligaments.

CLINICAL FINDINGS There is haemarthrosis and/or medial bruising and swelling. If there is an isolated rupture of the insertion to the meniscus, there is a capsule rupture as well and blood can

penetrate from the joint and cause bruising around the medial part of the knee. This causes a menisco-capsular lesion. The valgus stress test is positive if the rupture is complete. This is the most sensitive test and can verify a medial ligament rupture in more than 90 per cent of occurrences. The test should be done with a straight knee and is positive if there is a complete tear. With the knee flexed 20–25 degrees, the test is positive if the inner portion is ruptured. The latter positive test should raise the suspicion of injury to the medial meniscus, where the inner portion of the MCL is attached. Note! Since there are often associated injuries, examination must also include tests for cruciate ligaments, capsular structures and menisci.

INVESTIGATIONS Clinical examination is the most important tool for diagnosis and should include tests for all ligaments and other structures in the knee. X-ray is valuable to rule out fractures, in particular in growing or elderly athletes. MRI can verify the

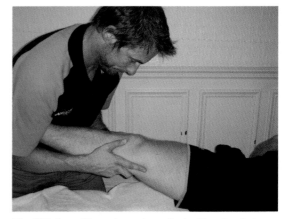

Fig. 108 A positive valgus stress test with extended knee indicates a complete MCL rupture

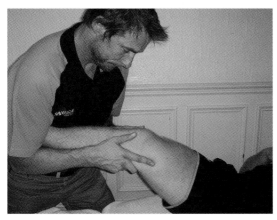

Fig. 109 A positive valgus stress test with flexed knee indicates a rupture of the inner portion of the MCL which inserts to the meniscus

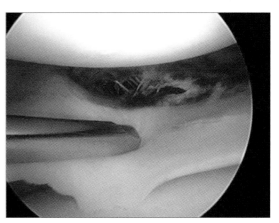

Fig. 110 Occasionally this injury occurs just at the insertion of the inner portion of the MCL to the medial meniscus. This injury must be treated with utmost caution

MCL tear in most cases but is more important for evaluating associated injuries.

TREATMENT An athlete with haemarthrosis and suspected MCL tear should be seen by an orthopaedic surgeon to consider arthroscopy. This procedure can verify the diagnosis and also deal with associated injuries that are often missed. Grade I-II injuries can most often be treated non-operatively, by a brace, but Grade III-IV may need surgery.

REFERRALS Refer to orthopaedic surgeon for further investigations to verify the extent of the injury. Physiotherapists will be involved in close collaboration with the surgeon.

EXERCISE PRESCRIPTION Cycling and swimming (not breast stroke) are good alternatives to keep up general fitness. Valgus stress to the knee should be avoided. Rehabilitation back to full sport usually takes three to six months depending on severity.

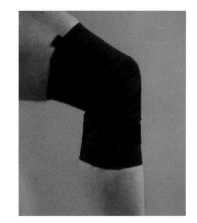

Fig. 111 A brace is useful to protect the knee during healing of an MCL tear

EVALUATION OF TREATMENT OUTCOMES

Monitor clinical symptoms and signs. Valgus stress test should be negative. Different functional knee scores for different sports are available to measure when the knee allows a return to full sport.

DIFFERENTIAL DIAGNOSES This is a straightforward diagnosis but associated injuries to the menisci, cartilage or cruciate ligaments should always be borne in mind.

PROGNOSIS Appropriate treatment will allow a return to professional sports within three months (non-operative) to six months (after surgery for Grade III-IV injury). The risk of re-rupture is low.

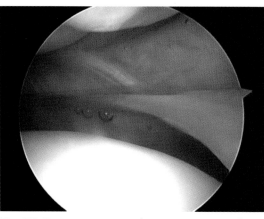

Fig. 112 Excision of the plica (seen by arthroscopy) usually relieves symptoms

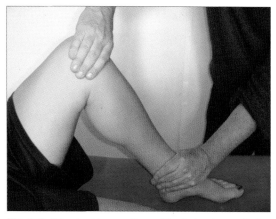

Fig. 113 Plica test is usually positive but not specific to this condition

SYMPTOMS There is gradual onset of diffuse or localised exercise-induced pain around the anterior part of the knee. Prolonged sitting and squatting often trigger the symptoms (positive movie sign). Walking down stairs is worse than up. Clicking or pseudo-locking during deep squats are common.

AETIOLOGY The medial plica is a vestigial tissue that many people have but with no symptoms. It connects the anterior fat pad with the medial knee joint capsule. Pain from an inflamed or fibrotic plica may either occur from direct contusions or sometimes as a result of sudden changes in training habits, such as an increase in intensity or amount of impact.

CLINICAL FINDINGS There is effusion and tenderness on palpation in the medial anterior joint line. The plica test is often positive.

INVESTIGATIONS X-ray can exclude fractures, OCD, osteochondral injuries and bone tumours. MRI can exclude soft tissue tumours and other localised soft tissue lesions but often miss the plica since it is commonly seen in unsymptomatic knees. MRI thus often underestimates chondromalacia and other superficial chondral injuries as well as many meniscal tears and medial plica syndrome. Ultrasound can be useful for differentiating functional tendon and ligament disorders such as jumper's knee or tendinosis around the knee. This condition is usually diagnosed and treated by arthroscopy.

TREATMENT Arthroscopic excision of the painful plica shows excellent outcomes.

REFERRALS These patients are very much helped by being evaluated clinically by their physician, surgeon and physiotherapist in close collaboration since there are many differential diagnoses (see anterior knee pain).

EXERCISE PRESCRIPTION Cycling and swimming are good alternatives to keep up general fitness. Running and jumping is usually allowed within a few weeks of surgery.

EVALUATION OF TREATMENT OUTCOMES
Normal clinical symptoms and signs.

DIFFERENTIAL DIAGNOSES Meniscus tear, chondral injuries, OCD, chondromalacia patellar, patella instability or mal-tracking, quadriceps insufficiency, Sinding-Larsen's syndrome, synovitis, PVNS, patellar tendon disorders, referred pain, secondary symptoms from ankle or back insufficiency, core instability and more.

PROGNOSIS Excellent but frequently these patients return with this painful condition in the other knee.

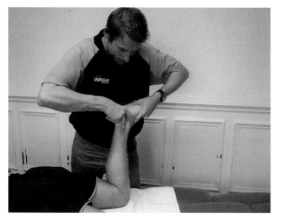

Fig. 114 Compression and rotation test provokes pain but cannot differentiate between a meniscus and a cartilage tear

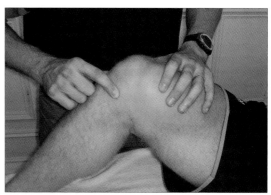

Fig. 115 Tenderness on palpation of the joint line indicates a local synovitis, often caused by an underlying cartilage or meniscal injury

SYMPTOMS Effusion and exercise-induced pain often combined with mechanical problems of locking, clicking, clunking or discomfort on impact (compression and rotation). This injury is common in sports such as football, rugby and other high-intensity contact sports but is also common, with no major trauma, as degenerative tears in older athletes or sedentary individuals.

AETIOLOGY In many cases this injury occurs from direct or indirect trauma or in association with other ligament injuries. It can occur from around 10 years of age and throughout life. Note! There are numerous ways the meniscus can rupture: horizontal, vertical, bucket handle or complex tears. The tear can be localised posteriorly, centrally or anteriorly, causing different symptoms and signs.

CLINICAL FINDINGS There is effusion in most cases. The compression rotation test is positive. There is often tenderness on palpation of the affected joint

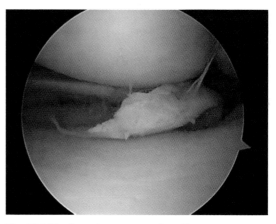

Fig. 116 Meniscus tear, as seen by arthroscopy

line and there are complementary tests for the same purpose. Note! Since there are often associated injuries, examination must include tests for ligaments, cartilage and capsular structures.

INVESTIGATIONS Clinical examination is the most important tool for diagnosis and should include tests for all ligaments and other structures in the knee. X-ray is valuable to rule out fractures and severe osteoarthritis. MRI can sometimes miss

10. MENISCUS TEAR *Cont.*

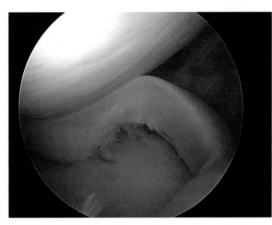

Fig. 117 Bucket handle tear of the meniscus, locking the knee from bending or extending

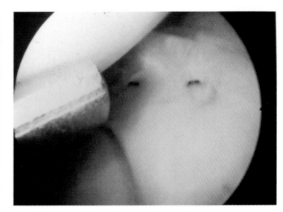

Fig. 118 A peripheral tear to the medial meniscus can be resutured

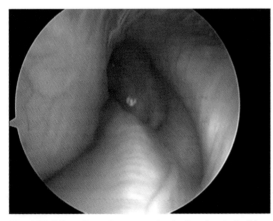

Fig. 119 Missed meniscoscapular lesion, healed with laxity, causing persistent knee instability

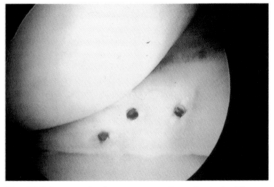

Fig. 120 A posterior horn tear can be refixated with meniscal arrows

significant meniscus injuries but is more important for evaluating associated injuries.

TREATMENT An athlete with effusion and suspected meniscus injuries should be seen by an orthopaedic surgeon to consider arthroscopy. This procedure can verify the diagnosis and deal with associated injuries. Meniscus injuries are trimmed or vaporised and partially excised. Loose bodies are excised. Meniscus injuries in the periphery can sometimes be sutured, which results in longer morbidity before a return to sport but better future protection for the knee. Meniscus re-implantation is experimental surgery and the long-term outcomes are not clear. Note: a meniscus tear should be treated for its symptoms. A non-symptomatic tear, seen on MRI, does not require surgery.

REFERRALS Refer to orthopaedic surgeon for further investigations to verify the extent of the injury. Physiotherapists will be involved in close collaboration with the surgeon.

EXERCISE PRESCRIPTION Cycling and swimming (not breast stroke) are good alternatives to keep up general fitness. Rehabilitation back to full sport usually takes a long time if micro-fracture is performed.

EVALUATION OF TREATMENT OUTCOMES
Monitor clinical symptoms and signs. Different functional knee scores for different sports are available to measure when the knee allows a return to full sport.

DIFFERENTIAL DIAGNOSES Cartilage injury, loose bodies, medial plica syndrome; all differentiated by arthroscopy.

PROGNOSIS Surgery (partial excision, timing or meniscus suture) will allow a return to professional sports in two weeks to several months. The knee will be more vulnerable to stress at the site of meniscus excision and in the long term, 10 to 20 years, the risk of developing local osteoarthritis is significant compared to a non-injured knee.

11. OSGOOD-SCHLATTER'S DISEASE

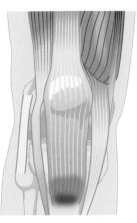

Fig. 121 Anatomical view of the location of Osgood-Schlatter's Disease

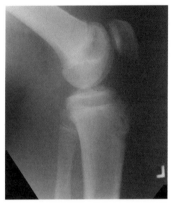

Fig. 122 Whilst the tibia apophysis is open, rapid growth can cause increased tension and localised inflammation until the growth plate is closed

SYMPTOMS There is gradual onset of localised exercise-induced pain and soreness at rest around the tuberositas tibia of the knee in a young growing athlete, usually 12 to 16 years old, without preceding trauma. It may be bilateral or affect the knees separately, depending on the growth of each leg.

AETIOLOGY The condition is caused by excessive stress to the growth plate (apophysis) where the patellar tendon inserts on the tibia. This condition typically occurs as a result of a sudden growth spurt and is aggravated by jumping and running. It is therefore often misunderstood as an over-use condition in sporty children.

CLINICAL FINDINGS There is localised tenderness on palpation over the tuberositas tibia, sometimes associated with swelling and a palpable lump.

INVESTIGATIONS X-ray defines the diagnosis and rules out rare bony tumours.

TREATMENT This temporary condition should be explained to the child and parents and treated by

suggesting temporary modifications in training. The pain will disappear when the growth plate closes.

REFERRALS Refer to physiotherapist for planning of a six to twelve months' modified return programme back to full sport.

EXERCISE PRESCRIPTION Avoid painful activities but do not advocate complete rest. It is important to keep these young athletes with their team or in their sport by participating in less painful activities so they don't lose contact and stop playing. Cycling, freestyle swimming and most low-impact activities are good alternatives to keep up general fitness.

EVALUATION OF TREATMENT OUTCOMES Normal clinical symptoms and signs.

DIFFERENTIAL DIAGNOSES Bone tumour (rare but must not be missed).

PROGNOSIS Excellent. However, since symptoms usually last a very long time, many young professional players are wrongly excluded from their team during a sensitive period of their development.

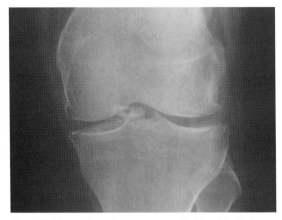

Fig. 123 X-ray of moderate osteoarthritis with slight reduction of joint space

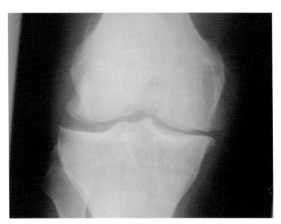

Fig. 124 X-ray of osteoarthritis grade IV with severe reduction of joint space and osteophytes

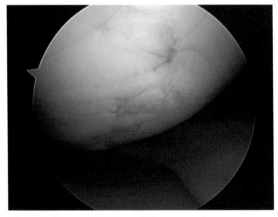

Fig. 125 Osteoarthritis grade II, as seen by arthroscopy. X-ray is normal

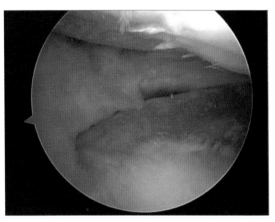

Fig. 126 Grade IV osteoarthritis affecting most of the medial weight-bearing surfaces of the knee

SYMPTOMS There is gradual onset of diffuse or localised exercise-induced pain and effusion of the knee. The knee is usually stiff and more painful in the morning than in the afternoon. In severe cases there is pain during rest. There are periods of better and worse symptoms. Clicking, crunching and pseudo-locking can occur. It usually affects the gait.

AETIOLOGY Osteoarthritis is a major problem for the general population and affects most weight-bearing joints. It is often secondary to previous trauma such as ACL ruptures and previous meniscus surgery. A typical patient is a footballer or rugby player who continues to play 10 to 15 years after an ACL reconstruction. Primary osteoarthritis is usually bilateral and hereditary. Osteoarthritis is a progressive disease affecting both the soft tissues and the cartilage of the knee joint. According to the Outerbridge scale, which is arthroscopic, osteoarthritis is graded from I (chondromalacia) to IV (bare bone) and correspondingly in a radiological score (as seen by X-ray) from 0-4.

CLINICAL FINDINGS Depends on the severity. There is effusion in around 70 per cent of cases. Deformation of the knee and protruding osteophytes can be found. A systematic and thorough approach in the clinical examination is crucial to a successful outcome. Tests of core stability, proprioception, muscle strength and balance and the flexibility of the entire kinetic chain must be thoroughly evaluated to assist in rehabilitation.

INVESTIGATIONS Weight-bearing x-ray can help to grade the severity but there could be major localised cartilage damage before X-ray will show a decreased joint space. Since this is a gradual disorder, many patients only seek medical advice in situations where the knee is particularly bad. Often meniscal tears suddenly occur, locking the knee or causing symptoms in an already sore knee. Arthroscopy is an excellent diagnostic tool to verify the extent and location of osteoarthritis as well as sorting out the meniscal problem. Shifting the load from a medial osteoarthritis to an unaffected lateral compartment may relieve symptoms over a long period of time.

TREATMENT There is no definite cure for this condition. However, there is a range of symptomatic treatments available: physiotherapy and exercise modification, NSAID, injections of synovial fluid derivates, cortisone, arthroscopic debridement, excision of loose bodies and trimming of blocking osteophytes, various forms of osteotomies for unilateral compartment osteoarthritis and, as an end range measure, knee replacement. A modern knee replacement will last for 10 to 20 years.

REFERRALS These patients are very much helped by being evaluated clinically by their physician, surgeon and physiotherapist in close collaboration.

EXERCISE PRESCRIPTION Cycling, walking, freestyle swimming and low-impact sports like golf are good alternatives to keep up general fitness.

EVALUATION OF TREATMENT OUTCOMES Monitoring of clinical symptoms and signs.

DIFFERENTIAL DIAGNOSES Meniscal tears, OCD, loose bodies, chondral injuries, reactive arthritis.

PROGNOSIS Fair-Poor. Due to the progressive development of symptoms, this condition often ends a sporting career.

Fig. 127 OCD could present as loose fragments locking the joint

SYMPTOMS There is gradual onset of diffuse or localised exercise-induced pain and soreness, often also at rest, usually in a young athlete without preceding trauma.

AETIOLOGY The aetiology is unknown but is often thought to be due to repetitive minor trauma. The sub-chondral bone goes into avascular necrosis and the overlying cartilage cracks. This condition often presents as a result of sudden changes in training habits, such as an increase in intensity or amount of impact. It is therefore often misunderstood as an over-use condition. It is graded I (softening of cartilage), II (cracks and fibrillation), III (partial loosening) or IV (loose fragment in the joint).

CLINICAL FINDINGS Symptoms depend on the grade and location of the OCD, from occasional soreness and minor effusion to a locked knee with major effusion.

INVESTIGATIONS X-ray taken in 20 degrees of flexion on weight bearing is valuable if the OCD is on the femur condyle. MRI will show subchondral oedema and is valuable to outline the extent of the injury. Arthroscopy should be performed to investigate the extent of the injury and treat it.

TREATMENT Depends on severity and location but usually involves arthroscopic surgery. Loose bodies are excised, frail edges are trimmed or vaporised and the bare bone area is micro-fractured or drilled

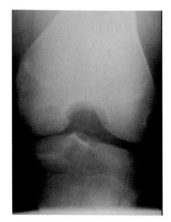

Fig. 128 OCD, as seen on X-ray

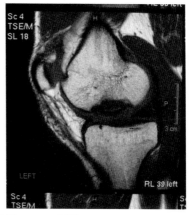

Fig. 129 The same OCD, as seen by MRI, with marked subchondral oedema

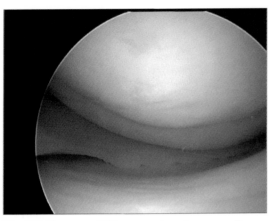

Fig. 130 The same OCD, as seen by arthroscopy. Even though the cartilage seems normal, the large, circular OCD is heavily undermined and soft on probing. It was treated successfully with micro-fracture

followed by non-weight-bearing exercise and physiotherapy over six to twelve months or more.

REFERRALS Refer to physiotherapist for planning of a six to twelve months' return programme back to sport. Refer to orthopaedic surgeon for arthroscopic treatment.

EXERCISE PRESCRIPTION No or low impact is allowed over the first months to avoid turning a lower grade OCD into a higher. Cycling and water exercises are good alternatives to keep up general fitness.

EVALUATION OF TREATMENT OUTCOMES
Normal clinical symptoms and signs and use repetitive X-rays, MRI and arthroscopy. Routine MRI may well show good healing and no bone oedema, whereas anthroscopy demonstrates that the fibrocartilage is soft and does not hold for impact. Cartilage-specific sequences on MRI are under development to improve this accuracy.

DIFFERENTIAL DIAGNOSES Meniscal tear (locking and effusion after sprain), osteochondral fracture or chondral injury (acute onset after direct trauma).

PROGNOSIS Unpredictable but many of these injuries respond well to micro-fracture. Since the injury usually takes a very long time to heal, many young professional players' careers are ended.

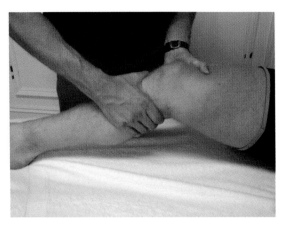

Fig. 131 A first time patella dislocation causes haemarthrosis and the clinical presentation is similar to that of an ACL rupture

SYMPTOMS The knee gives way (often with a loud popping sound) followed by immediate haemarthrosis and pain in the anterior part of the knee, preventing further activity.

AETIOLOGY The medial patella retinaculum ruptures, allowing the kneecap to migrate laterally. The kneecap can lock the knee in the flexed position by getting stuck outside the lateral femur condyle. The patella dislocates during a valgus hyper-extension sprain or from direct side trauma. The first time this happens the diagnosis is clear unless there is a spontaneous reduction. In many cases it is however a non-contact injury where the player loses their balance and twists the knee. This injury is often associated with other injuries to cartilage, menisci, capsule or ligaments.

CLINICAL FINDINGS There is intra-articular bleeding (haemarthrosis) in most cases. In first dislocations, if there is a retinaculum rupture, blood can penetrate from the joint and cause bruising around the medial anterior part of the knee. There is distinct tenderness on palpation around the patella. Since there are often associated injuries, examination must also include tests for cruciate ligaments, menisci and cartilage.

INVESTIGATIONS Clinical examination is the most important tool for diagnosis and should include tests for all ligaments and other structures in the knee. X-ray is valuable to rule out fractures, in particular in growing or elderly athletes. MRI or arthroscopy is important for evaluating associated injuries. Note! There is a high risk that the cartilage on the kneecap as well as on the femur condyle will have been damaged. The combination of ACL rupture and patella dislocation is also not uncommon.

TREATMENT A dislocated kneecap can be repositioned by gently extending the knee with the foot externally rotated to allow the kneecap to slide back into position. An athlete with haemarthrosis and suspected patella dislocation should be seen by an orthopaedic surgeon to consider early arthroscopy. This procedure can verify the diagnosis and deal with associated injuries that are often missed. Surgical repair of the medial retinaculum is only indicated in severe cases. If the injury reoccurs despite thorough physiotherapy other surgical options are available. These cases should be handled by a knee specialist.

REFERRALS Refer to an orthopaedic surgeon for further investigations to verify the extent of the injury. Physiotherapists will be involved in close collaboration with the surgeon.

14. PATELLA DISLOCATION *Cont.*

EXERCISE PRESCRIPTION Cycling and swimming are good alternatives to keep up general fitness. Valgus stress to the knee should be avoided so breast stroke is not recommended.

EVALUATION OF TREATMENT OUTCOMES Monitor clinical symptoms and signs. Different functional knee scores for different sports are available to measure when the knee allows a return to full sport.

DIFFERENTIAL DIAGNOSES This is a straightforward diagnosis but associated injuries to the menisci, cartilage or cruciate ligaments should always be borne in mind.

PROGNOSIS Good-Fair. Appropriate treatment will allow a return to professional sports within three (non-operative) to six months (after surgery).

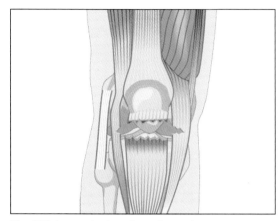

Fig. 132 Anatomic view of patella tendon rupture

Fig. 133 Clinical view of patella tendon rupture

SYMPTOMS Acute sharp pain to the anterior part of the knee and inability to walk and extend the knee. Patella tendon ruptures are rare.

AETIOLOGY This is an injury that typically occurs after previous cortisone injections to the area or when using anabolic steroids, which weaken the tendon. Long-term use of corticosteroids in rheumatic or other systemic ailments are also common backgrounds.

CLINICAL FINDINGS Inability to elicit force on knee extension. There is a palpable gap in the patella tendon, swelling and bruising and haemarthrosis.

INVESTIGATIONS Clinical examination is the most important tool for diagnosis and should include tests for all ligaments and other structures in the knee. MRI or ultrasound can verify the tear.

TREATMENT An athlete with suspected patella tendon tear should be seen by an orthopaedic surgeon for surgery.

REFERRALS Refer to orthopaedic surgeon for further investigations to verify the extent of the injury. Physiotherapists will be involved in close collaboration with the surgeon.

EXERCISE PRESCRIPTION After surgery, a braces is applied. After wound healing, cycling and swimming are good alternatives to keep up general fitness. Rehabilitation back to full sport usually takes around six months.

EVALUATION OF TREATMENT OUTCOMES Monitor clinical symptoms and signs. Different functional knee scores for different sports are available to measure when the knee allows a return to full sport.

DIFFERENTIAL DIAGNOSES This is a straight-forward but rare diagnosis. Because of haemarthrosis and give-way, it is sometimes mistaken for multi-ligament injury.

PROGNOSIS Good-Fair. The risk of re-rupture is very low but the long convalescence may sideline profesional athletes.

16. PATELLAR INSTABILITY OR MAL-TRACKING

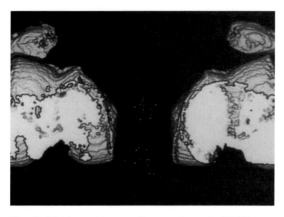

Fig. 134 Mal-tracking patellae, as shown by 3D CT scan

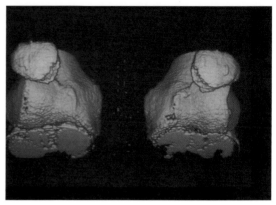

Fig. 135 Patella alta, as shown by 3D CT scan

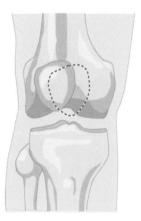

Fig. 136 Anatomic view of patellar mal-tracking

Fig. 137 Genu recurvatum, often seen in players with general joint laxity

SYMPTOMS The knee feels unstable or weak, or gives way in association with recurrent pain around the anterior part of the knee, with or without preceding trauma. It is particularly common in young female athletes.

AETIOLOGY This condition can be caused by inherited conditions such as patella baja or alta, genu valgus or muscle imbalance around the knee. It can develop after a previous patella dislocation.

CLINICAL FINDINGS Occasionally there is effusion but most commonly there are few clinical findings. An increased Q-angle and hyper-mobility can raise the suspicion of this diagnosis.

INVESTIGATIONS Clinical examination is the most important tool for diagnosis and should include tests for all ligaments and other structures in the knee. X-ray is valuable to rule out patella abnormalities. A three-dimensional CT scan taken at different knee angles can help measure the level of mal-tracking. MRI and arthroscopy may be important for evaluating alternative diagnoses. There is a high risk that cartilage on the kneecap as well as on the femur condyle will have been damaged if there was a previous dislocation. The combination of partial ACL rupture and patellar instability is not uncommon.

TREATMENT An athlete with anterior knee pain and recurrent instability of the patella should be seen by an orthopaedic surgeon and a physiotherapist. Most cases can be treated without surgery and with physiotherapy, working in particular on muscle strength and control of the entire kinetic chain. In cases with an increased Q-angle of over 20 degrees, surgical treatment with anterior medialisation of the tuberositas tibia may be indicated if physiotherapy fails.

REFERRALS Refer to orthopaedic surgeon for further investigations to verify the diagnosis. Physiotherapists should be involved in close collaboration with the surgeon.

EXERCISE PRESCRIPTION Cycling and water exercises are good alternatives to keep up general fitness. Valgus stress to the knee should be avoided so breast stroke is not recommended. Rehabilitation back to full sport usually takes around six months.

EVALUATION OF TREATMENT OUTCOMES Monitor clinical symptoms and signs. Different functional knee scores for different sports are available to measure when the knee allows a return to full sport.

DIFFERENTIAL DIAGNOSES Meniscus tear, chondral injuries, OCD, medial plica syndrome, chondromalacia patellae, quadriceps insufficiency, Sinding-Larsen's syndrome, patellar tendon disorders, referred pain, secondary symptoms from ankle or back insufficiency, core instability and more.

PROGNOSIS Good-Fair. Appropriate treatment will allow a return to professional sport within three (non-operative) to six months (after surgery).

17. PATELLAR TENDINOSIS

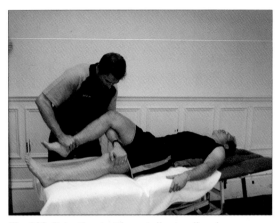

Fig. 138 Palpation test for patellar tendinosis

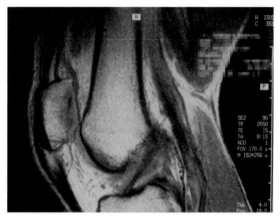

Fig. 139 Patellar tendinosis, as shown by MRI, in the most proximal and posterior part of the tendon insertion

SYMPTOMS Gradual onset of diffuse exercise-induced pain or ache around the proximal part of the patellar tendon. It is common in middle-aged runners and recreational athletes in racket sports.

AETIOLOGY Tendinosis is defined from histopathological findings as a free tendon condition with altered collagen structure, thickening of the tendon, re-vascularisation and increased cellularity. It can be looked upon as an active halt in an early healing stage and is an ongoing process, not a degenerative condition. The condition may or may not be symptomatic. A majority of complete Achilles tendon and rotator cuff ruptures show these changes. It is most often localised at the proximal, central and posterior part of the patellar tendon.

CLINICAL FINDINGS There is localised tenderness on palpation over the tendon, which often is thicker than the other side. There may be inflammatory signs with redness and increased temperature. Compare to the other side.

INVESTIGATIONS Ultrasound or MRI will show typical intra-tendinous findings.

TREATMENT This often chronic ailment may respond to conservative treatment in the early stages, including modification of training and muscle strengthening exercises that can be tried over three months. If this regime is not successful, surgery may be necessary to excise parts of the tendon. Cortisone injections should be administered only in rare exceptions, due to the high risk of later tendon rupture; indeed, NSAID and cortisone injection is one of the possible triggers of this ailment. Surgery is followed by a few weeks' partial immobilisation and a few months' rehabilitation before resuming sport. Weight bearing is usually allowed soon after surgery, avoiding plyometric activities.

REFERRALS Refer to orthopaedic surgeon for consideration of surgery. Refer to physiotherapist for planning of a three to six months' return programme back to sport.

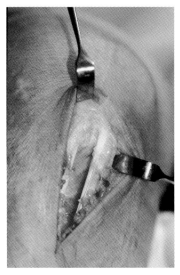

Fig. 140 Surgical excision of severe patellar tendinosis

EXERCISE PRESCRIPTION Cycling and water exercises (when the wound is healed) are good alternatives to keep up general fitness.

EVALUATION OF TREATMENT OUTCOMES

Monitor clinical symptoms and signs. Note that the injured tendon will remain thicker than the non-injured. Calf muscle performance should be similar to the other side. Objective tests for quadriceps strength and for flexibility and proprioception, such as the one-leg hop test, are strongly recommended before resuming full sport.

DIFFERENTIAL DIAGNOSES Tendinosis, tendinitis, bursitis, impingement from patella tip spur, meniscus tear, chondral injuries, OCD, medial plica syndrome, chondromalacia patellae, patellar instability or mal-tracking, quadriceps insufficiency, Sinding-Larsen's syndrome, fat pad syndrome, synovitis, referred pain, secondary symptoms from ankle or back insufficiency, core instability and more.

PROGNOSIS Good-Poor; in some cases this condition can be the beginning of the end for an elite athlete.

18. POPLITEUS TENOSYNOVITIS

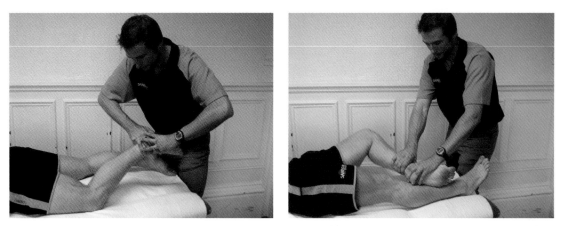

Fig. 141 Popliteus resistance test. Putting the leg in a figure-of-4 position opens up the lateral joint line for palpation

SYMPTOMS Gradual or acute onset of localised exercise-induced pain at the lateral posterior aspect of the knee with or without preceding trauma. It is most common in pivoting sports like football or rugby or in cross-country running.

AETIOLOGY This is an inflammatory response around the popliteus tendon in the posterior lateral intra-articular part of the knee. This condition typically occurs as a result of sudden changes in training habits, such as an increase in intensity or amount of impact, or after a direct impact, such as a kick.

CLINICAL FINDINGS There is tenderness on palpation in the posterior and lateral joint line over the femur condyle that is aggravated by a resistance test.

INVESTIGATIONS X-ray is normal. MRI may show superficial sub-chondral oedema and can usually exclude a lateral meniscal tear. Ultrasound is also helpful in the diagnosis. Repeating the clinical test before and after 1 ml of local anaesthetic is injected

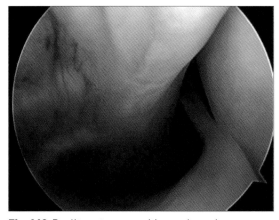

Fig. 142 Popliteus tenosynovitis, as shown by anthroscopy

into the most painful spot can usually help make the diagnosis clear.

TREATMENT This injury most often responds to conservative treatment, including modification of training and stretching exercises of the knee muscles. There is seldom an indication for surgery but in unclear situations, with effusion, arthroscopy may be needed to verify the diagnosis and administer a minor dose of cortisone.

REFERRALS Refer to physiotherapist for planning of a three months' return programme back to sport. Refer to orthopaedic surgeon if non-operative treatment fails.

EXERCISE PRESCRIPTION Most forms of exercise are allowed but temporary avoidance of jumping, twisting and pivoting activities may help.

EVALUATION OF TREATMENT OUTCOMES Normal clinical symptoms and signs.

DIFFERENTIAL DIAGNOSES Stress fracture (MRI differentiates), lateral meniscal tear (MRI or arthroscopy differentiate), iliotibial band traction syndrome (clinical differentiation and no effusion).

PROGNOSIS Excellent.

19. POSTERIOR CRUCIATE LIGAMENT TEAR (PCL)

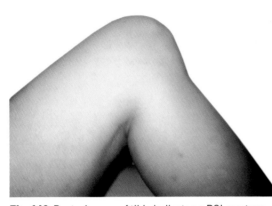

Fig. 143 Posterior sag of tibia indicates a PCL rupture

SYMPTOMS Immediate haemarthrosis and pain in the knee after a sudden hyper-flexion or hyper-extension sprain or direct tackle. It is common in contact sports such as football and rugby and other high-intensity sports.

AETIOLOGY The typical athlete suffers a hyper-extension or valgus rotation sprain during sport or after a direct impact to the anterior proximal tibia while the knee is flexed ('dashboard' injury). The thick ligament can rupture partially or completely. In growing athletes or after high-force trauma, the posterior tibia bone insertion can be avulsed. Note! This injury is often associated with injuries to cartilage, menisci, capsule or other ligaments.

CLINICAL FINDINGS There is intra-articular bleeding (haemarthrosis) in most cases. If there is a capsule rupture, blood can penetrate from the joint and cause bruising. The posterior drawer test is positive if the rupture is complete. Since there are often associated injuries, examination must also include tests for collateral ligaments, menisci and cartilage.

INVESTIGATIONS Clinical examination is the most important tool for diagnosis and should include tests for all ligaments and other structures in the knee. X-ray is valuable to rule out fractures, in particular in growing athletes or after high-impact trauma. MRI is valuable for evaluating associated injuries.

TREATMENT An athlete with haemarthrosis and suspected PCL tear should be seen by an orthopaedic surgeon to consider arthroscopy. This procedure can verify the diagnosis and deal with associated injuries that are often missed. An athlete with a complete PCL tear can usually return to full activity in most sports without surgical reconstruction. A PCL brace is very useful. However, individual considerations must be made. These injuries should be treated by a knee specialist.

REFERRALS Refer to orthopaedic surgeon for further investigations to verify the extent of the injury. Physiotherapists will be involved in close collaboration with the surgeon.

EXERCISE PRESCRIPTION After surgery, cycling and water exercises are good alternatives to keep up general fitness. Rehabilitation back to full sport usually takes around six months.

EVALUATION OF TREATMENT OUTCOMES Monitor clinical symptoms and signs. Different functional knee scores for different sports are available to measure when the knee allows a return to full sport. Recurrent pain is more common than subjective instability after a PCL injury has been thoroughly rehabilitated.

DIFFERENTIAL DIAGNOSES ACL rupture (initial posterior sagging will give a sense of anterior translation of tibia during Lachman or anterior drawer test and mislead the examiner).

PROGNOSIS Good-Fair. Surgery (PCL reconstruction) may be indicated in severe cases and will allow a return to professional sport within around six to nine months. Cartilage injuries and recurrent pain and effusion are common complications.

20. POSTERIOR LATERAL CORNER INJURIES

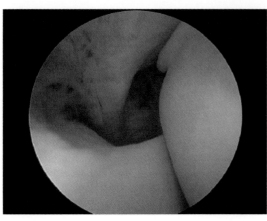

Fig. 144 A posterior lateral corner injury, reflected in the joint by separation of the popliteus tendon from lateral meniscus corner, as seen by arthroscopy

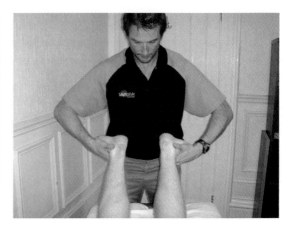

Fig. 145 A PLC injury and consequential laxity can be demonstrated by an increased external rotation of the foot with the knee flexed around 30 degrees (Dyer's test)

SYMPTOMS The symptoms are immediate haemarthrosis and pain in the posterior lateral corner of the knee. This injury is common in contact sports such as football and rugby. The diagnosis is often missed.

AETIOLOGY The typical athlete suffers a hyper-extension and varus rotation sprain during sport. The posterior lateral corner structures involve the capsule, the popliteus tendon and the lateral collateral ligament and can rupture partially or completely. This injury is often associated with other injuries to cartilage, menisci, capsule or other ligaments.

CLINICAL FINDINGS There is intra-articular bleeding (haemarthrosis) in most cases. If there is a capsule rupture, blood can penetrate from the joint and cause bruising. Dyer's test is positive. Since there are often associated injuries, the examination must include tests for collateral ligaments and menisci.

INVESTIGATIONS Clinical examination is the most important tool for diagnosis and should include tests for all ligaments and other structures in the knee. X-ray is valuable to rule out fractures. MRI is valuable for evaluating associated injuries.

TREATMENT An athlete with haemarthrosis and suspected posterior lateral corner injury should be seen by an orthopaedic surgeon to consider arthroscopy. This procedure can verify the diagnosis and deal with associated injuries. Surgery is often indicated but has to be determined individually and by a knee specialist. Surgery (reconstruction) will allow a return to professional sport within around six months. The reconstruction will protect the knee from further meniscus or cartilage injuries and restore function but it is technically difficult and a good outcome cannot be guaranteed. This injury is often missed if combined with an ACL tear. When the ACL has been reconstructed, rotational instability will remain.

REFERRALS Refer to orthopaedic surgeon for further investigations to verify the extent of the injury. Physiotherapists will be involved in close collaboration with the surgeon.

EXERCISE PRESCRIPTION Cycling and swimming (but not breaststroke) are good alternatives to keep up general fitness. Rehabilitation back to full sport usually takes around six months.

EVALUATION OF TREATMENT OUTCOMES Monitor clinical symptoms and signs. Different functional knee scores for different sports are available to measure when the knee allows a return to full sport.

DIFFERENTIAL DIAGNOSES ACL or PCL rupture.

PROGNOSIS Good-Poor. This is an injury that can halt a professional career.

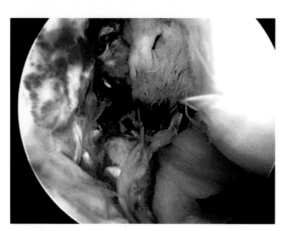

Fig. 146 A posterior medial corner injury, reflected in the joint by the capsule rupture, as seen by arthroscopy

SYMPTOMS The symptoms are acute posterior and medial knee pain and haemarthrosis, which is caused by bleeding from the ruptured posterior medial capsule. Since the capsule ruptures, the extent of bleeding is often underestimated. This injury is fairly uncommon but occurs in contact sports such as football, rugby and others.

AETIOLOGY The typical athlete suffers a hyper-extension and valgus rotation sprain. The capsule can rupture partially or completely. This injury is often associated with other injuries to the medial meniscus, cartilage or other ligaments, in particular the medial collateral ligament.

CLINICAL FINDINGS There is haemarthrosis in most cases. The capsule rupture will make blood penetrate from the joint and cause bruising. With the foot in internal rotation the posterior drawer test shows increased laxity if the rupture is complete but this injury is often missed clinically and found only during arthroscopy or MRI. Since there are often associated injuries, examination must also include tests for other ligaments, menisci and cartilage.

INVESTIGATIONS Clinical examination is the most important tool for diagnosis and should include tests for all ligaments and other structures in the knee. MRI can verify a capsule tear in most cases but this injury is often noted first on arthroscopy.

TREATMENT An athlete with haemarthrosis and suspected posterior medial capsule tear should be seen by an orthopaedic surgeon to consider arthroscopy. This procedure can verify the diagnosis and deal with associated injuries that are often missed. This injury may require early open or arthro-scopic surgery or bracing over six to twelve weeks.

REFERRALS Refer to orthopaedic surgeon for further investigations to verify the extent of the injury. Physiotherapists will be involved in close collaboration with the surgeon.

EXERCISE PRESCRIPTION Cycling and swimming (but not breaststroke) are good alternatives to keep up general fitness. Rehabilitation back to full sport usually takes around six months.

EVALUATION OF TREATMENT OUTCOMES Monitor clinical symptoms and signs. Different functional knee scores for different sports are available to measure when the knee allows a return to full sport.

DIFFERENTIAL DIAGNOSES PCL rupture.

PROGNOSIS There is very little data regarding the outcome of this particular injury.

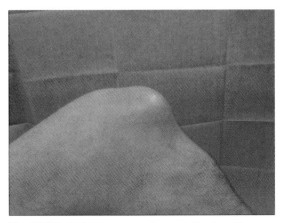

Fig. 147 Typical appearance of prepatellar bursitis

SYMPTOMS There is gradual or acute onset of localised swelling and inflammatory signs over the patella.

AETIOLOGY The bursitis can develop from a direct trauma and bleeding or from repetitive stress, when synovial fluid fills the bursa (housemaid's knee) or when pus from infected superficial skin wounds penetrates the bursa.

CLINICAL FINDINGS There is a localised tender and fluctuating swelling anterior to the patella but no effusion on the knee.

INVESTIGATIONS X-ray is normal. MRI or ultrasound will confirm.

TREATMENT If the swelling is caused by bleeding or temporary over-use (kneeling on hard ground) this injury responds to conservative treatment including cold and compression and avoidance of direct impact to the knee. There is seldom an indication for surgery. If it is caused by infection, antibiotics and open drainage of the bursa should be considered.

REFERRALS Refer to orthopaedic surgeon to determine the cause of the bursitis and treatment.

EXERCISE PRESCRIPTION Rest if the cause is infection. Otherwise most sports could be allowed, but avoid direct impact on the knee.

EVALUATION OF TREATMENT OUTCOMES Normal clinical symptoms and signs.

DIFFERENTIAL DIAGNOSES Soft tissue tumour (rare). Septic bursitis can develop into a much more dangerous septic arthritis by penetration of bacteria into the knee joint via the blood.

PROGNOSIS Good-Fair. Once the bursa has been affected, it will be more sensitive to further knocks and the bursitis can therefore recur independent of the initial cause.

23. RUPTURE OF THE QUADRICEPS OR HAMSTRING MUSCLES

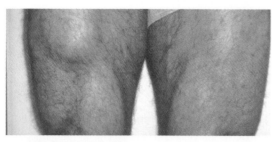

Fig. 148 Clinical view of quadriceps rupture in right leg

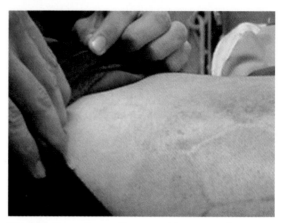

Fig. 149 Haematoma after a quadriceps muscle rupture. Note the mark of the football on the thigh. Apply ice and compression!

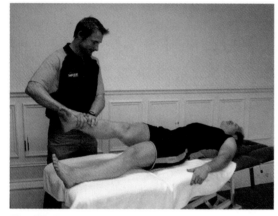

Fig. 150 Resisted strength test of rectus femoris hip flexion function

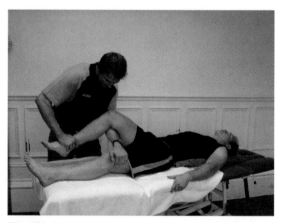

Fig. 151 Resisted strength test of quadriceps knee extension function

SYMPTOMS Sudden sharp pain most commonly affecting the quadriceps or hamstring muscles during activity. Often the athlete falls in the middle of a stride and cannot continue.

AETIOLOGY The tear can be partial (Grade I-II) or complete (Grade III-IV), often close to a musculo-tendinous junction and occasionally at the origins. The muscle can tear from sudden excessive strain, often during an eccentric contraction such as landing from a jump or push-off in sprinting.

CLINICAL FINDINGS There is tenderness on palpation around the rupture; sometimes there is a palpable gap in the muscle. Contraction of the muscle during a resistance test is painful and there is obvious weakness.

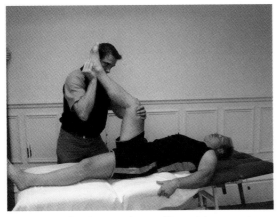

Fig. 152 Resisted strength test of hamstring muscles

INVESTIGATIONS Clinical examination is the most important tool for diagnosis and should also include tests for all ligaments and other structures in the knee. Ultrasound and MRI can be valuable to determine whether the tear is intra- or inter-muscular, which is important for treatment and prognosis.

TREATMENT Most muscle ruptures can be treated without surgery with immediate compression and ice, followed by gradual mobilisation and increased activity, guided by a rehabilitation programme, over three months. If the rupture is complete, surgery may be required. Also if the rupture and bleeding occur within its fascia, intra-muscular, surgical evacuation of the haematoma may be necessary.

REFERRALS Refer to orthopaedic surgeon for further investigations to verify the extent of the injury. Physiotherapists will be involved in close collaboration with the surgeon.

EXERCISE PRESCRIPTION Cycling and swimming are good alternatives to keep up general fitness.

EVALUATION OF TREATMENT OUTCOMES Monitor clinical symptoms and signs. Muscle strength and flexibility must be up to the same standard as the non-injured leg before allowing a return to full sport. An objective test in an iso-kinetic machine is recommended.

DIFFERENTIAL DIAGNOSES Tendon rupture, avulsion fracture of the origin or insertion.

PROGNOSIS A majority of these injuries will not cause long-term problems, subject to correct initial handling to reduce bleeding, and thorough rehabilitation. In rare cases, the bleeding may turn into calcification (myositis ossificans) and fibrosis, which may trap nerves or cause other local symptoms.

24. TIBIAL SPINE AVULSION FRACTURE

SYMPTOMS This injury is caused by a sprain and prevents continuation of sport in a young growing athlete usually below or just above 15 years of age. The symptoms are immediate haemarthrosis, which is caused by bleeding from the bone, and pain. This is an injury that is not uncommon in contact sports such as football or rugby and other high-intensity sports such as downhill skiing.

AETIOLOGY The typical athlete suffers a hyper-extension or valgus rotation sprain during sport. In some cases however it is a non-contact injury where the player loses their balance and twists the knee. The ACL avulses its insertion at the tibia spine since the bone is weaker than the ligament. Grade I injuries are not displaced; Grade II are but with the fragment still attached; Grade III is a displaced loose bony fragment. This injury is often associated with other injuries to cartilage, menisci, capsule or other ligaments.

CLINICAL FINDINGS There is haemarthrosis in most cases. If there is a capsule rupture, blood can penetrate from the joint and cause bruising. The Lachman test is positive in Grade III injuries but can be falsely negative in Grade I and II injuries. Since there are often associated injuries, examination must also include tests for collateral ligaments, menisci and cartilage. The compression rotation test is often positive due to the loose bony fragment.

INVESTIGATIONS Clinical examination is the most important tool for diagnosis and should include tests for all ligaments and other structures in the knee. X-ray is essential in growing athletes with a sus-pected ACL injury, to rule out this type of fracture. MRI or CT scans can be useful in unclear cases.

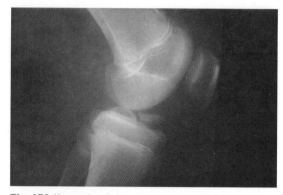

Fig. 153 X-ray showing avulsion of the tibia spine where the ACL is inserted

TREATMENT An athlete with haemarthrosis and suspected ACL tear should be seen by an orthopaedic surgeon to consider arthroscopy. This procedure can verify the diagnosis and deal with associated injuries that are often missed. In Grade III and in some Grade II injuries, the bone fragment can be re-fixated with a screw. Grade I injuries can be treated without surgery by being kept braced in extension for four to six weeks, followed by progressive rehabilitation.

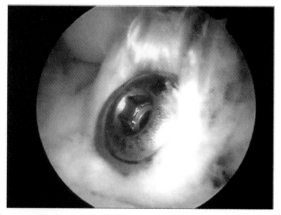

Fig. 154 Arthroscopic view of refixated ACL insertion and tibia spine

REFERRALS Refer to orthopaedic surgeon for further investigations to verify the extent of the injury. Physiotherapists will be involved in close collaboration with the surgeon.

EXERCISE PRESCRIPTION Cycling and water exercises are good alternatives to keep up general fitness. Rehabilitation back to full sport usually takes around six months.

EVALUATION OF TREATMENT OUTCOMES Monitor clinical symptoms and signs. Different functional knee scores for different sports are available to measure when the knee allows a return to full sport.

DIFFERENTIAL DIAGNOSES ACL rupture.

PROGNOSIS Surgery will allow a return to sport within around six months. The risk of re-rupture is low. Note! If the bony Grade II-III injury is missed, it will lead to chronic increased laxity and most often to the inability to perform pivoting sports due to functional instability.

EXERCISE ON PRESCRIPTION DURING INJURY TO THE KNEE

This table provides advice on forms of exercise that may or may not be recommended for athletes with different injuries. The advice must be related to the severity and stage of healing and take the individual's situation into account.

● This activity is harmful or risky.

◐ This activity can be done but with care and with specific advice.

○ This activity can safely be recommended.

	Running	Walking	Water exercises	Bicycling	Racket sports	Golf	Contact sports	Working-out	Home exercises
ACL TEAR	●	○	○	○	●	○	●	○	○
ANTERIOR KNEE PAIN	○	○	○	○	○	○	○	○	○
CARTILAGE INJURIES	●	○	○	○	●	○	●	○	○
CHONDROMALACIA PATELLA	○	○	○	○	○	○	○	○	○
GOUT: ARTHROPATHIES	●	○	○	○	○	○	○	○	○
ILIOTIBIAL BAND FRICTION SYNDROME	●	○	○	○	○	○	○	○	○
LCL TEAR	●	○	○	○	●	○	●	○	○
MCL TEAR	●	○	○	○	●	○	●	○	○
MEDIAL PLICA SYNDROME	○	○	○	○	○	○	○	○	○
MENISCUS TEAR	●	○	○	○	●	○	●	○	○
OSGOOD-SCHLATTER'S DISEASE	○	○	○	○	○	○	○	○	○
OSTEOARTHRITIS	●	○	○	○	●	○	●	○	○

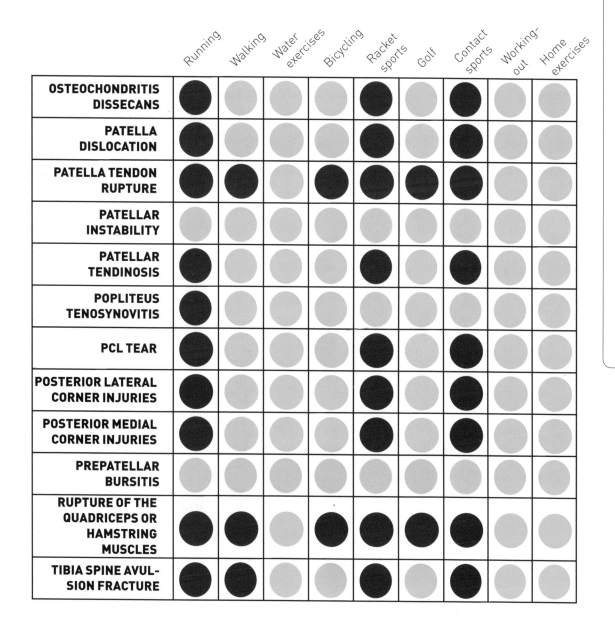

	Running	Walking	Water exercises	Bicycling	Racket sports	Golf	Contact sports	Working-out	Home exercises
OSTEOCHONDRITIS DISSECANS	●	○	○	○	●	○	●	○	○
PATELLA DISLOCATION	●	○	○	○	●	○	●	○	○
PATELLA TENDON RUPTURE	●	●	○	●	●	●	●	○	○
PATELLAR INSTABILITY	○	○	○	○	○	○	○	○	○
PATELLAR TENDINOSIS	●	○	○	○	●	○	●	○	○
POPLITEUS TENOSYNOVITIS	●	○	○	○	○	○	○	○	○
PCL TEAR	●	○	○	○	●	○	●	○	○
POSTERIOR LATERAL CORNER INJURIES	●	○	○	○	●	○	●	○	○
POSTERIOR MEDIAL CORNER INJURIES	●	○	○	○	●	○	●	○	○
PREPATELLAR BURSITIS	○	○	○	○	○	○	○	○	○
RUPTURE OF THE QUADRICEPS OR HAMSTRING MUSCLES	●	●	○	●	●	●	●	○	○
TIBIA SPINE AVULSION FRACTURE	●	●	○	○	●	○	●	○	○

v THIGH AND GROIN INJURIES

The figures below show the anatomical appearances of the groin and thigh from different angles with arrows indicating the locations of symptoms of particular injuries.

Patients with thigh and groin pain are usually not straightforward to diagnose and treat. In acute muscle rupture or trauma, it is of course easier. The patient's history is very important, since myriad conditions can cause pain in this region, ranging from referred pain from the lower back, vascular or neurological disorders, intra-pelvic or abdominal disorders such as gynaecological

Fig. 155 The groin area is very complex and groin pain can be caused by a variety of injuries

Fig. 156 Striking a ball repeatedly is a common cause of groin pain

problems, bowel ailments, prostatitis or hernias, muscle ruptures and tendon disorders or functional problems arising from poor core stability, to give just a few examples. A thorough clinical examination, followed by a systematic approach to the use of investigating tools such as ultrasound or MRI is essential for successful outcomes. These patients can travel between different health providers and become confused by the different advice and treatments given.

I must stress that in this book I deal only with musculo-skeletal causes of groin and thigh pain; if none of these causes fits with the symptoms, specialist advice should be sought. It is important to be systematic. In many of these conditions, associated or secondary problems from unilateral injuries are common. Many core stability problems cause tenderness at the insertion of the adductor longus muscles and around the symphysis so it is important to rule out whether these symptoms are primary or secondary. For example, a left knee injury, which causes limping or pain around that knee, may often result in contra-lateral right groin pain, due to the suddenly increased stress on that leg.

The history taken from the patient must include a description of the onset, type and location of the pain, details of previous injuries to the lower limbs and medical details about bowel or urinary diseases, neurological, gynaecological or back problems. If there is any suspicion that the symptoms may be caused by non-orthopaedic ailments, ask a relevant specialist for their advice. The type of pain and its triggers must be noted in detail. Note that secondary tightness of the muscles around the pelvis and hip is almost always associated. The clinical examination should include a functional provocation of the symptoms if possible. Ask the patient to demonstrate what causes most pain. The lower back must be examined from an orthopaedic and neurological perspective. Hip joint mobility, muscle flexibility tests and palpation of tender spots in the groin and thigh must be performed. X-rays are sometimes indicated but

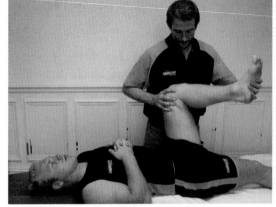

Fig. 157 Hip joint mobility test with external rotation. Compare with the other side

Fig. 158 Hip joint mobility test with internal rotation. Compare with the other side

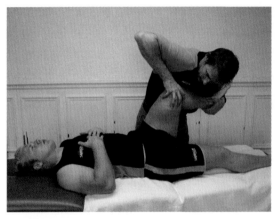

Fig. 159 Hip joint mobility test with compression can reveal injuries to the hip joint

must have a clear and relevant purpose such as suspected stress fracture or osteoarthritis, to avoid unnecessary or excessive exposure to radiation. MRI can be helpful but because of the complexity of the anatomy around the hip and groin, specific questions must guide the radiologist. Herniogram, hip arthroscopy and other sophisticated investigations may follow but again must be directed by logic.

Besides acute injuries, which are often relatively straightforward to handle, chronic groin pain can be handled as follows:

- Less than one month's duration: advice on modification of training, core stability tests and training if deemed necessary, NSAID if required, most conditions heal.

- More than one month's duration: refer to relevant specialist (orthopaedic surgeon, urologist, gynaecologist, general surgeon, physician) for advice and ask a physiotherapist for a functional evaluation. X-ray of the hip joints or relevant structures may be indicated.

- More than two months' duration: MRI or other specialist investigations may follow, guided by symptoms and signs and progression. Refer to relevant specialist for further investigation. Obviously professional athletes will not wait for two months.

- More than three months' duration: such patients are difficult to diagnose and require specialist treatment. Whatever the diagnosis, the absence from high-level sport is usually very long.

TRAINING OF THE CORE MUSCLES AND CORE STABILITY

This training requires a progressive programme, guided by a physiotherapist, since it includes a variety of complex manoeuvres, which often involve compensatory mechanisms. Slide boards, balls, wobble boards and other instruments may be used in parallel with functional sport-specific exercises such as dancing and martial arts. Strength training, stretching and functional exercises of specific muscle groups aim to restore a right–left leg balance and core stability that lasts. Limping, and injuries that move around the pelvic region, are signs of poor core stability. Recurrent pain in different locations, such as pain moving from the left groin, to the right groin, to the trochanter region and radiating down the hamstring muscles are other typical symptoms of poor core stability. The hip adductors and abductors and rotators are vital for core stability and their strength and flexibility can be trained in various ways. The iliopsoas muscles are the most important hip flexors and stabilisers of the lower back. Insufficiency or left–right imbalances of this

Fig. 160 Core stability exercises including martial arts are very important

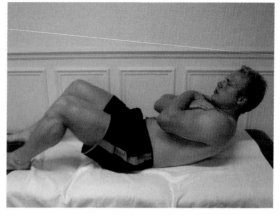

Fig. 161 Test of pelvic control can be tested by slow sit-ups and return to supine position

Fig. 162 The 'Charlie Chaplin' test provokes the lower lumbar vertebrae and the iliopsoas insertions

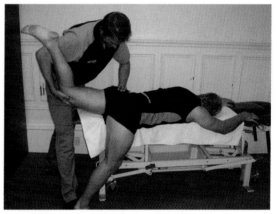

Fig. 163 Flexibility test and stretching of iliopsoas can be achieved effectively as demonstrated in this photo

muscle group can cause groin pain as well as lower back pain. A 'Charlie Chaplin' test is a simple test of iliopsoas muscle strength and screens for problems in the lower back. A disc prolapse or sciatica will make this test impossible but weak iliopsoas muscles will be identified. The flexibility of this muscle group can be improved with stretching.

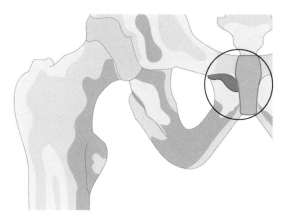

Fig. 164 Origin of the long adductor

SYMPTOMS Gradual onset of diffuse or localised exercise-induced pain at the insertion of the adductor longus around the symphysis. It can be associated with a slip, strain or split on a slippery football pitch. It is common in footballers, who usually complain of an inability to strike the ball with full power.

AETIOLOGY This is usually caused by excessive stress reaction or strain from jumping, twisting and plyometric or running exercises. Partial ruptures have also been discussed as a potential cause. The left and right leg anatomy can vary substantially in the same individual; therefore the symptoms may vary.

CLINICAL FINDINGS There is distinct tenderness on palpation over the most proximal part of the adductor longus tendon and its insertion, aggravated by contraction against resistance.

INVESTIGATIONS X-ray is normal. MRI may show intra-tendinous hyper-intensity and subchondral oedema. Ultrasound may show signs of tendinosis.

TREATMENT If it is the primary cause for the symptoms, this injury will most often respond to conservative treatment, including modification of training and stretching exercises. There is seldom any indication for immobilisation or surgery. The main clue to success is to realise whether the symptoms from the tendon are secondary to impaired core stability caused by another injury or the primary root of the symptoms.

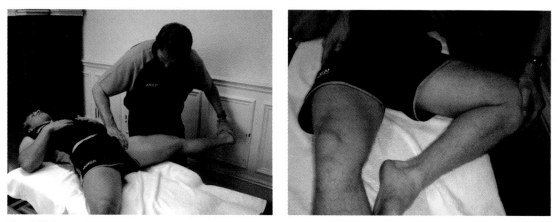

Fig. 165 Test of flexibility and strength of long adductor muscles can be evaluated whilst palpating the insertion

1. ADDUCTOR TENDONITIS/TENDINOSIS *Cont.*

REFERRALS Refer to physiotherapist for symptomatic treatment and planning of a three months' return programme back to sport. Refer to orthopaedic surgeon if non-operative treatment fails.

EXERCISE PRESCRIPTION Cycling and other low–impact activities are usually good alternatives to keep up general fitness.

EVALUATION OF TREATMENT OUTCOMES Normal clinical symptoms and signs.

DIFFERENTIAL DIAGNOSES It is important to be aware that myriad different conditions can cause these symptoms.

PROGNOSIS Excellent-Poor, depending on the cause.

2. HIP JOINT LABRAL TEARS

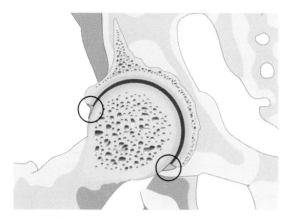

Fig. 166 Hip joint labrum

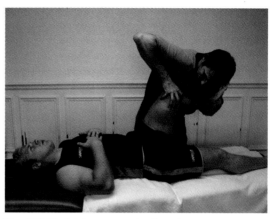

Fig. 167 Hip joint compression/rotation test

SYMPTOMS There is gradual onset of diffuse exercise-induced pain in the groin. Occasionally the patient experiences, and may be able to demonstrate, clicking from the groin in rotational movement. The hip joint is usually stiff and more painful in the morning than in the afternoon and rotational movements are most difficult. In severe cases there is pain during rest as well. There are periods of better and worse symptoms. Secondary muscular symptoms are very common around the glutei and trochanter regions. This injury is most common in relatively young and middle-aged footballers and rugby players.

AETIOLOGY Labral tears can be secondary to previous trauma. This diagnosis is one of many to be considered when a young, fit footballer has groin pain after intensive pre-season training or a tough game.

CLINICAL FINDINGS This depends on the severity. The patient's history and a systematic and thorough approach in the clinical examination are crucial for successful outcomes. Tests of core stability, proprioception, muscle strength and balance, flexibility and kinetic chain function must be thoroughly evaluated. Hip rotation and compression tests may provoke the symptoms.

INVESTIGATIONS X-ray is normal. MRI can occasionally indicate a labral tear. Arthrogram may be more successful in finding a leak from the joint that indicates a labral tear but carries a small risk of complications. Arthroscopy, also risky, is the best method to find and treat this condition.

TREATMENT A range of symptomatic treatments is available, from physiotherapy and exercise modification to NSAID, arthroscopic debridement and excision of loose bodies.

REFERRALS These patients are very much helped by being evaluated clinically by their physician, surgeon and physiotherapist in close collaboration. If this diagnosis is suspected, the patient should be referred to an experienced hip arthroscopist.

2. HIP JOINT LABRAL TEARS *Cont.*

EXERCISE PRESCRIPTION Cycling, walking, water exercises and low–impact sports like golf are good alternatives to keep up general fitness.

EVALUATION OF TREATMENT OUTCOMES Monitoring of clinical symptoms and signs, and X-ray.

DIFFERENTIAL DIAGNOSES It is important to be aware that different conditions can cause these symptoms.

PROGNOSIS Excellent-Poor depending on severity. Even if successfully operated, associated cartilage injuries can lead to osteoarthritis.

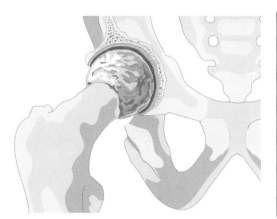

Fig. 168 Hip joint osteoarthritis, anatomic view

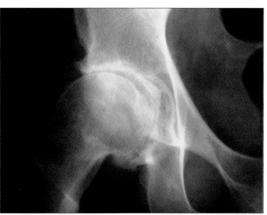

Fig. 169 X-ray of moderate hip joint osteoarthritis

SYMPTOMS There is gradual onset of diffuse exercise-induced pain in the groin. The hip joint is usually stiff and more painful in the morning than in the afternoon and rotational movements are most difficult. In severe cases, there is pain during rest. There are periods of better and worse symptoms. Secondary muscular symptoms are very common around the **glutei** and trochanter regions.

AETIOLOGY Osteoarthritis is a major problem for the general population and affects most weight-bearing joints. It can be secondary to previous trauma, and this is more common in footballers, ballet dancers and manual workers. Primary osteoarthritis is usually bi-lateral and hereditary. In the hip, this is a progressive disease affecting the soft tissues as well as the cartilage of the hip joint. For the cartilage, hip osteoarthritis is graded from 0–4 in a radiological score.

CLINICAL FINDINGS There is usually a restriction in rotation that when tested causes discomfort at the end range. Compare with the other side. Findings depend on the severity. If no structural pathological signs can be found, the problem may be functional, perhaps induced by poor core stability or referred from the back. The patient's history and a systematic and thorough approach in the clinical examination is crucial for a successful outcome. Tests of core stability, proprioception, muscle strength and balance, flexibility and so on must be thoroughly evaluated.

INVESTIGATIONS X-ray can help to grade the severity but there could be major cartilage damage before X-ray will show a decreased joint space, sclerosis and osteophytes. Since this is a gradual disorder, many patients seek medical advice in situations where the groin pain is particularly bad.

TREATMENT There is presently no cure for this condition. However there is a range of symptomatic treatments available, from physiotherapy and exercise modification to NSAID, arthroscopic debridement, excision of loose bodies and various forms of hip joint replacement. A replaced hip joint will last for 15–25 years before a replacement is required.

REFERRALS These patients are very much helped by being evaluated clinically by their physician, surgeon and physiotherapist in close collaboration.

EXERCISE PRESCRIPTION With appropriate advice and exercise the time until replacement can be significantly delayed. Cycling, walking, water exercises and low–impact sports like golf are good alternatives to keep up general fitness.

EVALUATION OF TREATMENT OUTCOMES Monitoring of clinical symptoms and signs and X-ray.

DIFFERENTIAL DIAGNOSES It is important to be aware that myriad different conditions can cause these symptoms.

PROGNOSIS Fair-Poor. Due to the progressive development of symptoms this condition often leads to so much restriction in mobility and pain that a hip joint replacement is required.

Fig. 170 Stretching of iliopsoas

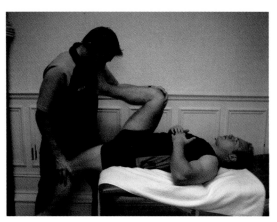

Fig. 171 Iliopsoas flexibility test

SYMPTOMS Gradual onset of diffuse or localised exercise-induced groin pain and occasionally lower back pain. A runner often complains that he cannot produce enough force in the stride forwards and a footballer cannot strike a ball properly. This condition can also present as low back pain.

AETIOLOGY This is secondary pain in the groin caused by a tight or cramping iliopsoas muscle, which blocks normal movements of the hip joint. The pain can be severe and radiate to the posterior thigh or medial femur. This condition typically occurs as a result of sudden changes in training habits, such as an increase in intensity or amount of impact in pre-season training, or as secondary to low back injuries.

CLINICAL FINDINGS There is tenderness on palpation over many structures around the groin area. Flexibility around the hip joint is decreased in all directions, in particular in extension. Iliopsoas flexibility is decreased and stretching of the iliopsoas may relieve or decrease the symptoms dramatically.

INVESTIGATIONS X-ray, MRI and other investigations are normal.

TREATMENT This problem responds to conservative treatment including modification of training and stretching exercises. Occasionally the player walks into the clinic in agony and leaves free of pain. However, if the symptoms are chronic the core stability has been affected and a long re-training period will be required. Furthermore, any underlying disc prolapse or instability must be addressed.

REFERRALS Refer to physiotherapist for functional rehabilitation.

EXERCISE PRESCRIPTION Stretching and strengthening exercises and core stability training are required. Otherwise full training can be resumed as soon as the symptoms subside.

EVALUATION OF TREATMENT OUTCOMES Normal clinical symptoms and signs. Similar flexibility in hip joint movement should be achieved on both legs.

DIFFERENTIAL DIAGNOSES It is important to be aware that different conditions can cause these symptoms.

PROGNOSIS Excellent.

5. NERVE ENTRAPMENT CAUSING GROIN PAIN

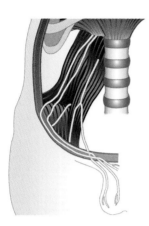

Fig. 172 Nerve distribution in the groin

SYMPTOMS Sharp, often radiating, pain in the groin, aggravated by stretching and exercise.

AETIOLOGY This pain is caused by entrapment of one of the nerves that branch to the groin: for example, the inguinal nerve. Since the left and right groins of an individual can vary substantially, from an anatomical point of view, symptoms can vary as well.

CLINICAL FINDINGS There is sometimes tenderness on palpation around the groin area but very few other clinical findings. If the affected nerve is found, Tinel's sign is positive (radiating pain is felt).

INVESTIGATIONS Most investigations are negative. MRI may in some cases show scar formations or neuromas that have caused the entrapment. Nerve conduction test may be valuable. Diagnostic blocking of the nerve with an injection of local anaesthetic may be useful to confirm the diagnosis.

TREATMENT If the duration of symptoms is less than one month, try symptomatic physiotherapy with stretching and local anti-inflammatory treatment.

REFERRALS Refer to physiotherapist for symptomatic treatment. Refer to surgeon if non-operative treatment fails, for consideration of further investigations or surgical nerve release.

EXERCISE PRESCRIPTION Maintain a normal training regime. There is no need to rest.

EVALUATION OF TREATMENT OUTCOMES Normal clinical symptoms and signs.

DIFFERENTIAL DIAGNOSES It is important to be aware that different conditions can cause these symptoms.

PROGNOSIS Excellent-Good, but the duration of symptoms may be very long even after successful surgical release.

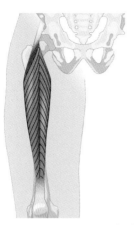

Fig. 173 Rectus femoris muscle, anatomic view

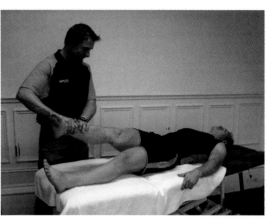

Fig. 174 Test against resistance causes pain and weakness

SYMPTOMS There is an acute onset of sharp tearing pain in the proximal anterior thigh or towards the anterior **iliac crest** during activity. This injury often occurs during intense activity in sports like tennis, squash or other sprinting and jumping sports.

AETIOLOGY This is usually a partial rupture of the insertion or proximal muscle bulk of the rectus femoris after excessive hip extension or eccentric contraction from push-off or landing.

CLINICAL FINDINGS There is tenderness on palpation over a localised area of the insertion of the muscle bulk. Resistance testing of the muscle in question will cause further pain. Jumping and landing on the forefoot with a straight knee is painful and hip flexion with straight knee against resistance and starting from maximal hip extension is very painful.

INVESTIGATIONS This diagnosis is made from the patient's history and clinical findings. Ultrasound or MRI can demonstrate the rupture and haematoma. These investigations are important if the initial diagnosis has been missed and can grade the rupture, which is important for rehabilitation and length of absence from sport.

TREATMENT In the acute situation, RICE. This injury most often responds to conservative treatment including modification of training and strength exercises over three months, which is the usual healing time. Partial weight bearing is usually allowed earlier.

REFERRALS Refer to physiotherapist for planning of a three to six months' return programme back to sport.

EXERCISE PRESCRIPTION Cycling, water exercises and other low-impact activities are good alternatives to keep up general fitness.

EVALUATION OF TREATMENT OUTCOMES Monitor clinical symptoms and signs. Strength and flexibility must be monitored objectively to be complete at the end of rehabilitation when compared with the other leg. The risk is otherwise high that the weaker muscle will re-rupture.

DIFFERENTIAL DIAGNOSES This is usually a straightforward diagnosis but still often missed.

LONG-TERM PROGNOSIS Excellent but re-ruptures are common due to a too-early return to sport and insufficient rehabilitation.

7. STRESS FRACTURE OF THE FEMUR NECK

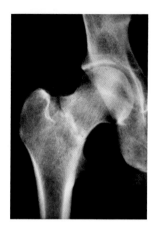

Fig. 175 X-ray of tension side stress fracture of the femur neck

SYMPTOMS Gradual or acute onset of diffuse or localised exercise-induced pain in the groin.

AETIOLOGY Stress reaction from excessive jumping or running exercises. Stress fractures in the femur neck are not as typical in osteoporotic or osteopenic patients as pelvic fractures. The location and type of fracture is important for the outcome: tension-side fractures may displace and cause major damage to the hip, leading to hip replacement in young athletes.

CLINICAL FINDINGS The athlete limps. There is pain on hip rotation and compression. Jumping and running on hard surfaces aggravates the symptoms. Secondary muscular symptoms around the groin are common.

INVESTIGATIONS This injury is often initially missed. If it is suspected, an X-ray may show the fracture. MRI will show localised bone oedema. CT can show the fracture line.

TREATMENT This injury must be treated with utmost care and the patient should not bear weight until the fracture is healed. Tension-side fractures should be operated on.

REFERRALS Refer to orthopaedic surgeon for consideration of surgery. If no surgery is indicated or after surgery, refer to physiotherapist for planning of a three to six months' return programme back to full sport.

EXERCISE PRESCRIPTION Cycling and water exercises are good alternatives to keep up general fitness.

EVALUATION OF TREATMENT OUTCOMES Normal clinical symptoms and signs and healing on X-ray.

DIFFERENTIAL DIAGNOSES It is important to be aware that different conditions can cause these symptoms.

PROGNOSIS Excellent-Good if the diagnosis is made early and if it is a side compression fracture, but poor if it is missed or if it is a tension-side fracture. Many tension-side fractures lead to displacement and, later, hip replacement.

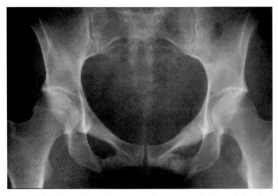

Fig. 176 X-ray showing stress fracture of the pelvic ring

SYMPTOMS There is gradual onset of diffuse or localised exercise-induced pain in the groin or pelvic area in a young anorexic athlete (often a female long-distance runner) or in elderly athletes with osteoporosis.

AETIOLOGY Stress reaction from excessive jumping or running exercises in fragile athletes. Stress fractures in the flat bones such as the pelvis are typical in osteoporotic or osteopenic patients.

CLINICAL FINDINGS Tenderness on palpation over affected bone. Eccentric jumping and running on hard surfaces aggravates the symptoms.

INVESTIGATIONS X-ray may be false-normal until callus formation, which in osteoporotic athletes may take a long time. MRI will show localised bone oedema.

TREATMENT This injury always responds to conservative treatment including modification of training until the fracture is healed.

REFERRALS If the athlete shows signs of anorexia or osteoporosis, bone density tests and referral to specialist should be made; the fracture reflects a multi-factorial disease. If this is a one-off injury, caused by sudden increase in training, refer to a physiotherapist for planning of a three months' return programme back to full sport.

EXERCISE PRESCRIPTION Cycling and water exercises are good alternatives to keep up general fitness. If osteoporosis or anorexia is causing the injury, specialist treatment is required and training must be substantially modified.

EVALUATION OF TREATMENT OUTCOMES Normal clinical symptoms and signs and X-ray.

DIFFERENTIAL DIAGNOSES It is important to be aware that these symptoms can be caused by myriad different conditions. Bone tumours and intra-pelvic ailments must be excluded.

PROGNOSIS Excellent-Good but the duration of symptoms may be very long. If anorexia is the cause, the prognosis is usually poor from a sporting point of view and the athlete should be told to abandon any attempts to reach elite level until the condition has improved.

9. SYMPHYSITIS

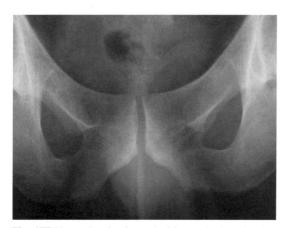

Fig. 177 X-ray showing irregularities and sclerosis of the symphysis

SYMPTOMS There is gradual onset of diffuse or localised exercise-induced pain in both the groin and around the symphysis. The symptoms are often vague and secondary muscular symptoms are very common, misleading the examiner.

AETIOLOGY This condition is thought to be a stress reaction from excessive jumping or running exercises but the exact aetiology is unknown. It typically presents as a result of sudden changes in training habits, such as an increase in intensity or amount of impact.

CLINICAL FINDINGS There is tenderness on palpation over the symphysis. However, this area is often tender in normal athletes, in particular footballers and other contact sport athletes. Pain can be provoked by repetitive jumping and attempts to strike a football hard with a straight leg.

INVESTIGATIONS X-ray may show fragmentation of the symphysis but this is also a common finding in asymptomatic players. MRI may show bone oedema but again this can be seen in asymptomatic players during the season. A bone scintigram may show localised increased uptake. Usually it takes a long time to reach this diagnosis.

TREATMENT This injury often responds to conservative treatment including modification of training and stretching exercises combined with core stability training.

REFERRALS Refer to a physiotherapist for planning of a six months' return programme back to sport. Seek advice from a urologist or gynaecologist if the symptoms are vague.

EXERCISE PRESCRIPTION Cycling and water exercises are good alternatives to keep up general fitness.

EVALUATION OF TREATMENT OUTCOMES Normal clinical symptoms and signs.

DIFFERENTIAL DIAGNOSES This is an unusual condition but one often suggested in referrals. Most pain in this area is secondary to core stability problems.

PROGNOSIS Good-Fair, but the symptoms can be very long-lasting.

EXERCISE ON PRESCRIPTION DURING INJURY TO THE THIGH AND GROIN

This table provides advice on forms of exercise that may or may not be recommended for athletes with different injuries. The advice must be related to the severity and stage of healing and take the individual's situation into account.

● This activity is harmful or risky.

◐ This activity can be done but with care and with specific advice.

○ This activity can safely be recommended.

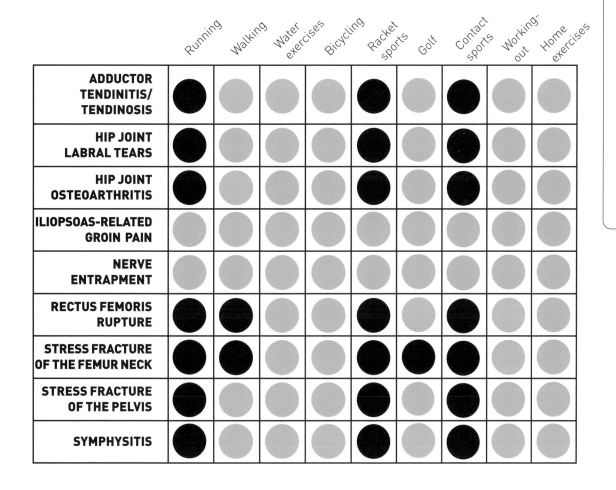

	Running	Walking	Water exercises	Bicycling	Racket sports	Golf	Contact sports	Working-out	Home exercises
ADDUCTOR TENDINITIS/ TENDINOSIS	●	○	○	○	●	○	●	○	○
HIP JOINT LABRAL TEARS	●	○	○	○	●	○	●	○	○
HIP JOINT OSTEOARTHRITIS	●	○	○	○	●	○	●	○	○
ILIOPSOAS-RELATED GROIN PAIN	◐	◐	◐	◐	◐	◐	◐	◐	◐
NERVE ENTRAPMENT	◐	◐	◐	◐	◐	◐	◐	◐	◐
RECTUS FEMORIS RUPTURE	●	●	○	○	●	◐	●	◐	○
STRESS FRACTURE OF THE FEMUR NECK	●	●	○	○	●	●	●	◐	○
STRESS FRACTURE OF THE PELVIS	●	◐	○	○	●	○	●	○	○
SYMPHYSITIS	●	○	○	○	●	○	●	○	○

vi WRIST AND HAND INJURIES

The figures below show the anatomical appearances of the hand and wrist from different angles with arrows indicating the locations of symptoms from the injuries.

Wrist and hand injuries are common in sports such as boxing, martial arts, snowboarding, skateboarding, tennis, ice hockey, hockey, handball, volleyball and similar sports. The importance of hand function is reflected in the

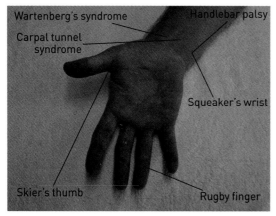

Fig. 178

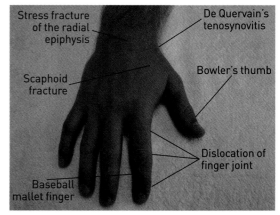

Fig. 179

Fig. 180 Boxing commonly causes hand and wrist injuries

existence of specialist hand surgeons and specially trained hand therapists who treat such injuries. The injuries listed below are just some of those that can affect the hand and wrist. If in any doubt, always consult a hand surgeon or other specialist.

1. BASEBALL MALLET FINGER

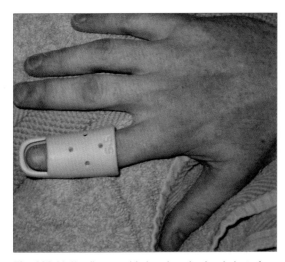

Fig. 181 Mallet finger - this bandage is simple but effective. It should be used for six weeks

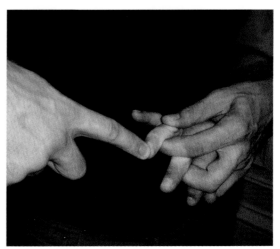

Fig. 182 Inability to extend distal phalang signifies a positive mallet test

SYMPTOMS There is localised pain and swelling around the distal inter-phalangeal (DIP) joint, which is difficult or impossible to extend fully. In chronic cases, pain and swelling may be absent but the inability to extend the distal phalanx remains.

AETIOLOGY This injury is a rupture of the most distal insertion of the extensor digitorum tendon at the DIP joint, often after a direct trauma to the tip of the finger from, for example, a basketball or volleyball.

CLINICAL FINDINGS There is tenderness on palpation over the DIP joint. The patient cannot actively extend the distal phalanx and cannot hold it extended against resistance.

INVESTIGATIONS X-ray may show a small avulsion fracture of the dorsal plate that corresponds to the tendon insertion. MRI or ultrasound may show the tendon rupture and haematoma.

TREATMENT If there is no fracture this injury usually heals by immobilising the distal phalanx in a 'mallet bandage'. If there is a fracture, re-fixing surgery is usually required.

REFERRALS Refer to hand specialist if there is a fracture on X-ray or if the diagnosis is unclear. A mallet bandage should be available to be applied on the field by the team medic.

EXERCISE PRESCRIPTION Usually the two or three adjacent fingers can be strapped together and normal activities may be continued throughout healing in some sports. However, in sports like boxing, martial arts and similar ones, six to eight weeks' absence may be needed. Running, cycling and water exercises (when the wound is healed after surgery) are good alternatives to keep up general fitness. Gym training can be maintained.

EVALUATION OF TREATMENT OUTCOMES

Normal clinical symptoms and signs. If there was a fracture, X-rays should show healing.

DIFFERENTIAL DIAGNOSES This is a clear clinical and sometimes radiological diagnosis.

PROGNOSIS Excellent, if treated appropriately. If it is missed, surgery can be performed at a later stage.

2. BOWLER'S THUMB

Fig. 183 If a bowling ball's hole is too small, it may cause 'bowler's thumb'

SYMPTOMS There is paraesthesia and decreased sensation in the thumb.

AETIOLOGY This injury is a compression **neuropathy** of the ulnar digital nerve of the thumb, for example from using a bowling ball with finger holes that one too small. A neuroma can develop, causing permanent symptoms.

CLINICAL FINDINGS Positive Tinel's sign and decreased sensation over the thumb. Compare with the other side.

INVESTIGATIONS This is a clinical diagnosis. An X-ray would be normal.

TREATMENT Avoid compression of the thumb temporarily, to see whether symptoms disappear. Adjust technique and size of finger holes to avoid further damage to the nerve.

REFERRALS If the symptoms persist, refer to hand specialist to consider surgical nerve release.

EXERCISE PRESCRIPTION Normal activities may be continued throughout healing in some sports. In precision sports like bowling, a period of less competing and training may be indicated. Running, cycling and water exercises (when the wound is healed after surgery) are good alternatives to keep up general fitness. Gym training can be maintained.

EVALUATION OF TREATMENT OUTCOMES Normal clinical symptoms and signs and a negative Tinel's sign.

DIFFERENTIAL DIAGNOSES This is a clinical diagnosis even though MRI might identify a neuroma.

PROGNOSIS Excellent, if treated appropriately. If it is missed, surgery can be performed at a later stage.

3. CARPAL TUNNEL SYNDROME

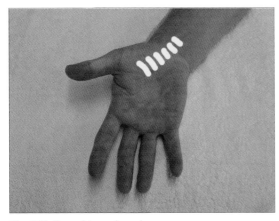

Fig. 184 Carpal tunnel syndrome

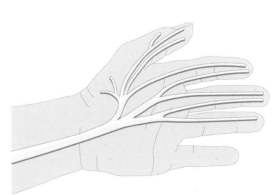

Fig. 185 Median nerve distribution in the palm of the hand and the wrist

SYMPTOMS There is paraesthesia of the radial three and a half fingers and pain around the wrist. Often, sleep is disturbed.

AETIOLOGY These symptoms are caused by chronic compression of the median nerve in the carpal tunnel by a hypertrophied flexor tendon retinaculum.

CLINICAL FINDINGS There is tenderness on palpation over the carpal tunnel and a positive Tinel's sign. In severe cases there is atrophy of the thumb muscles.

INVESTIGATIONS Nerve conduction test is usually positive.

TREATMENT NSAID and physiotherapy including stretching of the flexor muscles may be sufficient to relieve symptoms. The cause for the onset should be found and addressed. Surgery, with release of the retinaculum, is required in severe cases.

REFERRALS Refer to hand specialist if there is long duration of progressive symptoms or if the diagnosis is not clear. Physiotherapy, with exercises and stretching, is indicated.

EXERCISE PRESCRIPTION Most sports can be maintained but avoid static dorsi-flexion such as holding a handlebar on a bicycle. After surgery the symptoms are usually relieved almost immediately and most activities can be back to normal within six weeks. Running, cycling and swimming (when the wound is healed after surgery) are good alternatives to keep up general fitness. Gym training can be maintained.

EVALUATION OF TREATMENT OUTCOMES Normal clinical symptoms and signs and negative Tinel's sign.

DIFFERENTIAL DIAGNOSES This is a clear clinical diagnosis.

PROGNOSIS Excellent, if treated appropriately. If it is missed, surgery can be performed at a later stage.

4. DE QUERVAIN'S TENOSYNOVITIS

SYMPTOMS There is localised, sometimes intense exercise-induced pain and swelling over the radial part of the wrist. This is common in racket sports.

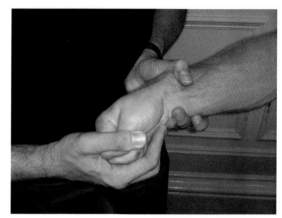

Fig. 187 Finkelstein's test is positive in de Quervain's syndrome but also in scaphoid fracture

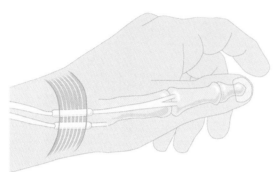

Fig. 186 de Quervain's syndrome of the wrist

AETIOLOGY These symptoms are caused by compression of the abductor pollucis longus and extensor pollucis brevis by swollen, inflamed or hypertrophied tendon sheaths.

CLINICAL FINDINGS There is tenderness on palpation over the radial part of the wrist and Finkelstein's test is positive.

INVESTIGATIONS Ultrasound investigation or MRI show para-tendinous fluid and occasionally two separate tendon sheaths. It is important to know this if surgery is required.

TREATMENT NSAID and physiotherapy including partial immobilisation of the wrist with strapping or a brace, to block ulnar deviation of the wrist and thumb **abduction**. Cortisone injections are often suggested but their side-effects must be considered.

Surgery for release of the tendon sheaths is indicated in severe or chronic cases.

REFERRALS Refer to hand specialist if there is long duration of progressive symptoms or if the diagnosis is not clear. Physiotherapy with partial immobilisation and training of hand muscle function is usually indicated.

EXERCISE PRESCRIPTION Most sports can be maintained but avoid static dorsi-flexion such as holding a handlebar on a bicycle. Moreover, technical aspects that may be causing the problems must be addressed, such as the size of the racket handle. After surgery the symptoms are usually relieved almost immediately and most activities can be back to normal within six weeks. Running, cycling and water exercises (when the wound is healed after surgery) are good alternatives to keep up general fitness. Gym training can be maintained.

EVALUATION OF TREATMENT OUTCOMES

Normal clinical symptoms and signs and negative Finkelstein's test.

DIFFERENTIAL DIAGNOSES This is a clear clinical diagnosis.

PROGNOSIS Excellent, if treated appropriately. If it is missed, surgery can be performed at a later stage.

5. DISLOCATION OF FINGER JOINT

SYMPTOMS There is intense localised pain and deformation (bayonet position, where distal phalanx is retracted over the dislocated joint by flexor tendons) of a meta-carpo-phalangeal (MCP), proximal inter-phalangeal joint (PIP) or distal inter-phalangeal (DIP) joint after direct trauma from a hard ball or a fall on a stretched-out finger.

AETIOLOGY One or more joints may dislocate and the joint capsule ruptures, causing bleeding and other soft tissue injuries.

CLINICAL FINDINGS There is tenderness on palpation and swelling over the deformed joint.

INVESTIGATIONS X-ray should be taken, to exclude fractures.

TREATMENT Repositioning of the joint can usually be done on the field by traction of the distal phalanx while holding the hand firmly.

REFERRALS Refer to hand specialist if there are multiple joint dislocations, if the joint pops back to a dislocated position or if this manoeuvre is very painful. Suspected fracture or complicated soft tissue injuries may require specialist treatment.

EXERCISE PRESCRIPTION Most sports can be maintained immediately after repositioning by strapping the adjacent fingers for support. After repositioning, the symptoms are usually relieved almost immediately and most activities can be back to normal within six weeks. Running, cycling and water exercises (when the wound is healed after surgery) are good alternatives to keep up general fitness. Gym training can be maintained.

EVALUATION OF TREATMENT OUTCOMES Normal clinical symptoms and signs.

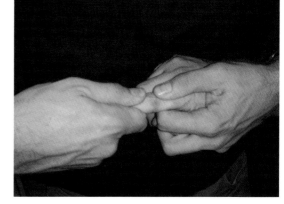

Fig. 188 Repositioning of dislocated finger joint

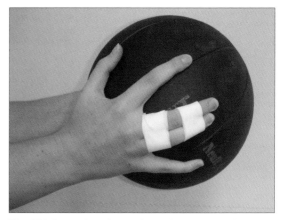

Fig. 189 Strapping of repositioned joint to nearby fingers allows an early return to sports

DIFFERENTIAL DIAGNOSES This is a clinical diagnosis but fractures and dorsal plate ruptures, which prevent repositioning, can complicate the outcome.

PROGNOSIS Excellent, if treated appropriately.

6. HANDLEBAR PALSY

Fig. 190 Professional cyclists who hold the handlebars too tightly over prolonged periods are typical victims of this syndrome

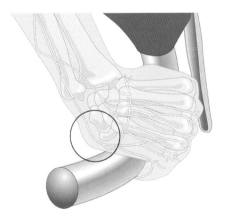

Fig. 191 Nerve distribution of paraestesia in handlebar palsy

Fig. 192 Froment's sign is positive in this syndrome

SYMPTOMS There is paraesthesia of the ulnar one and a half fingers and weakness and atrophy of the **intrinsic** hand muscles. It is common in cyclists and racket sport players.

AETIOLOGY These symptoms are caused by chronic compression of the ulnar nerve in Guyon's canal.

CLINICAL FINDINGS There is a positive Froment's sign and decreased sensation over the ulnaris nerve distribution area of the hand.

INVESTIGATIONS Nerve conduction test is usually positive.

TREATMENT Avoid further compression of the nerve by addressing technical aspects such as handlebar size and position, racket handle size, etc. NSAID and physiotherapy may be sufficient to relieve symptoms. A temporary brace may be useful. Surgery for release of the retinaculum is required in severe cases.

REFERRALS Refer to hand specialist if there is long duration of progressive symptoms or if the diagnosis is not clear. Physiotherapy with

6. HANDLEBAR PALSY *Cont.*

stretching and training of hand muscle function is indicated.

EXERCISE PRESCRIPTION Most sports can be maintained but avoid prolonged static dorsi-flexion such as holding a handlebar on a bicycle. After surgery the symptoms are usually relieved almost immediately and most activities can be back to normal within six weeks. Running, cycling and water exercises (when the wound is healed after surgery) are good alternatives to keep up general fitness. Gym training can be maintained.

EVALUATION OF TREATMENT OUTCOMES Normal clinical symptoms and signs and negative Froment's sign.

DIFFERENTIAL DIAGNOSES This is a clear clinical diagnosis.

PROGNOSIS Excellent, if treated appropriately. If it is missed, surgery can be performed at a later stage.

7. HYPOTHENAR SYNDROME

Fig. 193 Allen's test; compression of the ulnar artery causes pain and a sensation of coldness in the corresponding fingers

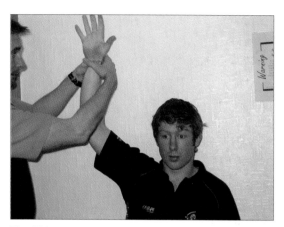

Fig. 194 Allen's test; release of pressure decreases symptoms

SYMPTOMS There is pain and a sensation of cold in the fingers. Often sleep is disturbed by pain. It is common in martial arts and lacrosse.

AETIOLOGY These symptoms are caused by spasm, thrombosis or aneurysm in the ulna artery in Guyon's canal.

CLINICAL FINDINGS There may be an ulceration of a distal finger tip and swelling around the base of the palm. Allen's test is positive.

INVESTIGATIONS Radiological intravenous investigation verifies the type and size of the blockage of the artery.

TREATMENT The cause for the onset should be found and addressed, possibly with better protection against direct trauma, bracing or changes in technique. Surgery may be required in severe cases.

REFERRALS Refer to hand specialist or vascular surgeon if there is long duration of progressive symptoms or if the diagnosis is not clear.

EXERCISE PRESCRIPTION Most sports can be maintained but avoid direct impact to Guyon's canal area. After surgery the symptoms are usually relieved almost immediately and most activities can be back to normal within six weeks. Running, cycling and swimming (when the wound is healed after surgery) are good alternatives to keep up general fitness. Gym training can be maintained.

EVALUATION OF TREATMENT OUTCOMES Normal clinical symptoms and signs and negative Allen's sign.

DIFFERENTIAL DIAGNOSES This is a difficult but clear clinical diagnosis.

PROGNOSIS Excellent-Good in most cases.

8. RUGBY FINGER

Fig. 195 In high impact sports such as rugby, where the hands are used, this injury is common

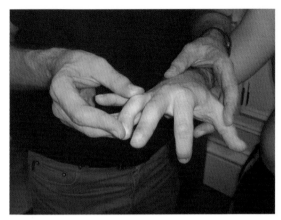

Fig. 196 Test for rugby finger

SYMPTOMS There is localised exercise-induced pain and inability to flex the DIP or PIP joint of the third finger.

AETIOLOGY These symptoms are caused by rupture of the volar plate with or without avulsion of a bony fragment or the flexor tendon insertion. It occurs when the finger is hyper-extended by force during an attempt to flex.

CLINICAL FINDINGS There is localised tenderness on palpation over the DIP or PIP joint of the ring finger and inability to flex the joints against resistance.

INVESTIGATIONS X-ray may show an avulsed bony fragment.

TREATMENT A stabilising bandage, brace or strapping should be applied. Surgery for repair of the volar plate is usually required followed by six weeks' immobilisation of the finger and physiotherapy.

REFERRALS Refer to hand specialist or orthopaedic surgeon if the pain is severe or if the diagnosis is not clear.

EXERCISE PRESCRIPTION Most sports can be maintained during healing. After surgery the symptoms are usually relieved almost immediately and most activities can be back to normal within six weeks. Running, cycling and water exercises (when the wound is healed after surgery) are good alternatives to keep up general fitness. Gym training can be maintained.

EVALUATION OF TREATMENT OUTCOMES Normal clinical symptoms and signs and good hand function. Compare with other hand.

DIFFERENTIAL DIAGNOSES This is a clear clinical diagnosis, verified by X-ray.

PROGNOSIS Excellent, if treated appropriately. If it is missed, surgery can be performed at a later stage.

9. SCAPHOID FRACTURE

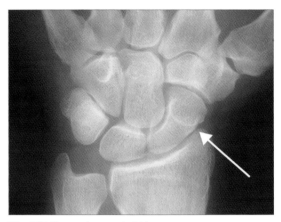

Fig. 197 X-ray of a scaphoid fracture

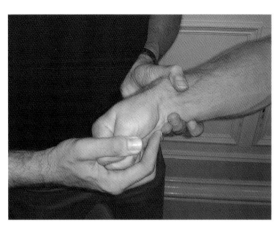

Fig. 198 Finkelstein's test is positive. There is tenderness on palpation in the 'snuff box'

SYMPTOMS There is localised pain and swelling over the medial base of the wrist. Wrist movement and gripping are painful. It is common in ice hockey, rugby, handball and similar sports.

AETIOLOGY These symptoms are caused by fracture of the scaphoid bone through trauma caused by a direct fall on to an outstretched hand or direct impact. The prognosis varies depending on whether there is vascular disruption leading to avascular necrosis.

CLINICAL FINDINGS There is localised tenderness on palpation over the 'snuff box' overlying the scaphoid, aggravated by Finkelstein's test.

INVESTIGATIONS X-ray may verify the fracture but undisplaced fractures are common and can easily be missed. A repeat X-ray two weeks later or MRI can help to diagnose this severe injury.

TREATMENT A stabilising cast, brace or strapping should be applied over six to twelve weeks depending on clinical findings and healing. Surgery for screw

fixation followed by six weeks' immobilisation is sometimes required.

REFERRALS Refer to hand specialist or orthopaedic surgeon for consideration of surgery.

EXERCISE PRESCRIPTION Most sports can be maintained during healing subject to an immobilised wrist. Usually athletes in sports where a brace is not allowed, such as rugby or soccer, will be off for around three months. Running, cycling and water exercises (when the wound is healed after surgery) are good alternatives to keep up general fitness. Gym training can be maintained.

EVALUATION OF TREATMENT OUTCOMES Normal clinical symptoms and signs and good hand function. Compare with other hand.

DIFFERENTIAL DIAGNOSES This is a clinical diagnosis, verified by X-ray but is still often missed.

PROGNOSIS Excellent, if treated appropriately unless avascular necrosis occurs. In such cases, repeated surgery may be necessary and the athlete can be out of competition either temporarily or permanently.

10. SKIER'S THUMB

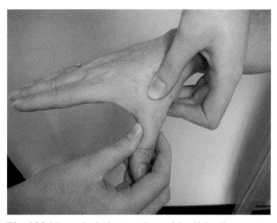

Fig. 199 Ulnar deviation test is positive if the ligament is torn

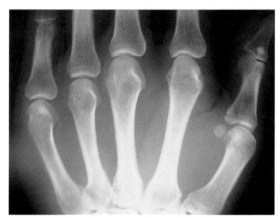

Fig. 200 Skier's thumb, as seen on X-ray, with an avulsion fracture of the ligament

SYMPTOMS There is pain and swelling over the ulnar aspect of MCP I after getting stuck or from a direct impact to the thumb during a fall. These symptoms are caused by rupture of the ulnar collateral ligament at the MCP I with or without avulsion of a bony fragment.

CLINICAL FINDINGS There is localised tenderness on palpation and inability to stabilise the MCP joint in an ulnar deviation test. Stener's complication results in soft tissue impinging into the joint, blocking the ligament from healing to the bone.

INVESTIGATIONS X-ray may verify an avulsed bony fragment.

TREATMENT A stabilising bandage, brace or strapping should be applied. Surgery for repair of the ulnar ligament is usually required, followed by six weeks' immobilisation and physiotherapy.

REFERRALS Refer to hand specialist or orthopaedic surgeon if this diagnosis is suspected or if the diagnosis is not clear.

EXERCISE PRESCRIPTION Most sports can be maintained during healing. After surgery the symptoms are usually relieved almost immediately and most activities can be back to normal within six weeks. Running, cycling and water exercises (when the wound is healed after surgery) are good alternatives to keep up general fitness. Gym training can be maintained.

EVALUATION OF TREATMENT OUTCOMES Normal clinical symptoms and signs and good hand function. Compare with other hand.

DIFFERENTIAL DIAGNOSES This is a clear clinical diagnosis but is still often missed.

PROGNOSIS Excellent, if treated appropriately. If it is missed, surgery can be performed at a later stage.

11. STRESS FRACTURE OF THE RADIAL EPIPHYSIS

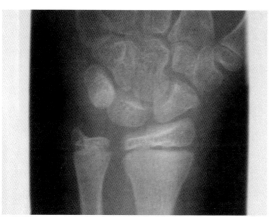

Fig. 201 X-ray of growing athlete's wrist can be considered normal and clinical diagnosis must overrule

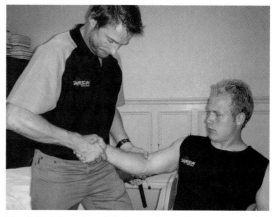

Fig. 202 A firm 'handshake test' usually causes pain if there is a stress fracture

SYMPTOMS There is exercise-induced pain and localised swelling over the distal radius. It is common in young gymnasts, soccer players and martial arts athletes.

AETIOLOGY These symptoms are caused by a stress fracture of the radial epiphysis from excessive tension-compression activities.

CLINICAL FINDINGS There is localised tenderness on palpation and pain on resisted dorsi-flexion-pronation or supination of the wrist, in a 'handshake test'.

INVESTIGATIONS X-ray is usually normal. Repeat X-ray after two weeks; MRI or bone scintigram verifies the diagnosis.

TREATMENT A stabilising bandage, brace or strapping on the wrist should be applied for two to four weeks. It is important to address what caused the injury to avoid further mistakes.

REFERRALS Refer to orthopaedic surgeon for immobilisation or if the diagnosis is not clear.

EXERCISE PRESCRIPTION Most sports can be maintained during healing but avoid direct impact on the wrist. After immobilisation the symptoms are usually relieved and most activities can be back to normal within six weeks. Running and cycling are good alternatives to keep up general fitness. Gym training can be maintained.

EVALUATION OF TREATMENT OUTCOMES Normal clinical symptoms and signs and good hand function. Compare with other hand.

DIFFERENTIAL DIAGNOSES This is a clear clinical diagnosis but is still often missed because of the normal first X-ray.

PROGNOSIS Excellent, if treated appropriately.

12. SQUEAKER'S WRIST

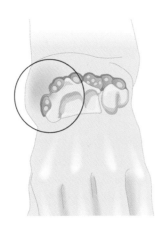

Fig. 203 Affected area of the wrist

SYMPTOMS There is exercise-induced pain and crepitation and swelling 6-8 cm proximal to Lister's tubercle at the wrist.

AETIOLOGY These symptoms are caused by a peri-tendinous bursitis between the first (abductor pollucis longus, extensor pollucis brevis) and second (extensor carpi radialis longus, extensor carpi radialis brevis) extensor compartments. This condition often affects rowers, weightlifters and squash players.

CLINICAL FINDINGS Fluctuating bursae and crepitation in wrist movements.

INVESTIGATIONS Ultrasound verifies the bursae.

TREATMENT NSAID and addressing what may have caused the bursitis. Cortisone may be injected into the bursae. Surgery for excision of the bursae may be indicated in severe cases.

REFERRALS Refer to hand specialist or orthopaedic surgeon if symptoms are severe or if the diagnosis is not clear.

EXERCISE PRESCRIPTION Most sports can be maintained. After surgery the symptoms are usually relieved almost immediately and most activities can be back to normal within six weeks. Running, cycling and water exercises (when the wound is healed after surgery) are good alternatives to keep up general fitness. Gym training can usually be maintained.

EVALUATION OF TREATMENT OUTCOMES

Normal clinical symptoms and signs and good hand function. Compare with other hand.

DIFFERENTIAL DIAGNOSES This is a clear clinical diagnosis, verified by ultrasound.

PROGNOSIS Excellent, if treated appropriately. If it is missed, surgery can be performed at a later stage.

Fig. 204 Tenosynovitis can occur around any of the extensor tendons

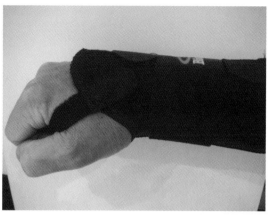

Fig. 205 A soft wrist brace may be helpful to reduce symptoms

SYMPTOMS There is acute or gradual onset of exercise-induced pain and swelling over the ulnar aspect of the wrist. Tenosynovitis can affect any tendon in any location.

AETIOLOGY These symptoms are caused by tenosynovitis and/or subluxation of the extensor carpi ulnaris tendon. It is common in tennis players, golf players, weightlifters and jockeys.

CLINICAL FINDINGS There is localised tenderness on palpation and on the ulnar aspect of the dorsal part of the wrist.

INVESTIGATIONS Ultrasound or MRI can verify the diagnosis.

TREATMENT Addressing the cause of this injury is vital, to avoid a chronic problem. A soft wrist brace may be helpful.

REFERRALS Refer to hand specialist or orthopaedic surgeon if this diagnosis is suspected or if the diagnosis is not clear.

EXERCISE PRESCRIPTION Most sports can be maintained during healing. Running, cycling and water exercises (when the wound is healed after surgery) are good alternatives to keep up general fitness. Gym training can be maintained.

EVALUATION OF TREATMENT OUTCOMES Normal clinical symptoms and signs and good hand function. Compare with other hand.

DIFFERENTIAL DIAGNOSES This is a clear clinical diagnosis but is often missed.

PROGNOSIS Excellent, if treated appropriately.

14. WARTENBERG'S SYNDROME

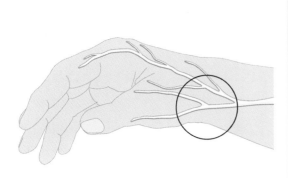

Fig. 206 Wartenberg's syndrome

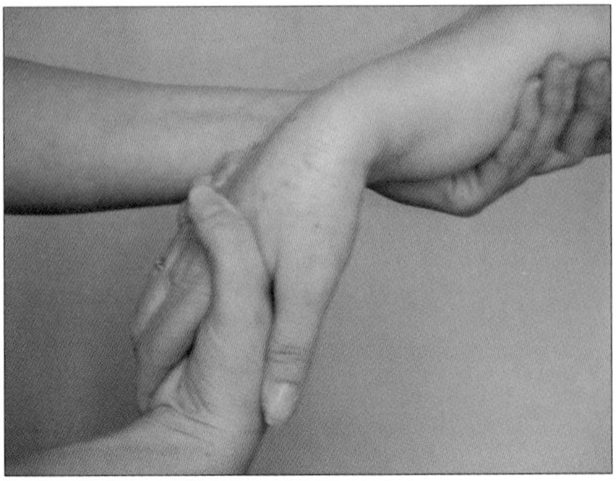

Fig. 207 Clinical test for Wartenberg's syndrome

SYMPTOMS There is a burning diffuse pain over the dorsal aspect of the thumb aggravated by pronation-supination and ulnar deviation.

AETIOLOGY These symptoms are caused by entrapment of a superficial branch of the radial nerve between the brachi radialis tendons. It is common in racket sports; wrist sweat bands have been suspected of causing this injury.

CLINICAL FINDINGS Pain is provoked on 'fisting' the hand, associated with ulnar and palmar flexion and hyper-pronation of the lower arm. Tinel's sign is often positive.

INVESTIGATIONS Injection of local anaesthetic relieves the symptoms.

TREATMENT Assessment of causative factors is essential. Physiotherapy may relieve symptoms. If there are severe or persistent symptoms surgical nerve release may be needed.

REFERRALS Refer to hand specialist or orthopaedic surgeon if this diagnosis is suspected or if the diagnosis is not clear.

EXERCISE PRESCRIPTION Most sports can be maintained during healing. After surgery the symptoms are usually relieved almost immediately and most activities can be back to normal within a few weeks. Running, cycling and water exercises are good alternatives to keep up general fitness. Gym training can be maintained.

EVALUATION OF TREATMENT OUTCOMES Normal clinical symptoms and signs and good hand function. Compare with other hand.

DIFFERENTIAL DIAGNOSES This is a clear clinical diagnosis but is often missed.

PROGNOSIS Excellent, if treated appropriately.

EXERCISE ON PRESCRIPTION DURING INJURY TO THE WRIST AND HAND

This table provides advice on forms of exercise that may or may not be recommended for athletes with different injuries. The advice must be related to the severity and stage of healing and take the individual's situation into account.

● This activity is harmful or risky.

● This activity can be done but with care and with specific advice.

● This activity can safely be recommended.

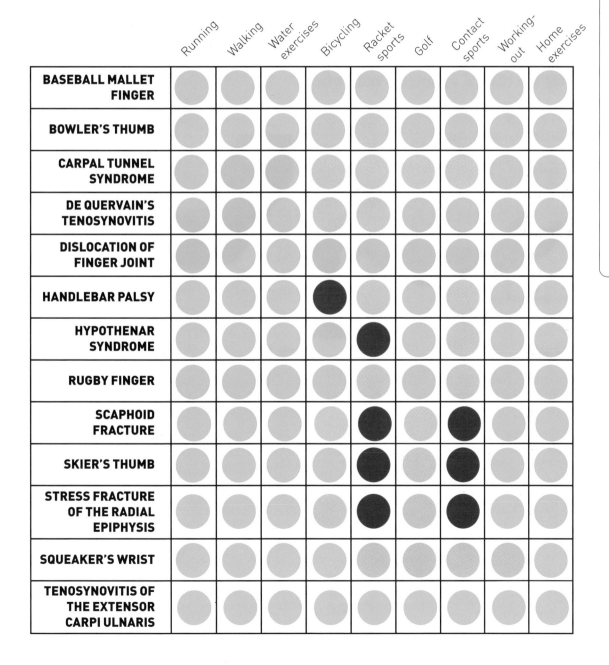

	Running	Walking	Water exercises	Bicycling	Racket sports	Golf	Contact sports	Working-out	Home exercises
BASEBALL MALLET FINGER	●	●	●	●	●	●	●	●	●
BOWLER'S THUMB	●	●	●	●	●	●	●	●	●
CARPAL TUNNEL SYNDROME	●	●	●	●	●	●	●	●	●
DE QUERVAIN'S TENOSYNOVITIS	●	●	●	●	●	●	●	●	●
DISLOCATION OF FINGER JOINT	●	●	●	●	●	●	●	●	●
HANDLEBAR PALSY	●	●	●	●	●	●	●	●	●
HYPOTHENAR SYNDROME	●	●	●	●	●	●	●	●	●
RUGBY FINGER	●	●	●	●	●	●	●	●	●
SCAPHOID FRACTURE	●	●	●	●	●	●	●	●	●
SKIER'S THUMB	●	●	●	●	●	●	●	●	●
STRESS FRACTURE OF THE RADIAL EPIPHYSIS	●	●	●	●	●	●	●	●	●
SQUEAKER'S WRIST	●	●	●	●	●	●	●	●	●
TENOSYNOVITIS OF THE EXTENSOR CARPI ULNARIS	●	●	●	●	●	●	●	●	●

vii ELBOW INJURIES

Elbow injuries are common in sports like boxing, martial arts, snowboarding, skateboarding, tennis, ice hockey, hockey, handball, volleyball and similar sports. The injuries listed below are just some of those that can typically affect the elbow. If in any doubt, always consult a specialist.

The figures below show the elbow from medial and lateral views with marking reflecting the location of symptoms for the injuries described. Note that some of these injuries can co-exist and secondary symptoms can occur that may blur the clinical symptoms and signs.

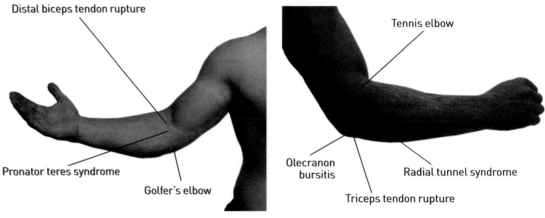

Distal biceps tendon rupture

Pronator teres syndrome

Golfer's elbow

Fig. 208

Tennis elbow

Olecranon bursitis

Radial tunnel syndrome

Triceps tendon rupture

Fig. 209

SYMPTOMS There is acute or gradual onset of exercise-induced pain around the elbow with recurrent locking or pseudo-locking or extension and flexion lag.

AETIOLOGY This is a cartilage injury in the elbow joint, which can occur by repetitive stress or direct impact, causing mechanical blocking and synovitis.

CLINICAL FINDINGS There is diffuse tenderness on palpation in the elbow joint.

INVESTIGATIONS X-ray and MRI may be normal unless there is a loose or uneven bony component.

TREATMENT Arthroscopic excision of the loose fragments.

REFERRALS Refer to orthopaedic surgeon if this diagnosis is suspected or if the diagnosis is not clear.

EXERCISE PRESCRIPTION Many sports can be maintained. Running, cycling and swimming are good alternatives to keep up general fitness. Gym training can be maintained.

EVALUATION OF TREATMENT OUTCOMES
Normal clinical symptoms and signs and good elbow function. Compare with other elbow.

DIFFERENTIAL DIAGNOSES OCD, synovitis (MRI and arthroscopy differentiate).

PROGNOSIS Excellent, if treated appropriately.

2. DISTAL BICEPS TENDON RUPTURE

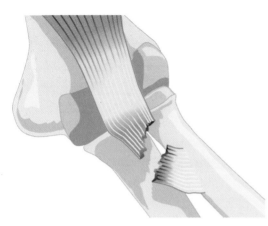

Fig. 210 Anatomical illustration of biceps tendon rupture

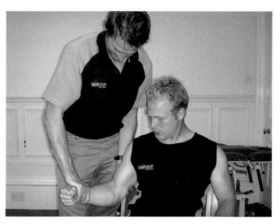

Fig. 211 Resistance test for biceps

SYMPTOMS There is acute pain in the elbow and sudden weakness in elbow flexion.

AETIOLOGY This is an acute injury, where the tendon usually ruptures close to the distal insertion at the radius during an excessive elbow extension or flexion manoeuvre.

CLINICAL FINDINGS Pain and weakness is provoked by resisting elbow flexion. There is often significant swelling, bruising and/or haemarthrosis.

INVESTIGATIONS X-ray should be taken, to rule out fracture of the elbow. MRI verifies the diagnosis.

TREATMENT A complete tear of the biceps tendon at this site usually requires surgical re-fixation in physically active people. A partial tear may be treated with partial immobilisation, since surgery can be performed later if healing does not occur.

REFERRALS Refer to orthopaedic surgeon if this diagnosis is suspected or if the diagnosis is not clear.

EXERCISE PRESCRIPTION Many sports can be maintained during healing but the inability to exert force from elbow flexion rules out most racket sports if the dominant arm is affected. After surgery most activities can be back to normal within 12 weeks. Running and cycling (when the wound is healed after surgery) are good alternatives to keep up general fitness. Gym training can be maintained.

EVALUATION OF TREATMENT OUTCOMES Normal clinical symptoms and signs and good elbow function, including strength and flexibility. Compare with other elbow.

DIFFERENTIAL DIAGNOSES This is a clinical diagnosis, verified by MRI, but fractures must be suspected.

PROGNOSIS Excellent, if treated appropriately.

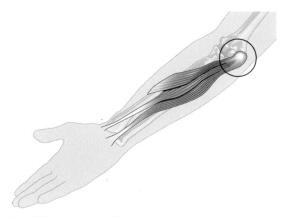

Fig. 212 Anatomical illustration of medial elbow flexor muscle origin

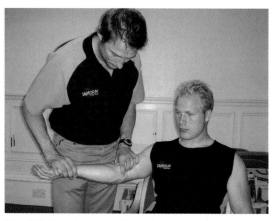

Fig. 213 Resistance test for extensor muscles and palpation at muscle origin

SYMPTOMS There is gradual onset of exercise-induced pain around the medial epicondyle of the elbow that is aggravated by hyper-extension.

AETIOLOGY This is an over-use type injury of unknown aetiology, often affecting the wrist flexor muscle origins at the medial epicondyle in racket sports players, javelin throwers and cricket bowlers. Despite the name, such injury to golfers is rare.

CLINICAL FINDINGS There is tenderness on palpation over the medial humerus epicondyle and pain and weakness is caused by resisted elbow hyper-extension.

INVESTIGATIONS X-ray and MRI are normal.

TREATMENT Temporary partial immobilisation avoiding hyper-extension may relieve symptoms. Address aspects such as bowling technique, errors in top spin or throwing, etc. Cortisone injections may be considered. A soft neoprene type of brace may decrease symptoms.

REFERRALS Refer to physiotherapist if this diagnosis is suspected or if the diagnosis is not clear.

EXERCISE PRESCRIPTION Many sports can be maintained during healing but the duration of symptoms is usually long. Running, cycling and swimming are good alternatives to keep up general fitness. Gym training can be maintained.

EVALUATION OF TREATMENT OUTCOMES Normal clinical symptoms and signs and good elbow function. Compare with other elbow.

DIFFERENTIAL DIAGNOSES Loose bodies, OCD, synovitis (MRI can usually differentiate).

PROGNOSIS Excellent, if treated appropriately.

4. LATERAL EPICONDYLITIS (TENNIS ELBOW)

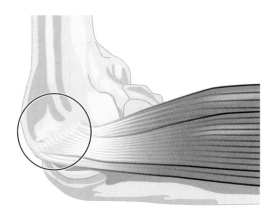

Fig. 214 Extensor muscle origin at lateral humerus condyle

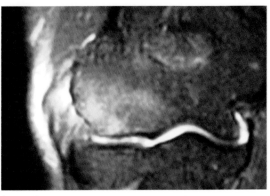

Fig. 215 Tennis elbow, as shown by MRI with surrounding bone oedema

SYMPTOMS There is gradual onset of exercise-induced pain around the lateral epicondyle of the elbow aggravated by hyper-flexion and supination of the wrist.

AETIOLOGY This is an over-use type injury of unknown aetiology, affecting the wrist extensor muscle origin at the lateral epicondyle in racket sports players, javelin throwers and cricket bowlers.

Despite the name, tennis players are an absolute minority of patients. And in further contrast with its name, there is no local inflammation.

CLINICAL FINDINGS There is tenderness on palpation over the lateral epicondyle and pain and weakness on a resisted Waiter test.

INVESTIGATIONS X-ray and MRI are normal.

TREATMENT Temporary partial immobilisation may relieve symptoms. Address bowling technique, errors in racket grip or throwing, etc. Recommend double backhand in tennis. Cortisone injections may be considered. A soft neoprene brace may decrease symptoms.

REFERRALS Refer to physiotherapist if this diagnosis is suspected or if the diagnosis is not clear. Only in persistent cases or when symptoms are severe is surgery (Homan's operation) needed.

EXERCISE PRESCRIPTION Many sports can be maintained. Running, cycling and swimming are good alternatives to keep up general fitness. Gym training can be maintained.

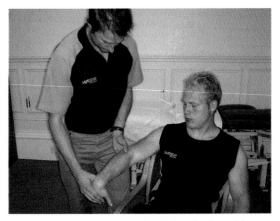

Fig. 216 Waiter's test – a resisted dorsiflexion of the wrist causes pain at muscle origin

EVALUATION OF TREATMENT OUTCOMES

Normal clinical symptoms and signs and good elbow function. Compare with other elbow.

DIFFERENTIAL DIAGNOSES Loose bodies, OCD, synovitis (MRI can differentiate). Referred pain from the cervical spine (examine the neck).

PROGNOSIS Excellent, if treated appropriately.

5. OLECRANON BURSITIS

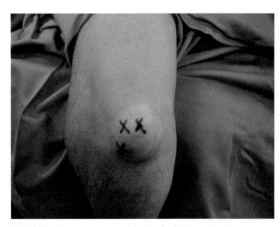

Fig. 217 Olecranon bursitis, typical appearance

SYMPTOMS There is gradual or acute onset of localised swelling and inflammatory signs over the olecranon.

AETIOLOGY It can occur after direct trauma and bleeding, from repetitive stress causing synovial fluid to fill the bursa, 'student's elbow' or pus in the bursa from infected superficial skin wounds.

CLINICAL FINDINGS Localised tender fluctuating swelling over the olecranon but no effusion of the elbow.

INVESTIGATIONS This is a clinical diagnosis. X-ray is normal. MRI or ultrasound will confirm the diagnosis. If septic bursitis is suspected tests for infections (temperature, CRP, ESR and bacterial cultures) must be performed.

TREATMENT If the swelling is caused by a bleeding or temporary over-use this injury responds to conservative treatment including ice and compression and avoiding direct impact. There is seldom any indication for surgery. If it is caused by infection antibiotics and/or open drainage of the bursa should be considered. In chronic cases, surgery may also be indicated for cosmetic reasons.

REFERRALS Refer to orthopaedic surgeon to determine the cause of the bursitis.

EXERCISE PRESCRIPTION Rest, if the cause is infection. Otherwise, most sports could be considered.

EVALUATION OF TREATMENT OUTCOMES Normal clinical symptoms and signs.

DIFFERENTIAL DIAGNOSES Soft tissue tumour (MRI can differentiate). Septic arthritis (elbow effusion and painful movement).

PROGNOSIS Good-Fair. Once the bursa has been affected, it will be more sensitive to further knocks and the bursitis can recur independent of the initial cause.

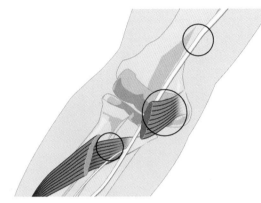

Fig. 218 Pronator teres muscles and median nerve branch

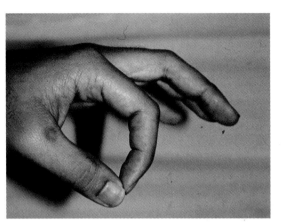

Fig. 219 Square test is positive in pronator teres syndrome

SYMPTOMS There is gradual onset of exercise-induced pain around the anterior proximal arm with paraesthesia of the radial three and a half fingers.

AETIOLOGY This is an injury often affecting the wrist in weightlifters, players in racket sports, javelin throwers and cricket bowlers. It is an entrapment of the median nerve between the two bulks of the pronator teres muscle or in some cases in the fascia between the pronator teres and flexor carpi radialis muscles.

CLINICAL FINDINGS There is a positive Square test.

INVESTIGATIONS X-ray and MRI are normal.

TREATMENT Stretching and correction of technique. Surgical nerve release in severe cases.

REFERRALS Refer to physiotherapist if this diagnosis is suspected or if the diagnosis is not clear. Refer to orthopaedic surgeon for consideration of surgery in severe cases.

EXERCISE PRESCRIPTION Many sports can be maintained. Running, cycling and swimming are good alternatives to keep up general fitness. Gym training can be maintained.

EVALUATION OF TREATMENT OUTCOMES Normal clinical symptoms and signs and good elbow function. Compare with other elbow. Square and Benedict's tests should be negative.

DIFFERENTIAL DIAGNOSES Radiating pain from the cervical spine (examine the neck).

PROGNOSIS Excellent, if treated appropriately.

7. RADIAL TUNNEL SYNDROME

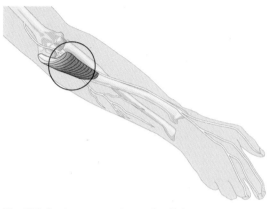

Fig. 220 Supinator muscles and radial nerve entrapment

Fig. 221 Pain on resisted extension of the middle finger

SYMPTOMS There is gradual onset of exercise-induced pain around the elbow.

AETIOLOGY This is an entrapment of the radial nerve between the supinator muscle bulks, often affecting players in racket sports and spin bowlers.

CLINICAL FINDINGS There is pain around the elbow on resisted extension of the middle finger. Tinel's sign is positive.

INVESTIGATIONS Nerve conduction test is positive.

TREATMENT Address bowling technique, errors in top spin or throwing, etc. Stretching and a soft neoprene brace may decrease symptoms.

REFERRALS Refer to physiotherapist if this diagnosis is suspected or if the diagnosis is not clear. If the symptoms are severe, refer to orthopaedic surgeon.

EXERCISE PRESCRIPTION Many sports can be maintained. Running, cycling and swimming are good alternatives to keep up general fitness. Gym training can be maintained.

EVALUATION OF TREATMENT OUTCOMES Normal clinical symptoms and signs and good elbow function. Compare with other elbow. Resistance test and Tinel's sign should be negative.

DIFFERENTIAL DIAGNOSES Loose bodies, OCD, synovitis (MRI can differentiate).

PROGNOSIS Excellent, if treated appropriately.

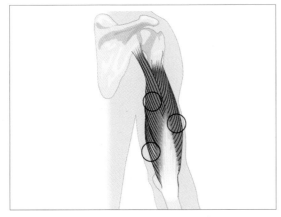

Fig. 222 Triceps muscle ruptures most often occur close to the musculo-tendinous junction

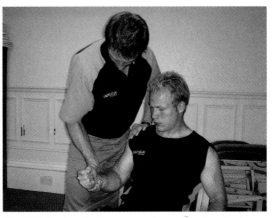

Fig. 223 Resisted elbow extension causes weakness and pain

SYMPTOMS There is acute onset of pain and bleeding around the triceps, tendor insection at the **olecranon** of the elbow, and loss of extension power.

AETIOLOGY This is an injury occurring from an excessive eccentric contraction or direct impact to the elbow, often affecting players in contact sports. Occasionally an avulsion fracture may occur.

CLINICAL FINDINGS There is tenderness on palpation over the olecranon and pain and weakness on resisted elbow extension.

INVESTIGATIONS X-ray and MRI are usually normal.

TREATMENT Partial tears can be treated with two to four weeks' immobilisation, followed by progressive rehabilitation over three months. A complete rupture requires surgical re-fixation.

REFERRALS Refer to orthopaedic surgeon if this diagnosis is suspected or if the diagnosis is not clear.

EXERCISE PRESCRIPTION Many sports can be maintained during healing but throwing manoeuvres are not allowed. Running and cycling are good alternatives to keep up general fitness.

EVALUATION OF TREATMENT OUTCOMES
Normal clinical symptoms and signs and good elbow function. Compare with other elbow.

DIFFERENTIAL DIAGNOSES Avulsion fracture, which is treated surgically.

PROGNOSIS Excellent, if treated appropriately.

EXERCISE ON PRESCRIPTION DURING INJURY TO THE ELBOW

This table provides advice on forms of exercises that may or may not be recommended for athletes with different injuries. The advice must be related to the severity and stage of healing and take the individual's situation into account.

● This activity is harmful or risky.

● This activity can be done but with care and with specific advice.

● This activity can safely be recommended.

	Running	Walking	Water exercises	Bicycling	Racket sports	Golf	Contact sports	Working-out	Home exercises
CARTILAGE INJURY AND LOOSE BODIES	○	○	○	○	○	○	○	○	○
DISTAL BICEPS TENDON RUPTURE	○	○	○	○	●	●	●	○	○
GOLFER'S ELBOW	○	○	○	○	○	○	○	○	○
LATERAL EPICONDYLITIS (TENNIS ELBOW)	○	○	○	○	●	○	○	○	○
OLECRANON BURSITIS	○	○	○	○	○	○	○	○	○
PRONATOR TERES SYNDROME	○	○	○	○	○	○	○	○	○
RADIAL TUNNEL SYNDROME	○	○	○	○	○	○	○	○	○
TRICEPS TENDON RUPTURE	○	○	○	○	●	●	○	○	○

Shoulder pain or instability are sometimes difficult to diagnose and treat unless caused by an obvious trauma. The patient's history is very important since myriad conditions can cause pain in this region, ranging from referred pain from the cervical spine, vascular or neurological disorders, muscle ruptures, tendon disorders, functional problems arising from poor posture or thoraco-scapular stability, to give just a few examples. A systematic approach to the use of investigating tools such as ultrasound or MRI is essential for a successful outcome. These patients often seek different health providers and can be confused by the advice and treatments given.

In this book, I deal only with the musculo-skeletal causes of shoulder pain and instability. It is important to be systematic in approach. In many of these conditions, associated or secondary problems from unilateral injuries are common. It is important to rule out whether these symptoms are primary or secondary.

The patient's history must describe the onset, type and location of the pain, details of previous injuries to the upper limbs or back and details about cardiovascular, neurological or rheumatic diseases. There are numerous non-orthopaedic conditions that may trigger shoulder pain. Heart ischaemia may well cause radiating pain to the left shoulder and liver disease to the right. In women, breast cancer and other rare diseases have to be considered. If there is any suspicion that the shoulder symptoms may be caused by non-orthopaedic ailments, ask a relevant specialist for advice.

The characteristics of pain and its triggering factors must be detailed. Note that secondary tightness of muscles around the shoulder, neck and upper back are almost always associated. A clinical examination should include a functional provocation of the symptoms if possible. Ask the patient to demonstrate what causes most pain. The shoulder must be examined both from an orthopaedic and a neurological perspective. Shoulder mobility and muscle flexibility must be investigated and palpation of tender spots performed. If X-rays are taken, there must be a clear and relevant reason, such as suspected stress fracture, osteoarthritis or tumour. MRI can be helpful but, because of the complexity of the anatomy around the shoulder, specific questions must guide the radiologist.

TRAINING OF SHOULDER AND ELBOW MUSCLES

The thoraco-scapular joint is stabilised by m latissimus dorsi, m levator scapulae, m rhomboideus, m trapezius, m serratus anterior, m pectoralis minor and m teres major. These muscles control the scapula movements that are vital for shoulder stability which is very important to restore the shoulder's function and after injury. Good posture is also essential for shoulder stability. Poor posture is unfortunately very common, and by itself can

Fig. 224 Poor posture, anterior view

Fig. 225 Poor posture, lateral view

Fig. 226 Good posture, anterior view

Fig. 227 Good posture, lateral view

cause shoulder pain. The figures on the previous page show the same player with poor (above) and improved posture (below). By inspection and identification of muscle atrophy, posture and thoraco-scapular movement, physiotherapists can cure most of the common shoulder pain conditions by advice and training.

The movement of the shoulder joint is controlled by complex muscle groups performing abduction (m deltoideus, m supraspinatus, m infraspinatus), adduction (m pectoralis major, m latissimus dorsi, m teres major, m deltoideus posterior), internal rotation (m subscapularis, m pectoralis major, m latissimus dorsi), external rotation (m infraspinatus, m teres minor), flexion (m deltoideus anterior, m pectoralis major) and extension (m latissimus dorsi, m teres major, m deltoideus posterior). Strength training of the shoulder muscles is absolutely essential in 'overhead' sports and elbow flexors (m biceps, m brachialis) and extensors (m triceps) should be included in this. Flexors (m flexor carpi ulnaris and radialis, m flexor digitorum superficialis and profundus, m pollicis longus) and extensors (m extensor carpi radialis and ulnaris, m extensor digitorum) of the wrist, as well as supinators (m biceps, m supinator) and pronators (m pronator teres) are also important. An upper limb

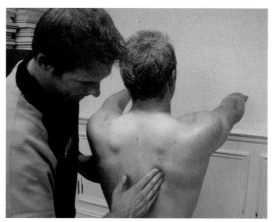

Fig. 228 Inspection, palpation and function test of thoraco-scapular articulation is very important

Fig. 229 The pectoralis muscles can be tested and strengthened in various ways

Fig. 230 Unilateral training for the latissimus dorsi muscles

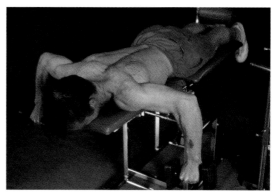

Fig. 231 Training of interscapular muscles can be done with dumbbells (as seen here) or cross-wires

Fig. 232 Tests to determine range of shoulder motion should demonstrate similar results on right and left side

training programme should always be associated with posture and core stability training. The figures on the previous page show examples of exercises that are important for shoulder function.

The shoulder has a very complex anatomy, with active and passive stabilisers. The four joints involved in shoulder control are the sterno-clavicular, acromio-clavicular, gleno-humeral and thoraco-scapular joints. The rotator cuff muscles are particularly important, as they are activated throughout gleno-humeral movements.

The figures below show the shoulder from posterior and anterior perspectives with numbers indicating the location of symptoms.

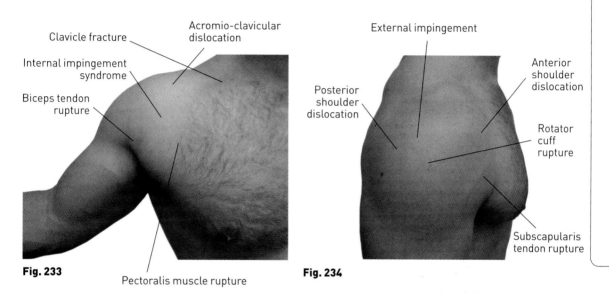

Clavicle fracture

Acromio-clavicular dislocation

Internal impingement syndrome

Biceps tendon rupture

External impingement

Anterior shoulder dislocation

Posterior shoulder dislocation

Rotator cuff rupture

Subscapularis tendon rupture

Fig. 233

Pectoralis muscle rupture

Fig. 234

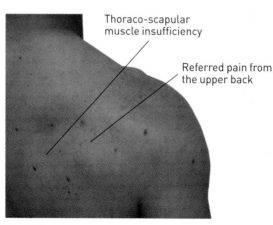

Thoraco-scapular muscle insufficiency

Referred pain from the upper back

Fig. 235

1. ACROMIO-CLAVICULAR DISLOCATION

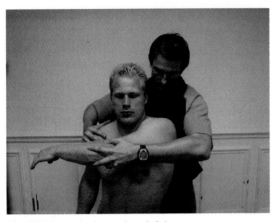

Fig. 236 Cross body test is painful

SYMPTOMS There is acute onset of localised swelling and pain over the acromio-clavicular joint with or without immediate deformation.

AETIOLOGY This injury can occur after a direct trauma or tackle to the shoulder or after a fall on to an outstretched arm. It is common in rugby, ice hockey or riding and cycling. A Grade I injury is a partial ligament tear; Grade II, one with added slight deformation or lifting of the distal clavicle end and easily reducible; Grade III, a complete tear with significant lifting, which is still easily reducible; Grades IV–VI, anterior or posterior dislocation that cannot be reduced and possibly a fracture.

CLINICAL FINDINGS There is localised tender and fluctuating swelling over the acromio-clavicular joint and, depending on the grade, a 'loose' clavicle end and typical deformation. Cross-body test is positive.

INVESTIGATIONS This is a clinical diagnosis. X-rays should be taken in different planes to rule out fracture and demonstrate the severity of dislocation by adding slight traction to the arm. MRI or ultrasound will confirm the diagnosis.

TREATMENT For Grades I-III this injury usually responds to conservative treatment including cold and compression and an 8-bandage to hold the acromio-clavicular joint in position for three to five weeks. There is seldom any indication for surgery for these grades. Some Grade III injuries and most Grade IV–VI injuries will require surgery. Surgery for this injury may not always be straightforward and should be handled by a shoulder specialist.

REFERRALS Refer to orthopaedic surgeon to determine the grade of injury and consideration of surgery. Refer to physiotherapist for functional assessment and rehabilitation.

EXERCISE PRESCRIPTION Many sports and activities, such as running and water exercises, can be maintained but avoid further direct or indirect trauma to the acromio-clavicular joint.

EVALUATION OF TREATMENT OUTCOMES Return to normal clinical symptoms and signs. Healing usually takes six weeks for Grades I–III but more severe injuries, requiring surgery, may bar a player from contact sports for three to four months.

DIFFERENTIAL DIAGNOSES Fractures must be ruled out, in particular upper rib fractures which can be complicated by pneumo-thorax or sternoclavicle injuries.

PROGNOSIS Good-Fair depending on the severity. Grade I and above will result in a persistent slight deformation but no loss of function.

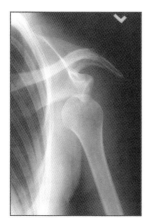

Fig. 237 X-ray showing a first time anterior dislocated shoulder

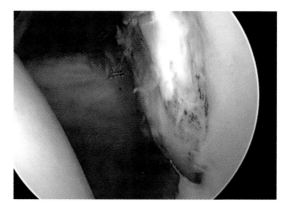

Fig. 238 Repaired anterior labrum (Bankart injury and repair) where the labrum has been refixed to the anterior edge of the glenoid with suture anchors

SYMPTOMS There is acute onset of localised swelling and pain over the anterior part of the shoulder with deformation, after an excessive external rotation and abduction trauma. This is the most common type of dislocation in sports (85-90 per cent). Movements of the arm cause pain and the patient will protect the arm in the 'Napoleon position'.

AETIOLOGY First dislocations occur after a forceful direct trauma or tackle to the shoulder or after a fall on to an outstretched arm. In the majority of cases, the arm is abducted and the shoulder is externally rotated. This is common in rugby, ice hockey, riding and cycling. In patients with lax shoulders or previous dislocations, dislocation can occur after much less trauma. The anteriorly dislocated humeral head causes a labrum tear of the anterior and inferior labrum, a Bankart injury, and a typical impression fracture, Hill Sachs lesion, on the posterior superior humeral head.

CLINICAL FINDINGS A first dislocation in a young athlete usually requires relaxation (under anaesthesia) to be repositioned, unless a team doctor is trained in the specific manoeuvres involved. After reposition, the apprehension test is positive, as well as the reposition test.

INVESTIGATIONS This is a clinical diagnosis. X-rays should be taken in different planes to rule out fracture and demonstrate the type of dislocation (to rule out rare cases of posterior dislocation). MRI is usually not required in the acute phase for the diagnosis but may be done in cases involving great trauma, to investigate associated injuries.

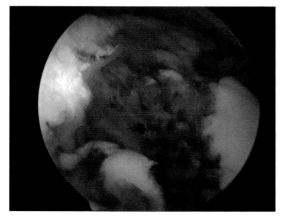

Fig. 239 Hill Sachs lesion, impression fracture of the humeral head, as seen by arthroscopy

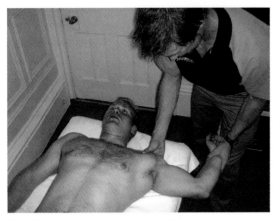

Fig. 240 Apprehension test is positive in chronic anterior instability

Fig. 241 Apprehension test can also be done in a sitting position if the patient is relaxed

TREATMENT Age and activity level is the most important factor in determining management. A rugby player younger than 25 years old will need surgery, a Bankart repair, followed by four to six months' rehabilitation, while a 40–year-old runner who has had a fall can most often be treated with stabilising training guided by a physiotherapist. In older age groups, associated injuries to the rotator

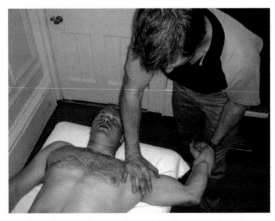

Fig. 242 Relocation test is positive if supporting the anterior capsule with the hand relieves apprehension

cuff and other structures are more common and may cause pain and need surgery for that purpose at a later stage. The risk of re-dislocation after surgery in the younger 'overhead' athletes is around 5 to 10 per cent with surgery but up to 100 per cent without.

REFERRALS Refer to orthopaedic surgeon to determine the diagnosis and for consideration of surgery. Refer to physiotherapist to start a six-month rehabilitation programme.

EXERCISE PRESCRIPTION Most sports and activities, such as cycling and cross-training, can be maintained but avoid further direct or indirect trauma to the shoulder. Running should initially be avoided since the shoulder will be sensitive to this type of impact and holding the arm still while running will cause secondary upper back and neck pain. Swimming should also wait for at least three months, though other water exercises are fine. The specific rehabilitation should aim at a full range of controlled motion, good posture and thoraco-scapular control after three months, followed by functional training for up to six months, before resuming sports like rugby.

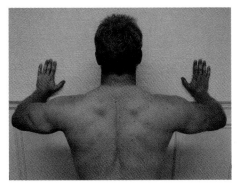

Fig. 243 The 'press against the wall' test is very useful to evaluate anterior shoulder instability (discomfort or pain and thoraco-scapular control (winging of scapulae)

EVALUATION OF TREATMENT OUTCOMES

Normal clinical symptoms and signs. The apprehension test should be negative. Functional strength, control and flexibility should be comparable with the other shoulder.

DIFFERENTIAL DIAGNOSES Fractures must be ruled out. Multi-directional and general joint laxity is a complicating factor that must be addressed before surgery.

PROGNOSIS Excellent-Fair, depending on the severity of the trauma. Multiple dislocations can lead to osteoarthritis in the long term.

3. BICEPS TENDON RUPTURE

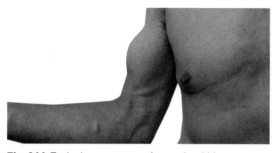

Fig. 244 Typical appearance of a proximal biceps tendon rupture - the 'Popeye sign'

Fig. 245 If resisted flexion with the arm externally rotated and straight elbow is painful or weak, a SLAP tear with biceps tendon pathology should be suspected

SYMPTOMS There is acute onset of pain over the anterior part of the shoulder with a lump typically forming at the mid-biceps from the retracted muscle bulk (the 'Popeye sign'). Usually the biceps longus tendon, originating from the anterior superior labrum, ruptures and the short biceps tendon originating at the coracoid is intact. This leaves some biceps function infact.

AETIOLOGY This injury often occurs in middle-aged or elderly athletes or after cortisone injections. The rupture can be partial, causing pain but no lump. If complete, the sudden lump on the mid-biceps is typical.

CLINICAL FINDINGS The typical deformation can be seen clearly on resisted elbow flexion. A proximal partial tear or subluxation gives a positive palm-up test.

INVESTIGATIONS This is a clinical diagnosis. MRI or ultrasound is usually not required for the diagnosis but may be done to investigate associated injuries.

TREATMENT Usually this injury is treated without surgery with gradual and progressive rehabilitation. Even though the long head of the biceps, subject to sufficient length and quality, can be re-inserted into the humeral head, the functional improvement may

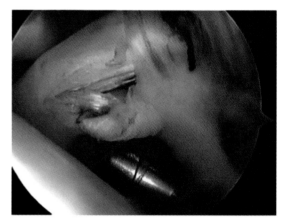

Fig. 246 Arthroscopic view of a partial biceps tendon rupture

be questionable. However, an associated, SLAP tear is not unusual and may require surgery.

REFERRALS Refer to orthopaedic surgeon to determine the grade of injury and for consideration of surgery. Refer to physiotherapist to start a three-month rehabilitation programme.

EXERCISE PRESCRIPTION Most sports and activities can be maintained, such as cross-training, working-out and running. The specific rehabilitation should aim at a full range of controlled motion, good posture and thoraco-scapular control, followed by functional training.

EVALUATION OF TREATMENT OUTCOMES

Normal clinical symptoms and signs. The apprehension test should be negative. Functional strength, control and flexibility should be comparable with the other shoulder.

DIFFERENTIAL DIAGNOSES Associated injuries must be ruled out. Due to its origin at the anterior superior labrum, a SLAP tear, with or without impingement, may complicate the situation and require surgery.

PROGNOSIS Good-Fair, depending on associated injuries.

4. CLAVICLE FRACTURE

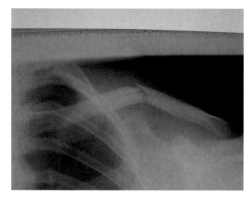

Fig. 247 X-ray of an uncomplicated clavicle fracture which will heal well in six to eight weeks with an 8-bandage

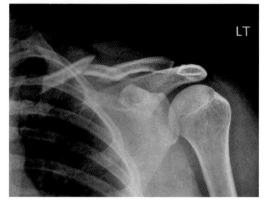

Fig. 248 X-ray of a clavicle fracture with intermediary fragments, complicated by nerve and vascular injury, requiring surgery

SYMPTOMS There is acute onset of localised swelling and pain over the anterior part of the shoulder, with typical deformation, after direct or indirect trauma, often in a young athlete.

AETIOLOGY It is common in rugby, ice hockey, riding and cycling.

CLINICAL FINDINGS A clavicle fracture is usually easy to diagnose since the patient refers to a 'crack' and can point to the fracture site where there is bruising, deformation and tenderness on palpation. Vascular complications (wrist pulse) and neurological complications (reflexes and sensation and power of the hand).

INVESTIGATIONS This is a clinical diagnosis. X-rays should be taken in different planes to demonstrate the fracture and the presence of intermediary fragments. MRI or CT are usually not required in the acute phase for the diagnosis but may be performed in cases involving great trauma to investigate associated injuries to underlying blood vessels or ribs or to the acromio-clavicular joint.

TREATMENT An 8-bandage, applied properly, will reduce the pain as well as holding the fracture in the best position for healing, which takes six to eight weeks. Only complicated cases will require surgery.

REFERRALS Refer to orthopaedic surgeon to determine the grade of injury and for consideration of surgery. Refer to physiotherapist to start an eight to twelve week rehabilitation programme back to full sport.

EXERCISE PRESCRIPTION Many sports and activities, such as water exercises and cross-training, can be maintained but avoid further direct or indirect trauma to the shoulder. Running should initially be avoided since the shoulder will be sensitive to this type of impact and holding the arm still while running will cause secondary upper back and neck pain. Swimming should also wait for around six weeks. The specific rehabilitation should aim at a full range of controlled motion, good posture and thoraco-scapular control after two months, followed by functional training for up to three months before resuming full sport.

EVALUATION OF TREATMENT OUTCOMES

Normal clinical symptoms and signs. Functional strength, control and flexibility should be comparable with the other shoulder.

DIFFERENTIAL DIAGNOSES Vascular or neurological injuries, sterno-clavicular or acromioclavicular joint dislocation and rib fractures should be ruled out.

PROGNOSIS Excellent-Good in most cases.

5. EXTERNAL IMPINGEMENT

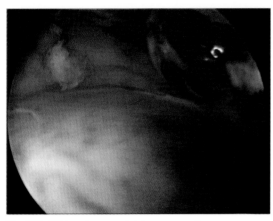

Fig. 249 After sub-acromial decompression, a very inflamed rotator cuff is revealed, explaining the symptoms of external impingement syndrome

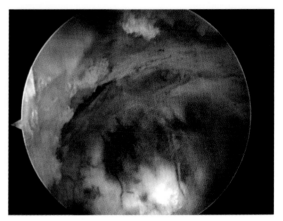

Fig. 250 Arthroscopic view of thick fibrotic bursa compressing the underlying rotator cuff

SYMPTOMS There is gradual onset of pain in the shoulder on overhead activity involving internal rotation and abduction. Typically, the pain is worst in one specific position or during a certain movement but often the shoulder gradually stiffens up, restricting abduction and rotation. It is painful to sleep on that side and movement becomes a problem.

AETIOLOGY External impingement is not a diagnosis but a symptom. It is usually caused by jamming of a scarred and inflamed bursae between the acromion and the rotator cuff.

CLINICAL FINDINGS The range of motion is usually decreased. External impingement is diagnosed by a positive Hawkin's test. Since an underlying rotator cuff tear can cause the bursitis, Jobe's test for the rotator cuff is often positive. In chronic cases there is often muscle atrophy.

INVESTIGATIONS This is a clinical diagnosis. X-rays should be taken in different planes to rule out bony pathology and anterior osteophytes. MRI is usually not helpful, since it is a static investigation

and the syndrome is a dynamic problem, but an underlying rotator cuff tear can be seen. Discussion with the radiologist is important.

TREATMENT The clue to success is the proper identification of the type of impingement and underlying cause. Arthroscopic evaluation and sub-acromial decompression, with or without repair of any underlying rotator cuff problem, is often required and must be followed by rehabilitation. In some cases physiotherapy is suffcient on its own. Cortisone injections should be used with care, since they will not cure a scarred and fibrotic bursae and can decrease the tensile strength of the rotator cuff, causing further ruptures and reducing the ability to repair.

REFERRALS Refer to physiotherapist and to orthopaedic surgeon to determine the diagnosis and for consideration of surgery. In almost all cases, a thorough rehabilitation programme, including specific treatment, thoraco-scapular control training, strength, flexibility and posture training is required with or without surgery.

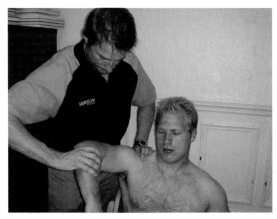

Fig. 251 Hawkin's test is positive if forced internal rotation with the arm in abduction causes pain

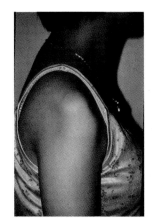

Fig. 252 Muscle atrophy can be caused by immobilisation, but also by nerve damage. This is a case of axillary nerve injury and complete wasting of the Deltoid muscle

EXERCISE PRESCRIPTION Most sports and activities without an overarm action are possible but secondary symptoms due to compensatory movements are common and must be addressed. Running should be avoided since the shoulder is sensitive to this type of impact and holding the arm still while running will cause secondary upper back and neck pain. Swimming is also unsuitable. The specific rehabilitation should aim at a full range of controlled motion, good posture and thoraco-scapular control after three months, followed by functional training before resuming sports such as rugby.

EVALUATION OF TREATMENT OUTCOMES Normal clinical symptoms and signs. Previously positive tests producing pain should now be negative. Functional strength, control and flexibility should be comparable with the other shoulder.

DIFFERENTIAL DIAGNOSES Nerve root compression from the cervical spine, frozen shoulder or post-traumatic damage to the axillary nerve can also cause similar symptoms and muscle atrophy.

PROGNOSIS Excellent-Good. Usually athletes in overhead sports can return to play within three months.

6. FROZEN SHOULDER

Fig. 253 Frozen shoulder causes mechanical block of movements in all directions

SYMPTOMS There is sudden or gradual onset of localised pain and stiffness in the shoulder, often in a middle-aged athlete, with no preceding trauma.

AETIOLOGY Frozen shoulder is a capsulitis of unknown origin that makes the shoulder freeze because of a gradually shrinking capsule. The onset can be dramatic; the patient wakes up with a stiff shoulder having had no previous problems. It is sometimes associated with general collagen disorders and diabetes.

CLINICAL FINDINGS The shoulder is passively restricted in movements in all directions. The condition is very painful.

INVESTIGATIONS This is a clinical diagnosis. X-rays should be taken in different planes to rule out bony pathology. MRI is usually not helpful since it is a static examination and the syndrome is a dynamic problem. Individual discussion with the radiologist is important.

TREATMENT A frozen shoulder is often said to be incurable but can heal within two years. That is not true: physiotherapy and occasionally arthroscopic release can improve the condition dramatically. NSAID can help in the initial stages. Each case needs to be discussed individually. Secondary problems in the neck and upper back are almost inevitable and must be addressed.

REFERRALS Refer to physiotherapist and to orthopaedic surgeon to determine the diagnosis and for consideration of surgery. In almost all cases, a thorough rehabilitation programme, including specific treatment, thoraco-scapular control training, strength, flexibility and posture training is required but symptoms should be expected to last a long time.

EXERCISE PRESCRIPTION Most sports and activities without an overarm action are possible but secondary symptoms due to compensatory movements are common. Running should be avoided since the shoulder will be sensitive to this type of impact and holding the arm still while running will cause secondary upper back and neck pain. Swimming is usually difficult but warm water can be helpful to release the shoulder. The specific rehabilitation should aim to achieve over time a full range of controlled motion, good posture and thoraco-scapular control.

EVALUATION OF TREATMENT OUTCOMES Normal clinical symptoms and signs. Range of motion, strength, control and flexibility should be comparable with the other shoulder.

DIFFERENTIAL DIAGNOSES Post-traumatic stiffness after surgery or immobilisation and external impingement syndrome can also cause these symptoms.

PROGNOSIS Fair-Poor in true frozen shoulder.

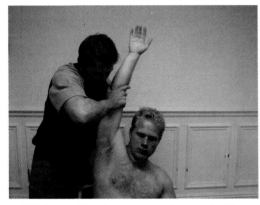

Fig. 254 Internal impingement can be provoked by letting patient's symptoms guide the examiner

Fig. 255 The 'apprehension test' should be done in different overhead positions - pain in a certain position reveals a positive impingement test

SYMPTOMS There is sudden or gradual onset of exercise-induced pain in the shoulder on overhead movements. Typically the pain occurs in one specific position or during one specific movement.

AETIOLOGY Impingement is not a diagnosis but a symptom. Internal posterior or anterior primary impingement can have a variety of causes, including loose bodies, partial flap tears of the rotator cuff or the labrum, synovitis or derive from functional instability as a secondary impingement. Primary impingement can lead to micro-instability.

CLINICAL FINDINGS Internal impingement is diagnosed from provoking the position that causes the pain in repeated tests – a positive internal impingement test. Since an underlying labrum tear can cause the same symptoms, an apprehension test, Jobe's test for the rotator cuff, SLAP tests, Gerber's lift-off test for the sub-scapularis tendon and the palm-up test for the biceps tendon must be evaluated. A clinical test that indicates an underlying multidirectional laxity is the sulcus sign. General joint laxity test should be ruled out. Functional tests such as the 'press against the wall' test and tests of thoraco-scapular control as well as a thorough examination of the cervical spine should complement the examination.

INVESTIGATIONS This is a clinical diagnosis. X-rays should be taken in different planes to rule out bony pathology. MRI is usually not helpful since it is a static examination and the syndrome is a dynamic problem. Discussion with the radiologist is important.

TREATMENT The clue to success is the proper identification of the type of impingement and its underlying cause. For internal and external impingement, arthroscopic evaluation and treatment is often required, followed by rehabilitation. For instability-related impingement, physiotherapy can often be the cure.

REFERRALS Refer to orthopaedic surgeon and physiotherapist to determine the diagnosis and for consideration of surgery. In almost all cases, with or without surgery, a thorough rehabilitation programme including specific treatment, thoraco-scapular control training, strength, flexibility and posture training is required.

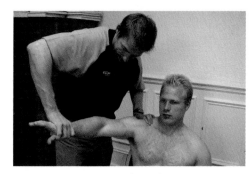

Fig. 256 A superior labrum (SLAP) tear can be provoked in many ways. If resisted flexion with the arm slightly abducted is weak or painful, a SLAP tear can be suspected

Fig. 257 Jobe's test is positive if there is resisted abduction and weakness with the arm internally rotated and slightly anterior (compare with other side). These are signs of a rotator cuff tear or, if there is pain, a sign of a partial tear and/or external impingement

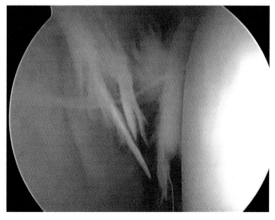

Fig. 258 Arthroscopic view of a partial rotator cuff tear

EXERCISE PRESCRIPTION Most sports and activities are possible but secondary symptoms due to compensatory movements and inappropriate muscle activity must be addressed. Running should initially be avoided since the shoulder may be sensitive to this type of impact and cause secondary upper back and neck pain. Swimming should also wait for around three months. The specific rehabilitation should aim at a full range of controlled motion, good posture and thoraco-scapular control, followed by functional training before resuming overhead sports.

EVALUATION OF TREATMENT OUTCOMES
Normal clinical symptoms and signs. Clinical tests should be negative. Functional strength, control and flexibility should be comparable with the other shoulder.

DIFFERENTIAL DIAGNOSES Multi-directional and general joint laxity is a complicating factor that must be addressed before surgery.

PROGNOSIS Excellent-Good. Usually, 'overhead' athletes are playing within three months after treatment.

Fig. 259 Multi-directional laxity is almost essential for some athletes. This does not require treatment. It is only defined as 'instability' if there are symptoms from the shoulder

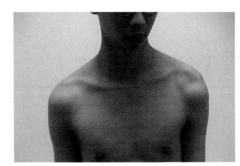

Fig. 260 A positive sulcus sign is related to multi-directional laxity - if there are symptoms from the shoulder as well, it indicates multi-directional instability

SYMPTOMS There is sudden or gradual onset of localised pain in the shoulder, usually during over-head activity. Typically, pain occurs in specific positions or during different movements. Sometimes there is a sense of weakness or instability.

AETIOLOGY Multi-directional laxity is a hereditary condition caused by a loose shoulder joint capsule. In many sports, such as ballet, gymnastics and figure-skating, this increased laxity is essential for performance. Some of these athletes may develop instability, which is a subjective problem.

CLINICAL FINDINGS A positive sulcus sign is the most important reflection of multi-directional laxity. General joint laxity may or may not co-exist. Functional tests, such as the 'press against the wall test', tests of thoraco-scapular control and a thorough examination of the cervical spine should complement the examination.

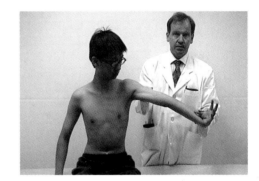

Fig. 261 If three major joints (for example, elbow, wrist and knee) are hypermobile, the patient has general joint laxity

INVESTIGATIONS This is a clinical diagnosis; a painful shoulder and a positive sulcus sign without preceding trauma are the main indicators of the diagnosis. MRI is not helpful since it is a static examination and the syndrome is a dynamic problem.

TREATMENT Multi-directional instability and related impingement can often be cured by physiotherapy. However, in this group of athletes other problems can co-exist and exercise fail to cure the symptoms.

REFERRALS Refer to physiotherapist. In almost all cases, a thorough rehabilitation programme including, thoraco-scapular control training, strength, flexibility and posture training is required. Refer to orthopaedic surgeon if this regime fails, in particular if trauma is involved.

EXERCISE PRESCRIPTION Most sports and activities without an overarm action are possible but secondary symptoms due to compensatory muscle activation are common and must be addressed. Swimming should also wait for around three months. The specific rehabilitation should aim at a full range of controlled motion, good posture and thoraco-scapular control by three months followed by functional training before resuming overhead sports.

EVALUATION OF TREATMENT OUTCOMES Normal clinical symptoms and signs. Sulcus sign will remain positive. Functional strength, control and flexibility should be comparable with the other shoulder.

DIFFERENTIAL DIAGNOSES Internal impingement caused by structural damage.

PROGNOSIS Excellent-Good. Usually athletes in overhead sports can return to play within three months.

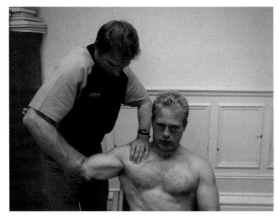

Fig. 262 Resisted adduction-flexion will be very weak if there is a complete rupture. Pain suggests a partial tear

SYMPTOMS Sudden onset of localised pain in the anterior part of the shoulder and upper arm after excessive abduction and external rotation such as in a rugby tackle. There is weakness on internal rotation and forward flexion.

AETIOLOGY The pectoralis muscle insertion at the upper humerus or muscle bulk can rupture partially or completely.

CLINICAL FINDINGS Clinical tests of resisting an internal rotation manoeuvre will identify the weakness and pain typical of a rupture.

INVESTIGATIONS This is a clinical diagnosis. MRI or ultrasound are helpful to delineate the extent of the injury.

TREATMENT A complete tear will require surgery while a partial tear can be treated with progressive rehabilitation over 12 weeks.

REFERRALS Refer to orthopaedic surgeon to consider surgery and to physiotherapist. In all cases a thorough rehabilitation programme, including specific treatment, thoraco-scapular control training, strength, flexibility and posture training is required.

EXERCISE PRESCRIPTION Most general activities are possible but secondary symptoms due to compensation and avoidance of pain are common and must be addressed. Running should initially be avoided since the shoulder will be sensitive to this type of impact and holding the arm still while running will cause secondary upper back and neck pain. Swimming should also wait for around three months. The specific rehabilitation should aim at a full range of controlled motion, good posture and thoraco-scapular control by three months followed by functional training for up to six months before resuming sports like rugby.

EVALUATION OF TREATMENT OUTCOMES
Normal clinical symptoms and signs. Functional strength, control and flexibility should be comparable with the other shoulder.

DIFFERENTIAL DIAGNOSES Fracture of proximal humerus or rib fractures in the area.

PROGNOSIS Good-Fair, depending on severity of the injury. Usually athletes in overhead sports can return to play within six to 12 months.

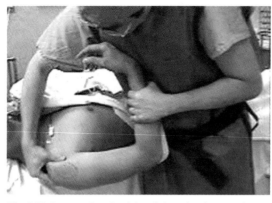

Fig. 263 A posterior shoulder dislocation is not only difficult to diagnose, it is also hard to reposition, and this often requires general anaesthetic

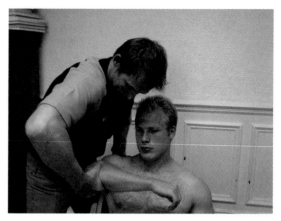

Fig. 264 Posterior drawer test is positive if there are injuries to the posterior labrum

SYMPTOMS There is acute onset of localised swelling and pain over the posterior part of the shoulder, with typical deformation, after an excessive trauma. This injury is more common in epileptics and alcoholics than in athletes.

AETIOLOGY This injury accounts for fewer than 5 per cent of shoulder dislocations. It is uncommon in sport but can occur from direct tackles or falls on an outstretched arm in rugby or American football.

CLINICAL FINDINGS A first-time posterior dislocation in a young athlete will usually need to be repositioned under relaxation (by anaesthesia). It is often mistaken for the more common anterior dislocation. After repositioning, the posterior drawer test and the reposition test are positive.

INVESTIGATIONS This is a difficult clinical diagnosis and is often missed. The active range of motion is grossly decreased. To find these rare cases of posterior dislocations, X-rays should be taken in different planes to rule out fracture and demonstrate the type of dislocation. MRI or CT are usually

helpful for the diagnosis and to investigate associated injuries.

TREATMENT Compared to anterior dislocations, this injury seldom requires stabilising surgery. If posterior instability causes discomfort it is felt during abduction and forward flexion. Physiotherapy is required to restore functional stability.

REFERRALS Refer to orthopaedic surgeon to determine the grade of the injury and for consideration of surgery. Refer to physiotherapist to start a six-month rehabilitation programme.

EXERCISE PRESCRIPTION Most sports and activities, such as cycling, cross-training and working-out, can be maintained but avoid further direct or indirect trauma to the shoulder. Running should be avoided since the shoulder will be sensitive to this type of impact and holding the arm still while running will cause secondary upper back and neck pain. Swimming should also wait for around three months. The specific rehabilitation should aim at a full range of controlled motion, good posture and thoraco-scapular control by three months followed by functional training for up to four to six months before resuming sports like rugby.

EVALUATION OF TREATMENT OUTCOMES

Normal clinical symptoms and signs. The posterior drawer test should be negative. Functional strength, control and flexibility should be comparable with the other shoulder.

DIFFERENTIAL DIAGNOSES Fractures must be ruled out. Multi-directional and general joint laxity is a complicating factor that needs to be addressed before any surgery.

PROGNOSIS Good-Fair depending on the severity.

11. POST-TRAUMATIC SHOULDER STIFFNESS

Fig. 265 Post-traumatic stiff shoulder causes mechanical block of movements in all directions

SYMPTOMS There is gradual onset of diffuse pain or ache, and stiffness in the shoulder after previous trauma or immobilisation.

AETIOLOGY This disorder has similar symptoms to frozen shoulder but has a traumatic background and can be treated much more aggressively. It is usually caused by fibrosis and scarring after a bleeding in or around the joint, which may affect either or both the gleno-humeral joint and the sub-acromial compartment.

CLINICAL FINDINGS The shoulder is passively restricted in movements in all directions. The condition is very painful.

INVESTIGATIONS This is a clinical diagnosis. X-rays should be taken in different planes to rule out bony pathology. MRI is usually not helpful since it is a static examination and the syndrome is a dynamic problem. However, there may be an underlying rotator cuff tear or bursitis.

TREATMENT Physiotherapy, after manipulation under anaesthesia and arthroscopic release, improves the condition dramatically. Secondary problems in the neck and upper back are almost inevitable and must be addressed.

REFERRALS Refer to physiotherapist and to orthopaedic surgeon to determine the diagnosis and for consideration of surgery. In almost all cases, a thorough rehabilitation programme, including specific treatment, thoraco-scapular control training, strength, flexibility and posture training is required after surgical release.

EXERCISE PRESCRIPTION Most sports and activities are possible but secondary symptoms due to compensation and avoidance of pain are common and must be addressed. Running should be avoided since the shoulder will be sensitive to this type of impact and holding the arm still while running will cause secondary upper back and neck pain. Swimming is usually difficult but warm water can be helpful to release the shoulder. The specific rehabilitation should aim to achieve over time a full range of controlled motion, good posture and thoraco-scapular control.

EVALUATION OF TREATMENT OUTCOMES
Normal clinical symptoms and signs. Previously positive tests should be negative. Functional strength, control and flexibility should be comparable with the other shoulder.

DIFFERENTIAL DIAGNOSES Frozen shoulder or nerve entrapment from the cervical spine.

PROGNOSIS Excellent-Good.

Fig. 266 Rugby is one of the sports where neck injuries are not uncommon, even if modern rules have tried to prevent them

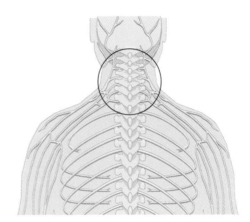

Fig. 267 Nerve root distribution C5-C7 to shoulder

SYMPTOMS There is usually exercise- or move-ment-related radiating pain and dysfunction of the shoulder, with or without preceding trauma and most often associated with discomfort or pain in the neck. Neurological signs from levels C5-C7 of the cervical spine may or may not be present in the shoulder, elbow and hand. The pain can also start as excruciating localised pain in the shoulder, with no clinical symptoms in the neck. In contact sports like rugby or after falls, acute injuries to the spine are always dangerous and must be dealt with immedi-ately at the highest possible level of expertise. Such injuries are not dealt with further in this book.

AETIOLOGY This is an entrapment of the C5-C7 nerve roots along the canals from the cervical spine. An underlying disc prolapse, spinal stenosis or instability from lysis or listesis may be involved. In rare cases tumours may be the cause.

CLINICAL FINDINGS The onset can be gradual and worsen by the day from a spinal stenosis, be

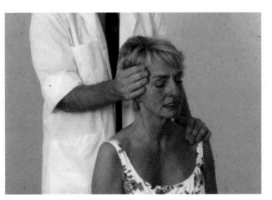

Fig. 268 If there is full, pain-free active/resisted range of motion and no distal neurological pathology, it is unlikely that the shoulder pain is referred from the cervical spine

intermittent from an unstable segment or acute from a prolapsed disc, even though a mix of clinical prob-lems may exist. The shoulder and range of motion of the cervical spine may be normal, which makes the diagnosis very difficult. Pain in the shoulder with normal clinical findings must raise suspicion of this injury. Whenever there is shoulder pain with distal symptoms in the arm, normal shoulder examination and no preceding trauma, the cervical spine must be examined thoroughly. Examine the neck by looking at the active range of motion in all directions, repeated against manual resistance and gentle compression tests that may or may not provoke symptoms.

INVESTIGATIONS This is a clinically difficult diagnosis. X-rays should be taken in different planes to rule out bony pathology. MRI is helpful for spinal stenosis and disc hernia but is usually not helpful if the pain is caused by dynamic instability problems. Individual discussion with the radiologist is important.

TREATMENT If problems in the cervical spine are suspected of causing the shoulder pain and dysfunction, they must be ruled out before any treatment to the shoulder is given.

REFERRALS Refer to physiotherapist and to neurosurgeon or spinal surgeon to evaluate the diagnosis and for consideration of surgery. In most cases a thorough rehabilitation programme including specific treatment, thoraco-scapular control training, strength, flexibility and posture training is required. In severe cases surgery is required.

EXERCISE PRESCRIPTION Some sports and activities may be possible but secondary symptoms due to compensatory movements are common and must be addressed.

EVALUATION OF TREATMENT OUTCOMES Normal clinical symptoms and signs.

DIFFERENTIAL DIAGNOSES Many shoulder injuries can cause neck problems and vice versa. The primary cause of the problems must be found.

LONG-TERM PROGNOSIS Excellent-Poor, depending on the underlying problem.

SYMPTOMS There is usually diffuse exercise or movement-related radiating pain and dysfunction of the shoulder, with or without preceding trauma.

AETIOLOGY Shoulder injuries often cause pain around the upper back and vice versa. Thoraco-scapular instability is an example of a functional problem that causes upper back and shoulder pain. Such dysfunctions can occur after a backwards fall to the ground or after immobilisation. Costo-verte-bral dysfunction can also cause similar symptoms.

CLINICAL FINDINGS Whenever there is shoulder pain but the shoulder appears normal on examination the cervical spine and upper back must be examined thoroughly. The active range of motion should be tested in all directions and repeated against manual resistance. Gentle compression tests may or may not increase suspicion. A 'press against the wall test' will reveal a gradually increasing winged scapula and 'angel manoeuvres' will reflect the control of the scapula, comparing left and right. A 'springing test' against the costo-vertebral joints may reveal problems that might be treatable with gentle manipulation.

INVESTIGATIONS This is a clinical diagnosis. X-rays should be taken in different planes to rule out bony pathology. MRI is usually normal. Individual discussion with the radiologist is important.

TREATMENT Depends on the underlying cause but most cases can be treated by exercise guided by a physiotherapist or chiropractor.

REFERRALS Refer to physiotherapist for a functional test of the upper back. A thorough rehabilitation programme including specific treatment,

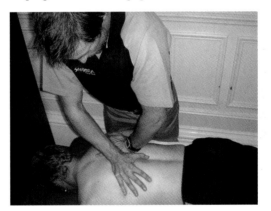

Fig. 270 Springing test against the costo-vertebral joints is often useful for diagnosis and therapy

thoraco-scapular control training, strength, flexibility and posture training is required.

EXERCISE PRESCRIPTION Most sports and activities are possible but secondary symptoms due to compensatory movements are common and must be addressed. Running and swimming may be possible. The specific rehabilitation should aim to achieve over time a full range of controlled motion, good posture and thoraco-scapular control.

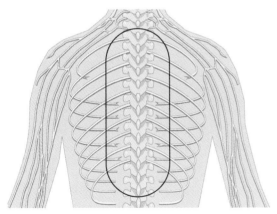

Fig. 269 Rotation of the upper back is often restricted or painful in one direction if the problems arise there

EVALUATION OF TREATMENT OUTCOMES
Normal clinical symptoms and signs. Previously positive tests should be negative. Functional strength, control and flexibility should be restored.

DIFFERENTIAL DIAGNOSES Many shoulder injuries can cause back problems and vice versa. The primary cause of the problems must be found. It is important not to forget non-musculo-skeletal causes of back pain, such as pneumonia, tumours, cardio-vascular problems or other internal ailments.

PROGNOSIS Excellent-Poor, depending on the underlying problem.

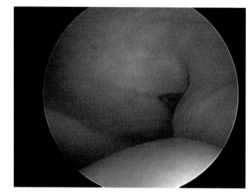

Fig. 272 Arthroscopic view of complete rotator cuff tear, missed by MRI but causing severe problems for the player

...uma to the
...injuries

...elated pain
...tion and in
...late that
...In many partial
...ondary impinge-
...ess.

...amatic, with
...jth from a direct or

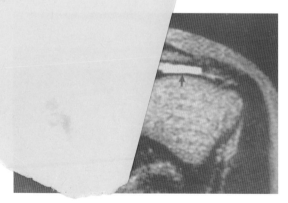

Fig. 273 MRI can sometimes demonstrate, as here, a complete tear of the cuff. However, partial tears are most common in active young players which are often difficult to find on MRI

indirect tackle. Development of symptoms in partial tears is more gradual. Tears may be under or upper surface flap tears, partial or complete avulsion tears from the humerus insertion, split tears in the mid-substance or a combination of degenerative and acute tears. The location of the tear may be posterior, lateral, medial or anterior. Thus, the symptoms may vary.

CLINICAL FINDINGS Since this injury often is associated with other injuries such as shoulder dislocations or SLAP tears, a broad range of clinical tests must be performed. The active range in all directions of shoulder motion should be tested (it is almost always decreased), repeated against manual resistance and compared with the other side. Jobe's test is positive in major or complete ruptures and internal impingement tests are positive in undersurface partial tears. Major tears are usually degenerative, affecting athletes over 40 years of age, while partial tears are common in younger athletes, but a severe tackle in rugby can tear a rotator cuff completely in a young player. In

14. ROTATOR CUFF RUPTURE *Cont.*

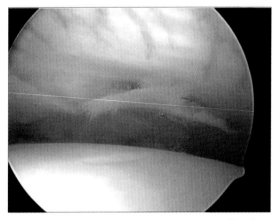

Fig. 274 Internal impingement from rotator cuff and SLAP tear flaps, as seen by arthroscopy

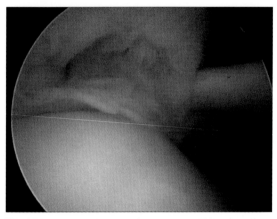

Fig. 275 Undersurface partial rotator cuff flap tear, close to biceps tendon

chronic cases, there is usually a restricted range of motion and muscle atrophy and secondary problems around the upper back and neck. Such rotator cuff tears may well be seen as a post-traumatic stiff shoulder.

INVESTIGATIONS This is a clinical diagnosis. Ultrasound or MRI is helpful when the tear is complete but often misses smaller or partial tears.

TREATMENT Physiotherapy, for restoration of thoraco-scapular control and posture, is essential. Arthroscopy is very valuable, both to investigate the extent of the injury and repair or treat tears.

REFERRALS Refer to physiotherapist and to orthopaedic surgeon to determine the diagnosis and for consideration of surgery. In almost all cases a thorough rehabilitation programme, including specific treatment, thoraco-scapular control training, strength, flexibility and posture training is required with or without surgery.

EXERCISE PRESCRIPTION Most sports and activities are possible but secondary symptoms due to compensatory muscle activation are common and must be addressed. Running and swimming are usually difficult but warm water can be helpful to release the shoulder. The specific rehabilitation should aim to achieve over time a full range of controlled motion, good posture and thoraco-scapular control.

EVALUATION OF TREATMENT OUTCOMES Normal clinical symptoms and signs. Jobes' test should be negative. Functional strength, control and flexibility should be comparable with the other shoulder.

DIFFERENTIAL DIAGNOSES Post-traumatic stiffness, frozen shoulder, SLAP tear, external impingement, non-orchopaedic disorders carrying referred pain.

PROGNOSIS Excellent-Poor, depending on the extent of the injury.

SYMPTOMS There is sharp impingement-type shoulder pain and weakness when trying to perform specific overhead activities, such as throwing a ball or serving in tennis.

AETIOLOGY The SLAP ligament (Superior Labrum Anterior to Posterior) is the superior part of the glenoid labrum. Besides stabilising and centring the humeral head to the glenoid, it stabilises the long head of the biceps tendon, which originates from the anterior part. When the SLAP ligament is damaged, the gleno humeral joint becomes unstable. SLAP injuries are common in many sports involving overhead activities, like rugby or tennis. It can also be caused by falling on to an outstretched arm. SLAP injuries are often associated with other injuries such as rotator cuff tears or Bankart lesions.

CLINICAL FINDINGS There are various clinical tests to verify the diagnosis. O'Brien's test, internal impingement tests and the 'palm-up' test are often positive. There are different types of SLAP tear and it is an injury that varies in severity. Additionally, it is seldom isolated, and for this reason the tests have to be done in the positions the athlete refers to as painful – a functional impingement test.

INVESTIGATIONS MRI, arthrogram and arthroscopy are most reliable to identify this injury.

TREATMENT Minor and stable SLAP tears are left to heal with physiotherapy and modified sporting activities. Unstable tears require either vaporisation or surgical refixation.

REFERRALS Refer to physiotherapist to assess thoraco-scapular control and muscle function. Refer

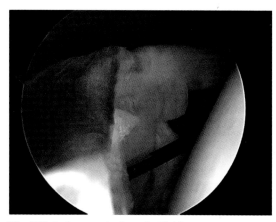

Fig. 276 Arthroscopic view of a SLAP tear

to orthopaedic surgeon if the pain/weakness is severe or if physiotherapy does not relieve symptoms.

EXERCISE PRESCRIPTION
This is an injury with which you can undertake virtually all non-overhead activities throughout the healing process. For this injury, a three- to four-month rehabilitation programme is usually sufficient before returning to overhead sport.

EVALUATION OF TREATMENT OUTCOMES
Clinical evaluation of symptoms.

DIFFERENTIAL DIAGNOSES The main problem is that this injury is often associated with impingement, caused by a variety of conditions such as a partial rotator cuff tear, partial subscapularis tendon tear, biceps tendon disorder or multi-directional instability. This frequently blurs the clinical presentation.

PROGNOSIS Excellent if appropriately diagnosed and repaired.

16. SUBSCAPULARIS TENDON RUPTURE

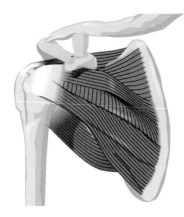

Fig. 277 Anatomical illustration of subscapularis tendon insertion to the anterior humeral head, where ruptures often occur

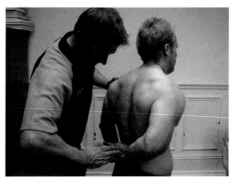

Fig. 278 If 'lift off' power is reduced or if pushing backwards with the arm is painful, there is a possible subscapularis tendon injury

SYMPTOMS There is acute or gradual onset of exercise-induced pain and weakness on internal rotation with the shoulder in a neutral position, and difficulty in reaching the lower back with the hand.

AETIOLOGY The onset can be dramatic and relate to an anterior shoulder dislocation caused by heavy tackling, for example in rugby.

CLINICAL FINDINGS Active forward flexion and external rotation is usually painful. Gerber's lift-off test is positive. There is tenderness on palpation in the anterior shoulder joint. Palm-up tests and SLAP tests are usually vaguely positive. Since this injury often affects many structures, a thorough clinical examination of these must also be undertaken.

INVESTIGATIONS This is a clinical though difficult diagnosis. Arthroscopy can confirm. X-rays should be taken in different planes to rule out fracture. MRI is helpful.

TREATMENT If there is a complete tear, surgical refixing is usually required but partial tears can be treated with progressive rehabilitation. Distal partial flap tears can cause impingement and require a thorough vaporation.

REFERRALS Refer to physiotherapist and to orthopaedic surgeon to determine the diagnosis and for consideration of surgery. In almost all cases, a thorough rehabilitation programme, including specific treatment, thoraco-scapular control training, strength, flexibility and posture training is required.

EXERCISE PRESCRIPTION Most sports and activities are possible but secondary symptoms due to compensatory movements are common and must be addressed. Swimming is usually difficult. The specific rehabilitation should aim to achieve over time a full range of controlled motion, good posture and thoraco-scapular control.

EVALUATION OF TREATMENT OUTCOMES
Normal clinical symptoms and signs. Gerber's lift-off test should be negative. Functional strength, control and flexibility should be comparable with the other shoulder.

DIFFERENTIAL DIAGNOSES A number of shoulder injuries can cause similar symptoms but Gerber's lift-off test is seldom positive if the subscapularis is not affected.

PROGNOSIS Excellent-Poor, depending on the severity of the injury.

17. THORACO-SCAPULAR INSTABILITY

Fig. 279 Winged scapulae are a sign of poor thoraco-scapular control

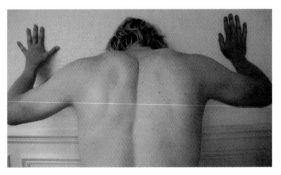

Fig. 280 Winging of scapula can be provoked by the 'press against the wall' test

SYMPTOMS There is anterior and or posterior shoulder pain and weakness in most active overhead and forward movements. A thrower cannot throw, a bowler cannot bowl, a tennis serve will be weak and boxers cannot hit hard.

AETIOLOGY This is secondary shoulder pain caused by dysfunction of the scapula, causing anterior shoulder instability, pain and weakness. It could be due to a (rare) thoracic longus nerve paralysis, where there would be spontaneous winging on forward flexion, but is more commonly due to an inter-scapular muscle insufficiency and poor control, causing progressive winging of the scapula over a short time, while pressing against the wall or lifting or carrying a light object.

CLINICAL FINDINGS Most shoulder joint tests are normal but pressing towards a wall gradually causes increased wing scapula and progressive anterior shoulder symptoms. In contrast with a thoracic longus nerve injury there is no immediate winging. Angel manoeuvres show poor thoraco-scapular control on the affected side.

INVESTIGATIONS This is a clinical diagnosis.

TREATMENT Physiotherapy, with thoraco-scapular training, cures this condition.

REFERRALS Refer to physiotherapist to determine the diagnosis. In almost all cases, a thorough rehabilitation programme, including specific treatment, thoraco-scapular control training, strength, flexibility and posture training is required.

EXERCISE PRESCRIPTION Most sports and activities are possible but secondary symptoms due to compensatory muscle activation are common and must be addressed. The specific rehabilitation should aim to achieve over time a full range of controlled motion, good posture and thoraco-scapular control.

EVALUATION OF TREATMENT OUTCOMES Normal clinical symptoms and signs. Press against the wall and angel manoeuvre tests should be negative. Functional strength, control and flexibility should be comparable with the other shoulder.

DIFFERENTIAL DIAGNOSES Many shoulder injuries can cause poor thoraco-scapular control as a secondary problem.

PROGNOSIS Excellent.

This table provides advice on forms of exercise that may or may not be recommended for athletes with different injuries. The advice must be related to the severity and stage of healing and take the individual's situation into account.

● This activity is harmful or risky.

● This activity can be done but with care and with specific advice.

○ This activity can safely be recommended.

	Running	Walking	Water exercises	Bicycling	Racket sports	Golf	Contact sports	Working-out	Home exercises
ACROMIO-CLAVICULAR DISLOCATION	●	○	●	○	○	○	●	○	○
ANTERIOR SHOULDER DISLOCATION	●	○	●	○	●	○	●	○	○
BICEPS TENDON RUPTURE	○	○	●	○	●	●	●	○	○
CLAVICLE FRACTURE	●	○	●	○	●	●	●	○	○
EXTERNAL IMPINGEMENT	○	○	○	○	●	○	○	○	○
FROZEN SHOULDER	●	○	○	○	●	○	○	○	○
INTERNAL IMPINGEMENT SYNDRONE	●	○	○	○	●	○	○	○	○
MULTI-DIRECTIONAL INSTABILITY	○	○	●	○	○	○	○	○	○
PECTORALIS MUSCLE RUPTURE	●	○	●	○	●	●	●	○	○

EXERCISE ON PRESCRIPTION DURING INJURY TO THE SHOULDER *Cont.*

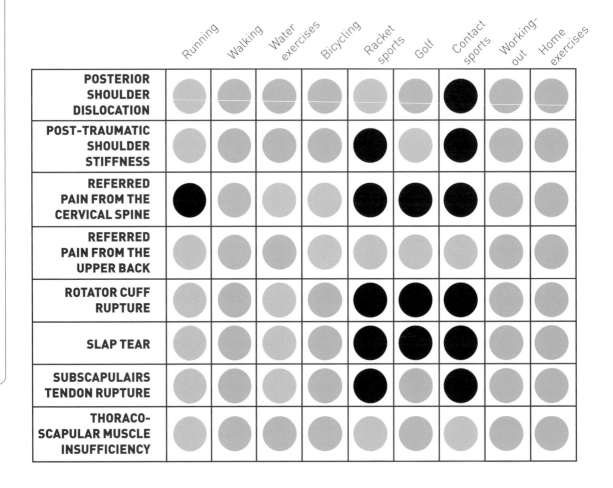

	Running	Walking	Water exercises	Bicycling	Racket sports	Golf	Contact sports	Working-out	Home exercises
POSTERIOR SHOULDER DISLOCATION	○	○	○	○	○	○	●	○	○
POST-TRAUMATIC SHOULDER STIFFNESS	○	○	○	○	●	○	●	○	○
REFERRED PAIN FROM THE CERVICAL SPINE	●	○	○	○	●	●	●	○	○
REFERRED PAIN FROM THE UPPER BACK	○	○	○	○	○	○	○	○	○
ROTATOR CUFF RUPTURE	○	○	○	○	●	●	●	○	○
SLAP TEAR	○	○	○	○	●	●	●	○	○
SUBSCAPULAIRS TENDON RUPTURE	○	○	○	○	●	○	●	○	○
THORACO-SCAPULAR MUSCLE INSUFFICIENCY	○	○	○	○	○	○	○	○	○

Abduction	to move a limb away from the central line of the body
Achilles tendon	the tendon that attaches the calf muscles to the heel bone
Adduction	to move a limb towards the central line of the body
Adductor longus	the strongest hip adductor muscle, which originates from the lower central pelvis bone and inserts on the lower medial femur
Adhesions	scarring between two structures after an acute inflammation
Aetiology	the science of the causes of an injury or disease
Aneurysm	excessive localised enlargement of an artery
Angel manoeuvre	moving arms to elicit diagnostic symptoms
Anorexia	psychological illness and altered self-perception causing an obsessive desire to lose weight by refusing to eat
Anterior cruciate ligament	one out of two cross-shaped ligaments in the knee joint that stabilise the knee during anterior-posterior translation and rotational movements
Arthroscopy	instrument allowing mini-invasive approach for joint visualisation, combining fiber-optic light source, movable camera lens and video link
Atrophy	waste of muscle bulk from immobilisation or other dysfunction
Avascular necrosis	cell death leading to collapse of bone caused by damaged blood supply

Avulsion	tearing away of a ligament or tendon or muscle complex from bone
Axillary nerve	nerve originating from the lower cervical spine (C5-C7) passing through the shoulder, supporting the motor function of the deltoid muscle and sensory function of the skin overlying the posterior-lateral part of the shoulder
Bone density	bone is a living organ and the tensile strength is dependent on several factors including the compactness or density as well as cell activity and structure. Bones normally get stronger by repetitive impact. Bone density can be measured with special scanners. A very low bone density often refers to pathologic weak bone called osteoporosis with increased risk of fracture at low impact.
Bursa	fluid-filled sac-like structure that decreases friction between structures. These are common around most joints.
Bursitis	inflammatory condition in a bursae that can be caused by increased mechanical friction, bleeding from trauma or infection
Calcaneus	the heel bone
Capsule	an enclosing, variably thick membrane that contains the joint structures
Capsulitis	inflammatory reaction to a joint capsule that can be caused by infection, repetitive trauma or reaction after surgery
Cartilage	a firm, flexible living structure outlining the superficial weight bearing areas of joints that gets its nutrition from the joint fluid
Cellularity	the number of cells in a structure. This does not necessarily mean active cells. For example, only 5 per cent of cells in an adult's tendon are active at any given time
Cervical spine	the structures enclosed by the top seven vertebrae from the skull down to the upper thoracic spine at shoulder level

Chondral	another word for cartilage
Chondromalacia	pathologic soft cartilage as probed during arthroscopy
Concentric muscle function	contraction of a muscle during shortening
Condyle	rounded process forming the end of a bone that articulates to another bone
Costo-vertebral	joint between costa (rib) and vertebrae (spine)
Crepitation	the action or sound of crackling or rattling
CRP	acute phase protein marker that increases early in the blood during infections or inflammation. Should normally be at a level < 10
CT scan	computerised tomography that may provide a three-dimensional bone structure and is used to evaluate fractures or bone tumours
Debride	to remove loose or inflamed soft tissue or inflamed structures during arthroscopy
Deltoid muscle	the thick triangular abductor muscle covering the shoulder
Distal	situated furthest away from the origin or centre
Dorsi-flexion	Flexion of the ankle resulting in the top of the foot moving towards the body
Dysaestesia	defective sensation of the skin or numbness
Eccentric muscle function	contraction of muscle during lenghtening
Effusion	increased joint fluid associated with intra-articular injuries, inflammation or infection
ESR	the sedimentation rate of red blood cells used to monitor ongoing infections or inflammations. Levels should normally be < 10
Eversion	turning the talo crural ankle joint inwards
External rotation	rotating the joint away from the centre of the body
Fascia	a thin sheath of fibrotic structure
Fasciotomy	cleaving of a fascia overlying a muscle compartment
Fast-twitch fibres	muscle fibres associated with capacity for quick contraction and high energy output necessary for sprinting or power lifting
Fat pad	fibrotic structure containing fat that absorbs impact or friction, such as under the heel bone or in the front of the knee joint

Femur	the thigh bone adjoining the hip and the knee
Fibrillation	fibrillation represents spontaneous activity on the part of single muscle fibres seen in dysfunctional muscles and in muscular disease
Fibrosis	thickening and scarring of connective tissue after injury
Fibula	lateral lower leg bone supporting rotation of the ankle and knee
Fibulo-calcanear ligament	commonly injured lateral ankle ligament originating from the lateral malleoli and inserting at the lateral calcaneal bone
Gout	metabolic disease causing increased uric acid production, associated with recurrent severe joint pain and swelling
Guyon's canal	the ulnar nerve and ulnar artery run through a tunnel known as Guyon's canal. This tunnel is formed by the pisiform and hamate bones and the ligament that connects them
Haemarthrosis	bleeding in joint usually associated with severe injury
Hernia	protrusion of an organ through weakening or rupture of the wall of the cavity
Histopathological	diseased structure as evaluated by histologic microscopic techniques
Hypermobility	increased mobility of a joint; can be general for all joints or affecting single joints
Hypertrophy	enlargement of an organ or structure such as a muscle from increase in cell size
Iliac crest	upper parts of the pelvic bone
Iliotibial band	the lower fascia-like band forming the distal insertion on to the proximal lateral tibia from the lateral thigh abductor muscles
Ilipsoas	a very powerful hip flexor muscle originating from the lower spine and inserting to the minor trochanter of the proximal femur
Internal rotation	rotating a joint towards the centre of the body
Intra-articular	inside the joint compartment

Intrinsic muscles	small muscles in the foot and hand abducting and adducting fingers and toes
Ischaemic	lack of oxygen due to strangulation of blood supply
Kinetic chain	all structures involved in the movement of a limb, such as ankle, knee and hip involved in movement of a leg
Labral tear	rupture of the ligament around, for example, the edge of the socket of the hip and shoulder joints
Lateral epicondylitis	erroneous labelling of a condition that implies an inflammation of the origin of the extensor muscles of the wrist at the lateral humerus epicondyle, so-called tennis elbow
Lateral malleoli	distal end of the fibula bone
Lateralisation	moving the structure away from the centre of the body line
Lavage	flushing out
Lister's tubercle	tubercle of the radius bone
Listesis	injury to the structures holding two vertebrae together, causing instability
Lysis	injury to one side of structures holding two vertebrae together, causing a rotational instability
Mal-tracking	non-optimal tracking of patella in the femur groove caused by structural imbalances
Maximal oxygen uptake	the oxygen uptake that maximally can be achieved in an individual; often referred to as endurance capacity and measured as ml of oxygen per kilogram of body weight per minute
Medial malleoli	the distal end of tibia
Medial plica syndrome	a pain condition caused by increased thickness, inflammation and friction from embryonic remains in the knee joint
Meniscus	shock-absorbing collagen structures in the medial and lateral parts of the knee
Metatarsal	bones between the ankle and the toes
Micro-fracturing	surgical technique including systematic cracking of small holes through the hard cortical bone

	to stimulate stem cells from the sub-chondral bone to reach the surface and stimulate cartilage repair
Morbidity	symptoms from injury not healed
MRI	magnetic resonance imaging, a technique that can image any body part in three dimensions
Necrosis	death of tissue
Neuroma	nerve tumour, usually benign
Neuropathy	abnormally sensitive nervous system
Non-dominant side	the limb that is not predominantly used for precision movements like writing or playing sport
Mal-union	incomplete healing due to instability or lack of bone-to-bone contact because of interfering fibrotic scar formation
NSAID	non-steroid anti-inflammatory drug, which frequently is used in sports to reduce symptoms of inflammation
OCD	osteochondritis dissecans is an avascular necrosis of the bone undermining the overlying cartilage in a joint, causing pain and effusion
Oedema	swelling of soft tissues
Olecranon	bony part of humerus in the elbow joint
Orthotics	used to correct alignment of the foot arch in the shoe
Osteid osteoma	bone tumour
Osteomyelitis	bone infection
Osteopenia	fragile bone due to immobilisation or inactivity
Osteophytes	bony spurs in or around the joint that are typical findings in the osteoarthritic process
Osteoporosis	pathologic decreased strength of bone associated with an increased risk of fracture due to low bone density common in post-menopausal women
Overhead sports	sports that include activities where the upper limbs are used around or above shoulder level
Palpation	examination of a body structure using the hands to feel
Paraesthesia	numbness and loss of sensation

Passive and active mobility tests	passive mobility tests are done by the examiner while active tests are executed by the examined athlete
Pathoanatomical correlate	the structural damage that is the cause of the symptoms
Periostitis	inflammatory reaction in the sheath surrounding the bone
Peroneus brevis	tendon originating at the fibula head and inserting at the base of the fifth metatarsal bone, flexing and everting the ankle joint
Peroneus tendons	peroneus brevis and longus
Phalanges	fingers and toes
Plantar fascia	the fascia connecting the short toe flexors to the heel bone
Plantar flexion	bending the ankle by contracting and shortening the ankle flexors
Plyometric	movement involving high eccentric impact, such as landing from high jumps
Posterior	situated at the back
Pronation	inward movement of the mid-foot or the wrist
Pronator teres muscle	Pronator teres is a forearm muscle that has two functions, pronation of the forearm assisting pronator quadratus and flexion of the forearm at the elbow joint
Proprioception	complex ability to control body position involving balance and core stability
Prostatitis	inflammatory reaction of the prostate gland in men caused by infection or tumour
Proximal	situated towards the centre of the body or attachment
Q-angle	angle imagined from the mid-thigh proximal to distal positioning and the proximal to distal patella tendon, normally below 20 degrees. If higher angle, there is increased risk of patella disorders including instability
Radius	forearm bone
Rectus femoris	most prominent of the quadriceps muscles, this muscle assists in hip flexion and knee extension

Resistance tests	involve active contraction of a muscle group while the examiner resists to test the strength
Retinaculum	connective tissue band that supports the stability and function of underlying tendons
Re-vascularisation	growth of new blood vessels after previous injury
Rheumatoid arthritis	chronic inflammatory disease
RICE	Rest, Ice, Compression, Elevation, comprising the concept of acute management of sport injuries
RoM	range of motion
Rotator cuff	muscle group controlling the fine-tuned movements of the shoulder, consisting of the subscapularis, supraspinatus and infraspinatus muscles
Rupture	tear
Scaphoid bone	medially located bone at the wrist important for stability and movements
Scapula	flat bone connecting and stabilising the shoulder joint to the posterior thorax
Scintigram	invasive investigation of bone turnover used to investigate bone conditions such as tumours or infections
Sesam bone	bone embedded in tendons such as the patella that enhances the biomechanical properties of joint function
SLAP test/tears	Superior Labrum Anterior-Posterior injuries are common in overhead sports. Specific clinical tests are used to diagnose these injuries
Slow-twitch fibres	muscle fibres that are mainly aerobic and predominant in muscles needed for endurance such as the soleus muscle
Spinal stenosis	thickening of the membrane surrounding the spinal cord, causing pain and compression of nerves
Sub-acromial impingement	impingement between the acromion bone and the rotator cuff common in elderly overhead athletes
Subluxation	mal-positioning of a joint due to lax joint capsule or functional instability
Sub-talar	space between the talus and calcaneus bones

Supination	outward movement of the ankle or wrist joints
Symphysis	cartilaginous and fibrotic "joint" between the two parts of the pelvic bones
Syndesmosis ligament	ligament structures holding together fibula and tibia throughout their lengths. There is an anterior and a posterior ligament holding the distal part of the bones together
Synovectomy	excision of pathologic synovia (joint capsule)
Synovitis	inflammation of the joint capsule
Talo-calcaneal coalition	fusion of the talus bone to the calcaneus bone
Talo-crural joint	joint between talus, fibula and tibia
Talo-fibular ligament	most commonly injured lateral ligament originating at the lateral malleoli and inserting at the lateral anterior part of talus
Talo-navicular coalition	fusion of the talus bone to the navicular bone
Tarsal tunnel	connective tissue band originating at the medial malleoli holding the flexor tendons, nerves and vessels in place during ankle movements
Tensile tissue strength	strength before tear
Tension-side/ compression-side	of bones predominantly affected by either tension or compression during loading
Thrombosis	blood clot forming in a vessel
Tibia	lower leg bone
Tibio-talar laxity	increased movement between the tibia and talus caused by a deltoid ligament rupture
Trochanter	any of several bone protuberances by which muscles are attached to the upper part of the thigh bone
Ulcerus cholitis	inflammatory disease affecting the large intestine, causing bleeding ulcers and severe dysfunction
Ulna	bone of the forearm
Ultrasound	investigation used on superficial structures such as tendons and muscles; treatment used to decrease inflammation
Uric acid	see Gout
Winged scapula	caused by either nerve paralysis to the long thoracic nerve or more commonly due to weakness or insufficiency of the inter-scapular muscles

REFERENCES

Bartlett R, Gratton C, Rolf C. *Encyclopedia of International Sports Studies*. Vol I–III. Routledge, UK & USA 2006.

Brukner P, Khan K. *Clinical Sports Medicine*. McGraw-Hill Book Co., Australia 1993.

Chan KM, Fu F, Mafulli N, Rolf C, Kurosaka M, Liu S. *Controversies in Orthopaedic Sports Medicine*. William & Wilkins Inc, 1998.

Chan KM, Micheli L, Smith A, Rolf C, Bachl N, Frontera W, Alenabi T. *FIMS Team Physician Manual*. 2nd Edition. International Federation of Sports Medicine, Hong Kong 2006.

Clain, A. *Hamilton Bailey's Physical Signs in Clinical Surgery*. 16th Edition. John Wright & Sons Ltd, Bristol 1980.

Peterson L, Renstrom P. *Sports Injuries: their prevention and treatment*. 3rd Edition. Martin Dunitz Ltd, 2001.

Rolf C (Ed). *Consensus Report I-III on the management of sports-related injuries*. Swedish Society of Sports Medicine, 1997–98. I, II, III.

NOTES

228

NOTES

NOTES